Ingram 12/11/03 26.00

SECRETS OF THE
PSYCHICS

SECRETS OF THE
PSYCHICS

Investigating
Paranormal
Claims

MASSIMO POLIDORO

Prometheus Books
59 John Glenn Drive
Amherst, New York 14228-2197

Published 2003 by Prometheus Books

Inquiries should be addressed to
Prometheus Books
59 John Glenn Drive
Amherst, New York 14228-2197
VOICE: 716-691-0133, ext. 207
FAX: 716-564-2711
WWW.PROMETHEUSBOOKS.COM

07 06 05 04 03   5 4 3 2 1

Library of Congress Cataloging-in-Publication Data

Polidoro, Massimo.
    Secrets of the psychics : investigating paranormal claims / by Massimo Polidoro.
       p. cm.
    Includes bibliographical references.
    ISBN 1-59102-086-7 (alk. paper)
    1. Parapsychology. I. Title.

BF1031.P75155 2003
133—dc21

2003010023

Printed in the United States of America on acid-free paper

Every attempt has been made to trace accurate ownership of copyrighted material in this book. Errors and omissions will be corrected in subsequent editions, provided that notification is sent to the publisher.

THIS BOOK IS DEDICATED TO A TRUE HERO,
AND A MAN WHO IS LIKE A SECOND FATHER TO ME,

JAMES RANDI

CONTENTS

PART 2. HISTORICAL INVESTIGATIONS

PART 3. INVESTIGATING PSYCHICS TODAY

CONTENTS

ACKNOWLEDGMENTS

This book is the result of many years of investigation and research. Most of the material here has been published previously in a scattering of journals, magazines, and books in both the United States and Europe. It is herewith collected, cleaned up, and updated for the first time.

First of all I would like to thank Piero Angela and James Randi without whom all this would most likely not have happened. I will be forever grateful to these two men for turning my dreams into reality. Thanks to Paul Kurtz, both for his constant help in starting the Italian skeptics group and for his encouragement in writing books for Prometheus.

Thanks to my good friend and partner in many of my investigations: Luigi Garlaschelli. What do you say, Gigi, is the time finally right for us to tell the world the striking adventure of the man without a cork leg?

Thanks to all my good friends at the Committee for the Scientific Investigation of Claims of the Paranormal (CSICOP), Prometheus Books, the *Skeptical Inquirer*, and the European Council of Skeptical Organizations

(ECSO) for their constant support, kindness, and humor: Jim Alcock, Jerry Andrus, Frederich W. Bach, Robert A. Baker, Rob Beeston, Barry Beyerstein, Amanda Chesworth, Kevin Christopher, Cornelis de Jager, Thomas Flynn, Kendrick Frazier, Martin Gardner, Ray Hyman, Barry Karr, Paul Kurtz, Martin Manher, Jill Maxick, Steven L. Mitchell, Joe Nickell, Lee Nisbet, Benjamin Radford, Wallace Sampson, Ranjit Sandhu, Amardeo Sarma, Michael D. Sofka, Bob Steiner, and Richard Wiseman.

Thanks to all my friends and colleagues around the world for the help, information, and cooperation they have given me through the years: José Alvarez, Alberto Angela, Luciano Arcuri, Susan Blackmore, Sandro Boeri, Richard Broughton, Monica Canclini, Marco Casareto, Christopher Clark, Michael H. Coleman, Livio Colombo, Sergio Della Sala, Chip Denman, Jeanine De Noma, Umberto Eco, Hilary Evans, Chiara Ferrari, Chris French, Gina Froelich, Mauro Gaffo, Laura Grandi, Michael Hutchinson, Lewis Jones, Stanley Krippner, Riccardo Mancini, Valeria Marietti, Tully McCarroll, Robert L. Morris, Carlo Musso, Matt Nisbet, Franco Ramaccini, Benjamin Radford, Mary A. Read, Cristian Riccardi, Gian Marco Rinaldi, Laura Rossetti, Ian Rowland, Linda Safarli, Tiziano and Cristina Sclavi, Michael Shermer, Silvan, Roberto Spampinato, Stefano Tettamanti, Anna Thurlow, Marina Trivellini, James Underdown, and Zofia Weaver.

Thanks to all my very good friends at Comitato Italiano per il Controllo delle Affermazioni sul Paranormale (Italian Committee for the Investigation of Claims of the Paranormal), whose precious work is deeply appreciated: Lucio Braglia, Simone Capeleto, Francesco Chiminello, Claudio Cocheo, Paola De Gobbi, Steno Ferluga, Andrea Ferrero, Matteo Filippini, Marino Franzosi, Silvano Fuso, Francesco Grassi, Francesca Guizzo, Riccardo Luccio, Claudio Marciano, Lorenzo Montali, Marco Morocutti, Adalberto Piazzoli, and Enrico Scalas.

Special thanks to my mother, Enrica, and to my sister, Elisa, for their constant encouragement and love.

And, finally, a very special thank-you to Elena: stand by me, from now on it's going to be even more fun . . .

IN SEARCH OF
PSYCHIC POWERS

*H*ow does one become a "psychic investigator"? Do you need to belong to some weird assembly or must you have experienced some mysterious happenings in your childhood? Frankly, I think the road is different for everyone. I can only speak for myself.

I was five years old when I first saw, on TV, that old Houdini movie with Tony Curtis; I was flabbergasted by the seemingly impossible exploits he performed. I decided that I had to know all about magic tricks, so I started to collect—and asked my parents to buy for me—anything that could be found on the subject. There wasn't much, really. Just a few books and some kits with simple tricks for kids. Then, one day, on a book I found the address of some American "magic dealers" (the existence of which I couldn't even imagine at that time!) and wrote to them immediately. I received magic catalogues and specialized magazines, and from then on my interest became more and more profound.

At some point I put together a series of tricks (among which there was obviously an escape in the style of Houdini) and started to perform my little act at the birthday parties of my schoolmates and on the stages of some local theaters. I may have dreamed of making a career out of my passion, but I realized that the things that I could do, though maybe surprising, were nothing like some of those "real" magical phenomena that one could sometimes see on TV.

I remember one afternoon, for example, when I saw a movie, *The Medusa Touch,* in which Richard Burton used the power of his mind to create disasters and kill his enemies. Though I understood that the movie was fiction, there was a brief documentary-like segment inserted in it which greatly impressed me. In this segment, "real" psychics could be seen moving objects or breaking glass plates with the power of their minds. Among them was the famous Nina Kulagina, of whom I had read somewhere. I remember that I was watching the movie with my dad and I immediately expressed my amazement at those fabulous powers. He was skeptical, however, and told me not to trust much what I saw on TV. His opinion was that, as impressive looking as they were, those things were probably not true.

Like any teenager, I was enormously fascinated by the world of the occult and the paranormal and by the incredible potential that it seemed to offer. I imagined that by practicing and exercising, anyone, including me, could learn to read minds or move objects with the power of the psyche. But for a while I lived in some confusion: on one side TV was telling me that these phenomena were absolutely authentic and proved by science; on the other, an important authority figure, my father, was telling me that these things were probably not so. How could they not be so? I still had fresh in my memory the TV appearances of that famous psychic who was able to bend spoons like butter: what was his name? Oh yes, Uri Geller. I had read his autobiography and he appeared to be sincere. Also, anybody who talked about the paranormal on TV or in books and magazines said that these things were true and perfectly validated: how could all these people be wrong? Was it possible for a book to contain information that was not true? And was my father the only one to have doubts?

PIERO ANGELA AND JAMES RANDI

One day when I was about fourteen, I entered a bookstore for my usual search of publications on the paranormal, and found a book by a TV science journalist whom I greatly admired, Piero Angela. To my surprise, the book, titled *Viaggio nel mondo del paranormale* (Journey in the World of the Paranormal), talked about parapsychology and promised to examine all psychic phenomena, including those claimed by Uri Geller. What induced me to invest my hard-earned savings in that book, instead of one on Nostradamus's prophecies, was the fact that on the back cover it stated that Angela's constant worry had been to avoid being fooled. "It is not possible," it said, "to go in search of new dimensions or new scientific theories by starting from mistakes, suggestions or frauds. This investigation of parapsychology aims to present precious material to those who are interested in psychic phenomena and wish to seriously inquire on the research presently going on in the field, instead of looking for some simple magical entertainment. This, in fact, is not a book for those who want to believe, but for those who want to understand."[1] Perfect, I thought. This was exactly what I was looking for.

That book really opened my eyes and mind to a new world. For the first time, I was helped to reason in a correct way; I could explain many things that, at first, had looked inexplicable; and, above all, I found out that one should not believe or doubt something only on the basis of instinct or according to the statements of some authority, but that first of all it is important to examine all the evidence in a critical way, trying to avoid suggestion, the wish to believe, or deception.

I lost one myth, Uri Geller, but found a new hero: James Randi. Angela devoted quite a lot of his book to telling about the adventures and investigations of this modern Houdini. The man was not a braggart, but really was a sensational person. After a career as a magic performer who had specialized in escapes like Houdini, his hero, he had devoted his time (also like Houdini, in the last few years of his life) to unmasking charlatans and frauds of the paranormal. That's it, I thought! Magic is a wonderful art and I will certainly continue to study it, but what I really want is to become like Houdini and Randi. I want to know all the secrets and the tricks of the charlatans in order to debunk them and, who knows, maybe along the way I could even stumble on some real, inexplicable phenomena.

Those were the dreams of a kid, but if I had considered them so, they would probably have remained just dreams. But I believed in them and did all I could to make them come true. In his book, Angela had published the address of CSICOP, the Committee for the Investigation of the Claims of the Paranormal. I immediately subscribed to its magazine, the *Skeptical Inquirer*. I knew English well, not only because I had studied it in school but, mainly because I had learned it by playing and singing Beatles songs.

Randi had been one of the founders of CSICOP and I wrote to him at the Committee's address, expressing all my admiration for his work and asking for information on Uri Geller (because I still could not perfectly explain the "spoon bending" demonstration). I did not really expect an answer. Can you imagine an American celebrity answering the letter of some Italian kid? For good measure, I also wrote to Piero Angela through RAI, the Italian state TV network, to compliment him on his book and to ask him what he thought of starting a committee like CSICOP in Italy.

It was summer and so I went on vacation with my parents, forgetting about the letters. When I got back I had a beautiful surprise: two letters were waiting for me in the mailbox, one was from Piero Angela and the other from James Randi! I was beside myself. Both congratulated me for my precocious interest in these subjects and for my critical approach and both hinted at something very interesting: yes, there was an idea of starting an Italian committee of skeptics. Angela had tried to do it about ten years earlier, right after his TV series on parapsychology and the publication of his book, but had not been able to transform the good will and support of the academic world into a viable project. Now he wanted to have another go at it, and was planning a meeting in Turin with all the Italian subscribers to the *Skeptical Inquirer* to see if something could be made of it. Randi said that he was coming to Italy to help Angela, his friend, found such a group, and he was looking forward to meeting me. In fact, he added, he had found some rare books on Geller and Houdini which he was going to bring me!

I could not believe it: just a few minutes before I had been a dreamer and now these people that I admired so much were talking to me like I was a peer.

I awaited in trepidation the day of the meeting, which took place in October 1988 in a Turin restaurant. Angela recognized me as soon as I entered the restaurant, maybe because I was the youngest there. Excited, I listened to him as he explained his ideas on the group of skeptics that he wished to create. He said that Randi could not be there because he had recently had minor surgery that prevented his traveling. He assured me, however, that Randi would certainly come to Italy in about a month for a new meeting.

Finally, the day of Randi's arrival in Italy came. I brought along a copy of his book *The Truth About Uri Geller*, hoping to have it signed, and a copy of the letters he had written to me: just in case he couldn't remember who I was. However, the moment I stepped forward, Angela introduced me. Randi smiled and shook my hand. He then opened his briefcase and took from it the books he had brought all the way from the United States for me. We started talking about séances and David Copperfield's illusions.

I had great expectations before meeting Randi and I was not disappointed. He was just as dynamic and charismatic as he seemed from his books and from what people like Angela had told me.

The meeting ran late and I realized that my chance to speak with Randi again was quickly waning. The following day he had to be in Rome with Piero Angela to tape some TV shows and then he would have to fly back to the United States. I wondered when I would see him again. Somehow I found the courage to tell Randi that I would love to go to Rome with them. Both Randi and Angela liked the idea and invited me to be their guest. Again, I was amazed, but I still didn't know what was coming.

I sat between Randi and Angela on my first airplane ride and then spent three beautiful days in Rome with them. I went to the RAI studios, saw for the first time how TV shows were produced, and even played Randi's accomplice for a particular illusion he was going to perform live. We also paid a visit to Silvan, Italy's greatest magician and another of my

Fig. I.1. The author and James Randi in Rome,
a few days after their first meeting. (Massimo Polidoro Collection)

boyhood heroes. On the last day of Randi's stay in Italy we went for dinner at Piero Angela's home in the beautiful hills of Rome. When the other guests left, Randi and Angela left for some private talking and I chatted for a while with Piero's son, Alberto, then a paleontologist and today a familiar figure on Italian TV.

"Massimo, could you join us?" asked Randi from another room.

"You know," said Angela, when I sat down on a couch in front of them, "I have been talking with Randi; I had asked him to look closely at you during these three days; you appear to be very smart and I wanted to know if it is worthwhile to help you. Randi told me that you have proved to be quite alert and can do some good reasoning." Now I understood all those little puzzles and tricks that Randi had asked me to solve.

"Our proposal is this," continued Angela. "What would you think of going to the U.S. with Randi, to become his apprentice and learn to investigate psychic powers? Oh, and of course I would sponsor your trip.

... Don't consider this a gift; I see it as an investment. You don't have to answer now, but what do you think?"

It was like a genie had appeared from Aladdin's lamp and asked: "Would you like to transform your dreams into reality?"

I am sure you can guess what my answer was.

EXPLORING PSYCHIC POWERS

My apprenticeship with Randi started immediately, in the most intense way possible. During the first seven days I spent with him we visited Germany, Austria, France, and England: sometimes to attend a congress, to visit some mysterious place (Stonehenge, the Père-Lachaise Cemetery), or to tape for a TV special. I was grateful for that TV show, because it gave me an opportunity to be involved in the experimental examination of a series of psychic claims.

The program was titled "Exploring Psychic Powers Live!" and it was going to be aired on June 7, 1989, from Los Angeles, on the Fox Network, and live in many other places as well (Europe, Australia, Canada, and South America).

A publicity campaign a few months before that date was started and, among other things, a lot of flyers were printed and distributed in various cities. "We're looking for a few good psychics," said the front page, and Randi's eyes stared at the reader. "Does someone in your city have what it takes to claim this check?" continued the flyer inside. The check was signed by Randi for the sum of $100,000 and was payable to anyone who could demonstrate genuine psychic powers under controlled conditions (see figs. I.2 and I.3).

When we reached Los Angeles the selection had already taken place and the claimants reduced to twelve. The scientific commission that was going to evaluate the performances of the psychics included Stanley Krippner, then president of the Parapsychological Association, and Ray Hyman, a statistician, psychologist, and one of the best critical experts in parapsychology.

Fig. I.2. "We are looking for a few good psychics" says the cover of this promotional leaflet produced for the "Exploring Psychic Powers Live!" TV show. Randi's watching you. (Massimo Polidoro Collection)

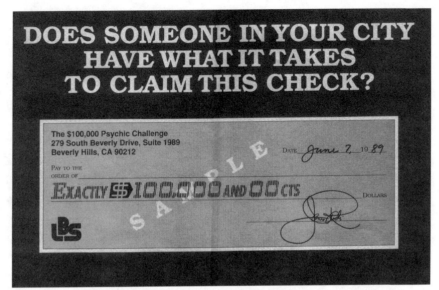

Fig. I.3. The inside of the leaflet, with a reproduction of the
$100,000 check that was going to be awarded to anyone
who could prove his psychic powers. (Massimo Polidoro Collection)

The first claimant was an astrologer, Joseph Meriwether, who claimed he was able to guess correctly the astrological sign of a person if he had the chance to speak to him or her for only a few minutes. He was presented with twelve people one by one, each with a different astrological sign and all within three years of the same age. Meriwether was obviously not allowed to ask questions regarding their birth dates, and all subjects were asked to remove any object (rings, chains, badges, and so on) that would indicate their astrological sign. In the TV studio there were twelve big posters with all zodiacal signs and, during the show, each person was asked to sit in front of the sign that Meriwether thought was correct. By previous agreement, if ten of the people were assigned to their actual signs, Meriwether would win $100,000. The late Bill Bixby, who was cohosting the show with Randi, asked that if any were not seated in front of their correct sign, to stand up and come forward. All twelve stood up; Meriwether had scored zero matches.

It was then time for Barbara Martin, a psychic who claimed to be able to read auras. The experiment designed to test this claim was quite original: since Martin claimed that auras surround the body for a "thickness" of at least five inches, volunteers were placed, unseen by the psychic, behind some large screens. All ten subjects had been chosen by Martin as having a clearly visible aura and she had agreed in advance that the auras would be visible above the screens: this way she would be able to tell whether or not a person was standing behind each screen.

It was then randomly decided how many of the subjects actually stood behind the screens, which were numbered one through ten. It was calculated that, just by chance, she could guess five out of ten correctly. To demonstrate genuine psychic powers, she had to guess at least eight correctly. Martin slowly studied the front of each screen and then proclaimed that a person was standing behind each and every screen. A show of hands revealed that someone was behind only four of them.

Forrest Bayes, a dowser, claimed he could locate water even when this was inside a bottle and the bottle sealed in a cardboard box. He was presented with twenty numbered and sealed boxes and each box was placed under a small wooden bridge on which Bayes would walk and try to feel the presence or absence of water through his divining rod. At the end of the procedure he announced that eight boxes contained water: in fact, only five did.

Another quite clever experiment was designed to test the claims of Sharon McLaren-Straz, a psychometric psychic. In psychometry, a psychic is said to receive all kinds of personal information and details about the owner of an object just by holding the object. In order to avoid vague and ambiguous statements by the psychic, which would be extremely difficult to evaluate, a variation of the test was suggested, on which the psychic promptly agreed. She was presented with twelve watches and twelve keys, all mixed up. She had to match the watches with the keys belonging to the same owner. By prior agreement, she had to match nine out of twelve correctly to win. She succeeded in matching only two sets.

Furthermore, throughout the program a classic ESP test was being performed: psychic Valerie Swan sat at a table for the whole two hours, trying to guess the identity of Zener cards (a set of 250 cards, each with one of five

Fig. I.4. Massimo Polidoro and James Randi in 1989,
on the "Exploring Psychic Powers Live!" set.
(Massimo Polidoro Collection)

specific symbols: a circle, a plus sign, wavy lines, a square, or a star) on which an experimenter was concentrating. Out of the 250 trials, she had agreed that she had to get 82 correct calls to win the $100,000. Her final score was 50—the exact number that would be expected by chance!

The show also had its *coup de theatre*. Just a few days before going on air, the producers revealed to Randi that a surprise guest had been invited on the program: Uri Geller. This would have been fine if he had allowed his claimed powers to be tested, like the other psychics. However, Geller agreed to participate on the show only if he was allowed to promote himself without having to prove anything. When he heard about this, Randi was ready to quit the program, but agreed to remain on the condition that, during the show, he was allowed to reproduce each and every one of Geller's demonstrations, to show the audience that anyone could do the same things.

Geller bent a key, deflected a compass's needle, and made some radish seeds germinate in the palm of his hand. Then Randi repeated exactly the same demonstrations under the same circumstances. For his finale, however, Geller announced that he was going to shock the whole wide world. He was going to fix broken watches and house appliances directly in the homes of the viewers who, by the way, could announce the success of the experiment by calling the show (a 900 number, of course). A couple of calls from viewers whose stopped watches had started again were aired and Geller challenged Randi to explain the phenomenon.

Randi smiled and, without addressing Geller directly, asked the director of the show to air a tape that he had brought with him. In that tape you could see a certain "young psychic from Italy" who, during a live radio show taped only a couple of days before in Phoenix, Arizona, was receiving calls from listeners who had their broken watches fixed. As you may have guessed, I was that "psychic" and, as we shall see later in this book, the watches had not been fixed thanks to some supernatural intervention which I could not produce, but because of a very worldly mechanical effect.

Just one month after my departure from Italy, I thus found myself face to face with my fallen idol, but standing beside a true hero of ration-

Fig. I.5. James Randi. (James Randi Educational Foundation)

Fig. I.6. (From left) Piero Angela, James Randi, and Massimo Polidoro at the 1996 First World Skeptics Conference in Buffalo, New York.

ality. When the show ended, Geller approached me and applauded me on the way I had bent a spoon during the show (a feat that, thanks to Randi, I had finally been able to master). I thanked him and said that I was just a student: he was the real master of this kind of thing. He acknowledged my thanks with a wink and then he promised that, one day, we would sit at a table to chat as old friends.

I heard from Geller again a few years later, when he had his lawyers inform me that he would take me to court if I did not cease immediately to be critical of his demonstrations.[2]

Notwithstanding this kind of threat, neither Randi nor I have ever stopped saying what we think about pseudoscientific claims made by people who play with the feelings, health, and lives of those who turn to them in desperation.

Those days in Los Angeles represented my initiation into the scientific investigation of claims of the paranormal; a practice that, sometimes, inevitably became what Carl Sagan aptly called the "fine art of baloney detection." I spent over a year in the United States studying and working with Randi, then returned to Italy. There I worked to have the Italian Committee for the Investigation of Claims of the Paranormal (CICAP) grow while I studied to earn a degree in psychology. During those years, I also led dozens of other investigations and experiments on paranormal claims (most of which are collected in the fifteen books I have published so far in Italy).

In the following pages you will find a selection of some of these studies and investigations; in a couple of these I have been helped by my good friend Luigi Garlaschelli. Luigi, or Gigi as we call him, is a chemist at the University of Pavia and has become one of the most accomplished critical experts in the field of "miracles" and "supernatural phenomena." Among other things, Garlaschelli, along with colleagues Sergio Della Sala and Franco Ramaccini, developed a close approximation of the substance known as the "Blood of St. Januarius," which liquifies during religious ceremonies in Naples, and published his results in *Nature* magazine.[3] We have worked together in countless investigations during the past ten years or so: traveling all over Italy and abroad in search of strange phenomena, visiting haunted houses, attending sacred and mysterious rites, attending séances, testing the claims of all sorts of psychics, from astrologers, healers, telepaths, seers, and dowsers, to firewalkers and those who sleep on beds of nails!

NOTES

1. Piero Angela, *Viaggio nel mondo del paranormale* (Journey in the World of the Paranormal) (Rome: Garzanti Editore, 1978), back cover. My translation.

2. What had apparently upset him was an investigation I did on one of his TV appearances, where it was possible to see something that one was probably not supposed to see (see chap. 13).

3. To read more about Garlaschelli's work, go to his Web site at http://chifis.unipv.it/garlaschelli/.

PART 1

THE PSYCHOLOGY
OF
PSYCHIC DECEPTION

CHAPTER ONE

IT'S ALL
IN THE MIND

On the Mechanisms of Deception
in Psychic Fraud

*I*t frequently happens that the media introduces to the public extraordinary people who claim to possess some fantastic psychic ability. They may read minds, move objects only by thinking, read newspapers with their fingertips, levitate, or perform other marvels. Often, in such cases, the psychic is accompanied by some sort of scientific validation, which means that one or more scientists have observed him or her under scientific conditions and have reached the conclusion that his or her powers are genuine.

A problem arises when one examines the last 130 years in the history of psychical research. A striking fact that emerges, in fact, is that there are countless examples of cases in which scientists, even celebrated ones, have been duped by some clever trickster.[1] The obvious question, then, is: Are scientists always the best-suited persons to conduct investigations in the area of psychical research?

They most certainly are, but they should not work alone in this field, especially when they deal with subjects apparently gifted with some fantastic ability. As Martin Gardner clearly pointed out: "Scientists are the easiest persons in the world to fool. It's not hard to understand why. In their laboratories the equipment is just what it seems. There are no hidden mirrors or secret compartments or concealed magnets. If an assistant puts chemical *A* in a beaker he does not (usually) surreptitiously switch it for chemical *B*. The thinking of a scientist is rational, based on a lifetime of experience with a rational world. But the methods of magic are irrational and totally outside a scientist's experience."[2]

For this reason, scientists involved in the examination of psychics should seek the advice of those expert in the techniques and psychology of deception, who are usually competent magicians themselves.

The aim of this chapter is to better acquaint the reader with the many psychological stratagems used by fake psychics to convince their audience that they really possess psychic powers. To begin with, we will consider an account of a session with a fictional, self-proclaimed psychic, Ugo Tomato. Although Tomato does not exist in reality, the account is based on various, similar accounts of actual psychic sessions—sometimes the descriptions have been reported word for word. This exercise will make it possible to dissect the account, attempting to understand what often happens during such "experiments."

A Session with a Psychic

Ugo Tomato is a twenty-eight-year-old Italian who achieved quite a success by demonstrating his psychic abilities in telepathy and psychokinesis. He appeared to be able to accomplish extraordinary feats: move objects without touching them, bend forks and nails, read messages sealed in boxes, dematerialize his body, and so on.

In an experimental session for a group of scientists in Pavia, Italy, Tomato recently gave some examples of his powers. After stating that he was tired, thus excusing himself in case something did not work, he explained that how well his powers work depends on the mental attitude of his audience. If people are with him, he said, all sorts of things happen; if they are not with him, nothing happens.

Tomato claims he first noticed his strange abilities after experiencing a severe electric shock as a child. He kept his powers to himself, but continued practicing them and finally decided he should use them to make his living. Inevitably, he started to attract the attention of parapsychologists, who were interested in studying his singular abilities.

Tomato asked for metal objects, like keys, cutlery, and pens. He gathered many such objects on a tray, started to pick up one or another, then selected a key. He held the key in his fist and concentrated hard. After a couple of minutes he opened his hand but nothing had happened. He was encouraged by the experimenters and agreed to try a different experiment. He asked a researcher to make a simple drawing on a pad, while he turned his back to her. He also asked the others present in the room to look at her drawing and concentrate on it without whispering what it was.

When the drawing was finished, he asked for the pad to be turned face down and then he turned back again. He closed his eyes, concentrated, and drew on his pad a simple geometric house. The researcher turned up her drawing which also showed a simple house. Tomato appeared to be enthusiastic about his success and the researchers also were impressed by it.

A new telepathic test was suggested. A previously prepared drawing, sealed in an envelope, was presented to Tomato. Would he be able to guess it? He drew a simple sun, but canceled the test when he noticed that the drawing (a sun, in fact) could be seen through the envelope. His honesty was, nonetheless, appreciated.

Finding a pack of cards lying around, he asked someone to shuffle them, since he said he was not very good at this sort of thing. He then asked the researcher to try to divide the pack of cards into two piles, red and black, without looking at them. At that moment, he stood up, as if he felt something. He turned to the tray with the metal objects and looked through it to see if anything had happened to the keys. But nothing had.

The card experiment was resumed. The cards were dealt in two piles, face down. However, when turned over, it could be seen that they were almost perfectly divided in blacks and reds. Tomato congratulated the researcher who had dealt the cards since, he felt, he must have strong psychic abilities, too.

He then looked again at the tray and appeared to be surprised. A couple of keys and a spoon in it were bent. Tomato explained that sometimes things happen even when he is not paying attention. Probably, he said, some kind of "energy" liberated during the successful experiment with the cards influenced the keys somehow. As for the nature of his powers, he could not say exactly, but he felt they came from "an outside source," "some kind of external intelligence."

He then tried again to bend a spoon but without success. This, he said, showed that it was not a trick which would always work. He asked for some metal object to be put close to the spoon and then tried again. This time, the spoon bent upwards. He then held a fork which melted into two pieces. The experimenters were quite impressed with what they had seen.

Tomato repeated that he was genuine and asked those present to search him, in case someone thought he had some hidden instrument with which he could cause the bendings. Before he left, a last phenomenon occurred. A noise was heard, caused by a small toy falling to the floor, apparently out of nowhere. One of the researchers recognized it as a toy, long thought lost, that belonged to his child.

There have already been various attempts to describe the psychological stratagems used by charlatans to convince experimenters that they really have psychic powers.[3] This work, then, will attempt to summarize and, when possible, amplify all these previous works in a singular list of psychological stratagems. There are at least twenty-six different strategies, divided into five main processes: (1) how to be believable; (2) how to limit and thwart the controls; (3) how to perform seeming miracles; (4) what to do in case something goes wrong; and (5) how to distort memories.

How to Be Believable

The Psychic Creates a Believable Claim

To avoid arousing too many doubts in the observers, the psychic usually tries to present a claim that, although being paranormal, can be considered true by those ready to believe in this sort of thing. For example, in a telepathy test, where the psychic has to guess the identity of hidden cards, if the psychic correctly indicates a number of cards slightly above that expected from chance, it is considered a success. Thus, a pseudopsychic who finds a way to gain information on the cards by normal means may decide to correctly identify a number above that expected from chance but never all of the cards, since this might look too suspicious. In the example above, Ugo Tomato had a researcher divide a pack of cards into two piles. This is a standard magic trick by which a person other than the performer can divide the cards into blacks and reds without realizing how he did it. To make it believable as a psychic demonstration, however, Tomato had to mess up the demonstration a bit, by having some wrong cards appear in the two piles.

The Powers Come from a Force Outside the Psychic

Usually, psychics claim that the powers they possess are given to them by supernatural forces not under their control. Mediums usually say that it is the spirits who guide them and suggest the ideal conditions for their manifestations (namely, sitting still in a dark room). Astrologer Jean Dixon claimed that her prophecies came from God; self-styled psychic Uri Geller stated that his powers came from a flying saucer called "Spectra." In this way, tricksters like Ugo Tomato can impose their conditions on the tests without appearing to be artificial: "*They* want it so," they explain. Also, this allows prophets, for example, to make any kind of wild prophecy without worrying too much about it being correct or not. As James Randi pointed out, one of the "rules" of astrologers and the like is the following, "Credit God with your success, and blame yourself for any incorrect interpretations of his divine messages. This way, detractors have to fight God."[4]

The Psychic Appears Modest and Humble

A psychic will make sure his voice sounds sincere and he constantly apologizes "if nothing works." This inevitably makes the audience watching him want him to succeed. In this way, as in the Tomato example, an experimenter may feel motivated to help him and inadvertently overlook one control or another.

The Psychic Pretends to Be Amazed by His Own Powers

This is one of the best ways to lend authenticity to a demonstration. At the beginning of the test the psychic appears unsure of his success in a certain experiment. He may claim to be tired, like Tomato. This is a direct consequence of the second strategy; since his powers come from a force outside him, the psychic does not know if they always work. However, when the experiment works, the obvious reaction is to be amazed and thrilled by the results.

The Consistency of the Phenomenon with Previously Reported Ones Appears as Strong Evidence of Its Genuineness

In the heyday of spiritualism, it frequently happened that "materialized figures" were discovered to be the same mediums, or their accomplices, dressed up as ghosts. Instead of dismissing materializations as mere tricks, every time a new medium was caught being disguised as a "ghost," believers considered it a further proof of the authenticity of the phenomenon. "Since this always happens," spiritualists reasoned, "there must be a reason for it." A theory was then put forward, according to which, when a spirit wants to materialize, "he needs to borrow organic matter from the material world, and thus he takes it from the medium."[5]

The Psychic May Produce a Claim
that the Individual Wants to Believe

A psychic may exploit people's physical and emotional needs. Wiseman notes, for example, how a pseudopsychic may claim to possess psychic healing powers, in the hope of motivating an ill individual to believe in him.[6] Also, mediums may exploit the need for comfort in individuals who have recently suffered a bereavement, by promising some form of communication with deceased friends and relatives.

Participants Are Credited with Paranormal Powers

Another strong way to involve participants and make them feel motivated is for the psychic to claim that they too possess paranormal powers. He can accomplish this by presenting a demonstration in which the participant appears to be in charge of the results while, in reality, it is the psychic who controls the game. An Italian psychic, Gustavo A. Rol, used to present a demonstration with playing cards, in which a spectator appeared to be able to separate black cards from red ones without looking (the same demonstration as in the Tomato story above). This is one of the classics of magic. It is a trick, invented by magician Paul Curry, called "Out of This World," in which the performer only has to briefly touch the cards in a very natural way for it to work. People who witness this trick inevitably go away convinced that they were the only ones who handled the cards and got the astonishing result. Randi comments, "Bear in mind that people so flattered are apt to get a bit gushy and relax just a mite more than ordinarily. Blame for a failure can be assigned to them by the same token."[7]

How to Limit and Thwart the Controls

The Result of a Demonstration Is Not Stated in Advance

This is one of the oldest rules of magicians: never say in advance what you are going to do. How useful to a fake psychic this rule can be is very clear. If an audience does not know what is going to happen, they do not know what to look for, and this makes it impossible to apply useful controls or postulate possible normal solutions until the demonstration is over—when, usually, it is too late.

The Original Goal Is Switched and the New Goal Is Accepted

Whenever the experimenter knows what kind of demonstration the psychic is going to present, the psychic can still escape the controls by presenting a slightly different demonstration from the one intended. An experimenter, for example, may ask a psychic to break a spoon with her powers (a feat which the latter is known for) and hand her a checked spoon; the psychic, however, bends the spoon instead of breaking it. This switching of goals can be accepted by the experimenter, since the phenomenon is quite similar. Breaking a spoon, however, requires a specially "gaffed" spoon, while bending it only requires special manipulatory skills and can be accomplished almost instantaneously.

The Psychic Creates Chaos

This is the golden rule which allows the psychic to divert attention away from the requested test. The psychic may: start an experiment and then stop it because he lacks the needed "concentration"; start a different demonstration then stop for a while to "recharge" and talk a lot, then return again to the original one; and so on. In the Tomato story, this ruse is quite evident. The psychic starts an experiment with cards, but suddenly stands up for no apparent reason and examines the cutlery on a tray: nothing has happened. He then returns to the cards and later it is discovered that some of the spoons on the tray have bent. Using actions or suggestions to relax observation of the original intended action, then, the psychic may be able to divert the attention of the observers. In this way, he can perform the so-called dirty work (that is, the trick) for a demonstration, while the attention of the participants is concentrated on a different feat. At the other extreme, still with the object of distracting the observers' attention, the psychic can make use of a strategy labeled "monotony": in brief, he takes a very long time before attempting any form of trickery, thus lessening the individual's vigilance.[8]

The Psychic Exploits Controls Applied at Inappropriate Times

Very often, the psychic may be able to prepare the trick for a fake demonstration long before the experiment starts. For example, he may be invited onto a television show where he knows he will be asked to duplicate the drawing sealed in an envelope. By getting to the television station early, he may be able to get close to the envelope (even only for a few seconds) and, by means of various techniques available to magicians, get access to its content. In this case, even before the show starts, the psychic already knows what drawing is in the envelope and, when he is on the air, he only has to act the role of the uncertain psychic, who attempts a guess and then acts excited when the envelope is opened and the drawings are seen to correspond. In the story of Ugo Tomato, the materialization from nowhere of the toy could have been accomplished by similar means. For example, the psychic may be picked up and taken to the laboratory by an experimenter who uses his own car; in this case, the psychic has only to reach under the seat of the car, while unseen, and may often find lost objects, like earrings or toys. A long time after this ride, the psychic (or his accomplice) may throw in the air the object while people are distracted, and claim it is an "apport."[9]

The Psychic Exploits Ineffective or Removable Controls

During the 1970s, when self-proclaimed psychic Uri Geller became famous, there were many imitators, especially children, who claimed that they too could bend metal objects with the power of their minds. A common test used by parapsychologists in such cases was to present the child with a test tube, inside which was a piece of metal; the tube was usually closed (though not sealed) with a cork. It was very easy for the children to take advantage of a moment when the experimenter was distracted to remove the cork, bend the metal, and close the tube; it only takes a few seconds. It should be noted that no one has ever been able to bend a piece of metal (or anything else) inside a properly sealed test tube.

The Subject Is Allowed to
Suggest Tests and Conditions for Tests

By suggesting test conditions, the psychic can set limits within which he can operate. In the 1870s the celebrated medium Daniel Dunglas Home became very popular for his spectacular feats and for the fact that he was never caught cheating (as opposed to all of his colleagues). This is not surprising, knowing the conditions under which Home operated. He did not subject himself to any kind of restraint or control, although sometimes he made it appear that he did. Actually, it was he who dictated the conditions. He could choose the participants in his séances, and turn away those he felt were too skeptical. He decided what was going to happen and in what kind of light. And of course he justified his impositions by claiming that it was the spirits who wanted it so.[10]

HOW TO PERFORM SEEMING MIRACLES

The Psychic Appears Incapable of Fraud

To induce in the observers the idea that a psychic is performing real miracles, he first needs to convince his audience that he cannot and, above all, *would not* want to cheat. Some experts of the paranormal are convinced that fakers possess a sort of "physique du role." A faker, according to such experts, should be: adult, extremely intelligent, and well educated.

If he does not fit this idea of a trickster, then he must be real. There have been countless cases in which children, peasants, or uneducated people have been credited with real psychic powers only because it was thought that they could not possibly be able to fool a cultured person. The truth is quite different, as psychical history shows. It may be sufficient to remind the reader that the whole Spiritualism movement was started by two little girls, Margaret and Kate Fox, who snapped their toes to create noises that were quickly attributed to the spirits. It was only after forty years, when Spiritualism had gathered millions of followers, that the Fox sisters revealed the hoax and, as expected, very few acknowledged that they had been fooled by such simple tricks.[11]

The Psychic Fails to Pass Tests Designed to Determine If the Necessary Skill Is Present

James Randi gives a clear example of this: "In France, recently, Jean-Pierre Girard was tested for strength by his mentor, Charles Crussard, to see if he could physically bend the bars that he seemed to be bending psychically. Crussard reported that Girard was not able to do so, no matter how hard he tried!"[12] The subject's failure to pass such a test should prove him honest to the experimenter. In passing, it may be noted that later Girard was proved to have used trickery in his act.

The Psychic Appears to Have No Motivation to Deceive

A common belief among certain parapsychologists is that a person may decide to become a fake psychic because he seeks money or fame. No other motivation is considered to be sufficient. Thus, if the psychic does not ask for money, and does not look for fame, the fact is presented as strong proof of the genuineness of his powers. In Italy, the already mentioned Rol never asked for money for his performances and did not look for publicity in the media. The facts that he was already rich and that, thanks to his private demonstrations, he had become very powerful and almost a cult figure among various artists, intellectuals, and scientists

(Federico Fellini, for example, was said to be one of his best friends and admirers), did not seem a sufficient motivation for cheating to Italian experts in the paranormal.[13]

The Psychic Uses Familiar Objects

The use of everyday objects, sometimes borrowed, greatly enhances the impact of an effect, as illustrated in the Tomato episode: first, because an everyday object, better if borrowed, easily convinces an audience that it is authentic and not gimmicked in any way; and second, because the audience can identify with an everyday object and will automatically assume that the item is free from deception. As Harris notes, "Many magicians use gimmicked apparatus for certain effects. Because the apparatus used consists of natural looking objects, handled every day by most of us, we do not suspect that there could be gimmickery involved. To further enhance this psychological subtlety all the magician needs to do is borrow his gimmicked wares from an accomplice planted in the audience."[14]

The Psychic Uses Simple Methods

The best way for a psychic never to be caught cheating is to avoid using gimmicks (i.e., special apparatus that allows some kind of trickery). Instead, it is better to rely on simple methods, based only on psychological deceptions. For this reason, mediums that were caught hiding cheesecloth (generally used to fake ectoplasm) in their clothes or luggage had a hard time justifying themselves, while mental mediums, who maybe relied on psychological techniques like "cold reading," were far better off.[15] A very famous trick, used by some psychics to convince an audience they can read minds, relies on this kind of psychological deception. The psychic asks the audience to think of a simple geometrical figure and then to think of a second simple geometrical figure inside it: he then draws what he "receives" from the audience and, most of the time, he is correct. The trick lies in the fact that, given this kind of instruction, most of the time people will think of a circle inside a triangle or vice versa.

The Psychic Never Uses the Same Method
to Fabricate the Same Kind of Phenomena

An old dodge of conjurors is: "Never repeat a trick; or, if you do, use a different method." The reason is that, when someone watches a trick for the first time, he does not know what to look for and is easily deceived. This advantage is lost, however, if the trick is performed a second time. The only solution, in this case, is to use a different method to accomplish the same result. It is generally not known that there are, for example, many different ways to move a table or to bend a spoon, each one suitable for certain kinds of conditions.

The Great Fake Psychics Are Improvisers

A really good pseudopsychic is able to produce phenomena in almost any situation. A quick mind and a good knowledge of the techniques and psychology of deception are all that are needed. Sometimes, only a quick mind is sufficient. In one of the early tests of telepathy, in 1882, fake psychic G. A. Smith and his accomplice, Douglas Blackburn, were able to fool some researchers from the Society for Psychical Research. In a 1911 confession, Blackburn described how they had to think fast and frequently invent new ways for faking telepathy demonstrations. Once, for example, Smith had been swathed in blankets to avoid the exchange of signals between him and Blackburn. Smith had to guess the identity of a drawing and Blackburn secretly drew it on a cigarette paper. When Smith exclaimed, "I have it," and projected his right hand from beneath the blanket, Blackburn had transferred the cigarette paper to the tube of the brass projector on the pencil he was using. When Smith asked for a pencil, Blackburn gave him his. Under the blanket, Smith had concealed a luminous painted slate, which in the dense darkness gave sufficient light to show the figure on the cigarette paper. Smith only needed to copy the drawing.[16]

Regarding fraud detection, magician Harry Houdini noted, "It is manifestly impossible to detect and duplicate all the feats attributed to fraudulent mediums who do not scruple at outraging propriety and even decency to gain their ends. . . . Again, many of the effects produced by them are impulsive, spasmodic, done on the spur of the moment, inspired or promoted by attending circumstances, and could not be duplicated by themselves."[17]

What to Do in Case Something Goes Wrong

Failure Is Proof of Genuine Paranormal Powers

It is a general conviction among some psychic researchers that "if it is a trick it always works." Thanks to this false belief, then, a pseudopsychic is not only excused when something in his demonstration does not work, but is credited with real psychic powers *because* it did not work. It is claimed, in fact, that this kind of phenomena only work in a sporadic and unpredictable fashion, and the subject cannot produce them on command or on a regular basis. A pseudopsychic, then, has a great advantage over a straight magician; the latter must always perform "miracles" to avoid being booed off stage; the former, however, is allowed to "pass" when conditions are not ideal or an audience is "too skeptical."

Skeptics Produce "Negative Vibrations"

The subject does not do well when persons with a skeptical attitude are nearby. In consequence, phenomena are inhibited unless the skeptics can be turned away. Thus people who could watch a demonstration and not be biased toward belief are turned away. As has frequently been shown, believers tend to distort their memories of a psychic demonstration, while skeptics tend to correctly recall a demonstration, even when it appears to support the existence of paranormal powers.[18]

Any Trickery Detected May Be
Attributed to the Subject's Desire to Please

One of the greatest mediums that ever lived, Eusapia Palladino, was also, possibly, the one most often caught at cheating (see chapter 3). However, her experimenters were quick to explain that she could not help herself, and the fault rested on the observers who did not prevent her from doing so. Of course, this is an immensely powerful tool for a fake psychic. It means that when he is not caught cheating, the phenomenon must be real. However, when he is caught it is not his fault, since he has a "compulsion to cheat" to please the observers. Some other psychic researchers, in trying to explain undoubted fraud by a psychic, instead of admitting the unreliability of that psychic, and rejecting all previous work done with him, prefer to believe that the psychic acted "unconsciously."

Any Trickery Detected May Be Considered Proof of Genuine Powers

Sometimes an experimenter notices, in a test with a medium or a psychic, some quite suspicious movement or action that could help the psychic to perform his feats by normal means. However, in many such cases, experimenters decide that this is further proof of the reality of the phenomenon. They simply explain that, since the ruse appeared too crude for it to be mistaken (i.e., there was no doubt that it was a move used to fake a demonstration), the psychic must have made it involuntarily, since it would have been too easy to spot it.

How to Distort Memories

Many researchers have shown that eyewitness testimony in relation to psychic demonstrations is generally unreliable and can lead to wrong conclusions. There are many factors that can influence the reliability of the eyewitness testimony, and the pseudopsychic can take advantage of this situation.[19]

The Psychic Is Elusive

The claims are always vague and never specific in advance of a demonstration. As said above, this makes it impossible for the observer to know what to look for and, futhermore, after the demonstration it will be impossible to remember exactly what went on, especially if the demonstrations took place in "well-designed chaos" (see above).

The Psychic Often Recapitulates
What Happened to Alter Memories

If the psychic declares that he never touched a key when it bent, that's what people will remember.[20] It will be completely forgotten, for example, that the psychic moved the key from one spot to another, because that movement is considered insignificant. In reality, that may be the moment when the trick took place. Also, a psychic may perform the same demonstration several times, using a different technique each time. Statistician Perci Diaconis, in explaining the "bundle of sticks phenomenon," noted, "the weak points of one performance are ruled out because they were clearly not present during other performances. The bundle of sticks is stronger than any single stick."[21]

CONCLUSIONS

After this review of the various strategies used by fake psychics to simulate real paranormal powers, you may feel better defended against psychic fraud. However, you should not think that you are now immune to fraud, since this is not possible. Even great experts in psychic deception are not totally immune to this kind of fraud. What one can do, however, is to use this knowledge in a useful way to examine mysterious stories of psychic demonstrations. As a start, you could begin by reading again the account of the experiments with the fictional Ugo Tomato and see if you can spot his methods. Then you could direct your attention to real descriptions of claimed psychic feats. This kind of material will probably be seen with different eyes now, and many previously overlooked details may assume a new meaning.

NOTES

Adapted, with permission from Sergio Della Sala (ed.), *Mind Myths* (Chichester, U.K.: John Wiley & Sons, 1998). Copyright 1998 by John Wiley & Sons, Ltd.

I would like to thank Prof. Sergio Della Sala and Dr. Luigi Garlaschelli for their kind help and assistance.

1. See Harry Houdini, *A Magician Among the Spirits* (1926; reprint, New York: Arno Press, 1972); John Mulholland, *Beware Familiar Spirits* (1938; reprint, New York: Charles Scribner's Sons, 1979); James Randi, *The Truth about Uri Geller* (Amherst, N.Y.: Prometheus Books, 1982), and *Flim-Flam!* (Amherst, N.Y.: Prometheus Books, 1982); Martin Gardner, *Science: Good, Bad and Bogus* (Amherst, N.Y.: Prometheus Books, 1981); R. Brandon, *The Spiritualists: The Passion for the Occult in the Nineteenth and Twentieth Centuries* (New York: Alfred A. Knopf, 1983); T. H. Hall, *The Enigma of Daniel Home* (Amherst, N.Y.: Prometheus Books, 1984) and *The Medium and the Scientist* (Amherst, N.Y.: Prometheus Books, 1984); and my *Viaggio tra gli spiriti* (Journey Among the Spirits) (Carnago, Va.: Sugarco, 1995); *L'illusione del paranormale* (The Paranormal Illusion) (Padova: Franco Muzzio Editore, 1998); *Il grande Houdini* (The Great Houdini) (Casale Monferrato: Piemme, 2001); *Il trucco c'è* (Here's the Trick!) (with Mariano Tomatis) (Padova: CICAP, 2003).

2. Gardner, *Science: Good, Bad and Bogus*, p. 92.

3. See U. Fuller, *Confessions of a Psychic* (Teaneck, N.J.: Karl Fulves, 1975) and *Further Confessions of a Psychic* (Teaneck, N.J.: Karl Fulves, 1980); Randi, *Truth about Uri Geller* and *Flim-Flam!*; David Marks and Richard Kamman, *The Psychology of the Psychic* (Amherst, N.Y.: Prometheus Books, 1980); Ben Harris, *Gellerism Revealed* (Calgary, Alb.: Micky Hades International, 1980); and Richard Wiseman, "Modeling the Stratagems of Psychic Fraud," *European Journal of Parapsychology* 10 (1994): 31–44.

4. James Randi, *The Mask of Nostradamus* (New York: Scribner's, 1990).

5. A. C. Holms, *The Facts of Psychic Science* (New York: University Books, 1969).

6. Wiseman, "Modeling the Stratagems of Psychic Fraud," pp. 31–44.

7. Randi, *Flim-Flam!* p. 196.

8. D. Fitzkee, *Magic by Misdirection* (Oakland, Calif.: Magic Ltd., 1945).

9. Fuller, *Further Confessions of a Psychic*.

10. Hall, *The Enigma of Daniel Home*. See also my *Viaggio tra gli spiriti*.

11. Brandon, *The Spiritualists*. See also my *Viaggio tra gli spiriti*.

12. Randi, *Flim-Flam!* p. 37.

13. For a complete critical examination of Rol's performance, see Mariano Tomatis, *Rol: Realtà o Leggenda* (Rol: Reality or Legend?) (Rome: Avverbi, 2003).

14. Harris, *Gellerism Revealed*, p. 11.

15. R. Hyman, "Cold Reading: How to Convince Strangers That You Know All About Them," *Zetetic* 1 (1977): 18–37.

16. D. Blackburn, "Confessions of a Telepathist: Thirty-Year Hoax Exposed," *London Daily News*, September 1, 1911.

17. Harry Houdini, *A Magician Among the Spirits* (New York: Harper & Brothers, 1924; reprint, New York: Arno Press, 1972), p. 245.

18. See W. H. Jones and D. Russell, "The Selective Processing of Belief Disconfirming Information," *European Journal of Social Psychology* 10 (1980): 309–12; Richard Wiseman and R. L. Morris, "Recalling Pseudo-Psychic Demonstrations," *British Journal of Psychology* 86 (1995): 113–25.

19. Richard Wiseman, "Witnesses to the Paranormal: How Reliable?" in *The Encyclopedia of the Paranormal*, ed. G. Stein (Amherst, N.Y.: Prometheus Books, 1996), pp. 829–34.

20. Fuller, *Confessions of a Psychic*.

21. P. Diaconis, "Statistical Problems in ESP Research," in *The Skeptic's Handbook of Parapsychology*, ed. P. Kurtz (Amherst, N.Y.: Prometheus Books, 1985), p. 572.

CHAPTER TWO

WHEN I WAS A PSYCHIC . . . FOR AN HOUR

*T*he psychic looks at us from the television screen and says: "Take out your broken watches and your cutlery and bring them close to the television set. I will try to make something happen in your own homes! The broken watches will start ticking again and the cutlery will bend. Also, look out, because other strange phenomena may happen. The chandelier may swing or the TV may go off. . . ."

The psychic then attempts to make the hands on the TV host's watch move backward, using his "psychic powers." While doing this, he invites the viewers to concentrate on their watches, trying to fix them. Suddenly, on the host's watch we see that the time has gone back two hours! Now it is time to check if something has happened in the homes of the viewers. They are invited to call the TV station and tell their experiences. Phone lines start ringing and miracles are reported with each call: a watch, stopped for many years, now runs perfectly; another one has jumped ahead one hour; a Rolex watch, the whole inside mechanism of which had to be replaced for an estimated cost of nearly $1,000, now works regularly; a clock, broken for twenty-five years and rusty, is behaving strangely: the second hand runs at twice the usual speed and the minute hand goes backward; two watches, still for ten years and declared dead by a watchmaker, now work perfectly; another watch, which had been working perfectly, has now stopped dead; a one-hundred-year-old clock, quiet for many years, now works irregularly; a watch collector has seen three of his stopped watches start working again. Twenty-four more calls follow from people reporting that their broken watches are fixed!

But that's not all: dozens of other people call to say that their spoons, forks, and keys have bent; a glass of water has begun to boil; a TV set has gone off; and much, much, more (see table 1).

The episode described here took place in 1992 when, as a guest on a popular Italian TV show, "L'Istruttoria" (The Inquest), I had a chance to test a theory I was rather curious about.

Posing as a "psychic" with the complicity of the show's host, I intended to duplicate a demonstration that, during the 1970s, had brought fame to a man who claimed to possess real psychic powers: the Israeli Uri Geller.

For a few years, Geller had been able to convince many people, including a few scientists, that he could bend keys and forks, guess drawings closed in sealed envelopes, and predict future events with only the power of his mind; but various investigators could find no scientific basis for his claims.[1]

One of the most convincing performances of this charismatic character was, in fact, the apparent ability to cause strange phenomena to happen directly in the houses of TV viewers; after this happened several times, as dozens of phone calls could testify to each time, the most obvious conclusion for most of the people was that the phenomenon had to be real. Geller could not have so many stooges.*

The paranormal, however, may have nothing to do with this demonstration. The explanation, in fact, could lie more easily in an interesting effect of mass suggestion, as demonstrations by magicians such as Milbourne Christopher and James Randi have shown. This was not the first

---

*A "stooge" in technical magic terms is a hidden accomplice.

TABLE 1. PHENOMENA REPORTED BY VIEWERS OF "L'ISTRUTTORIA" DURING AN HOUR OF BROADCASTING

City	Phenomena	Notes
Cesate (MI)	3 watches restarted	stopped for at least 4 years
Arezzo	a watch runs briefly	stopped for more than 100 years
Senago (MI)	a watch starts again	stopped for two months
Perugia	a clock works again	"broken"
Cagliari	2 watches restarted	stopped for 10 years
Cuneo	watch jumps six hours ahead	it was stopped
Roma	watch restarted	stopped for years
Milano	watch restarted	"broken"
Prov. Parma	a clock runs an hour	broken two years prior
Napoli	a watch runs briefly	stopped for years
Milano	a clock goes backward	stopped for 25 years
Prov. FR	watch runs fast	"broken"
Milano	watch restarted	stopped for 2 years
Bari	a clock runs fast	stopped for 2 years
Alghero	watch (Rolex) restarted	saved on expensive repairs
Prov. MI	two spoons are misplaced	also a stopped watch starts
Fidenza	watch jumps an hour ahead	stopped for months
Napoli	2 watches restarted	stopped for a long time
Roma	a watch restarted	"broken"
Mazzara del Vallo	a key has bent	not the one held in the hand
Catania	watch goes back and forth	stopped for two years
Modena	a bent spoon straightens up	the TV set goes off
Torino	4 pieces of cutlery bend	
Prov. Bari	a fork bends "by itself"	
Imperia	a glass of water "boils"	it had already happened
Cuneo	a spoon bends	a watch is stopped
Trieste	a spoon bends	it had already happened
Napoli	a watch restarts	stopped for a long time
Cagliari	a watch breaks up	
Firenze	nothing happened	
Cagliari	a pendulum-clock has stopped	

time I had posed as a psychic to test this theory. In 1989, James Randi asked me to claim psychic powers on a radio show to demonstrate during the "Exploring Psychic Powers Live!" TV show how anyone could duplicate this phenomenon by the clever use of suggestion. I did as he said, went on the show, and claimed that, while I was talking, incredible things would start happening in the houses of the listeners.

After only five minutes, about twenty people called reporting the strangest things: a television set had turned on all by itself, a cat was behaving strangely, a picture had fallen from the wall, a lamp had exploded, a book on spiritualism had fallen from the table, the whole computer network of a lawyer's office had blown out, and much more.[2]

There was nothing extraordinary about those things; they happen normally but nobody pays much attention or ever thinks that they must be psychic occurrences; however, after the listeners had been alerted by me, any event happening while I was talking was easily going to be interpreted by the most suggestible people as an apparent psychic phenomenon.

PERSUASION IN ACTION

We are obviously facing some of the major principles of persuasion: Robert B. Cialdini has summarized very clearly what they are and how they work.[3] The principles are: the reciprocity principle; the authority factor; the motivation and coherence principle; the shortage principle; the sympathy principle; and the social confirmation principle. What they have in common are: the almost automatic process by which their power can be activated; the consequent easy exploitation of this power by someone who knows how it works; the elegant and parsimonious way by which these tools lend themselves to be used. Let's see how these principles apply to the situations described above.

First of all, the operator sets the stage: that means that he tries to present himself to the public as a believable person. In my case, the speaker told the listeners at the beginning of the radio broadcast that some Italian universities were conducting experiments on my powers; on

TV, I was able to demonstrate my claimed powers by bending and breaking a spoon, by correctly guessing a drawing sealed in an envelope, and by making some radish seeds germinate in my hand. In other words, I had "offered" something solid to the viewers, an apparent, convincing demonstration of extraordinary powers. The reciprocity principle says that we have to reciprocate what somebody presents to us; in this case, the TV viewer, in exchange for my demonstration, could have been led to listen with more willingness to what I had to say.

Furthermore, in both cases my claims were not confuted or doubted by the hosts: both expressed their belief in their reality and pretended they were very puzzled. This way, I was drawing from the authority factor, a principle whose strength has been clearly shown by Stanley Milgram.* Owing to the sense of compliance toward authority, which is profoundly rooted in human beings, a spectator may well have surrendered to the judgment of the hosts and undertaken the same attitude of wonder that they had toward my claims. At this point, the message we wanted to get through, namely, that I had real psychic powers, was already appearing as a consistent hypothesis by a considerable portion of the viewers.

---

*In 1963, Stanley Milgram began a set of experiments which would test the extent to which ordinary people would obey an authority figure, even when the orders conflicted with their individual morals or beliefs. Milgram prepared an environment where an individual was instructed by a person, who was believed to be a scientist, to administer shocks to an individual (really an actor who was not harmed at all) strapped into a chair when that individual answered questions incorrectly. The shocks varied in intensity and became stronger as the subject in the chair answered incorrectly. Before he conducted his experiments, Milgram surveyed a group of experts and students, asking what results they expected the experiment to produce. The consensus was that most subjects would stop in the mid-range of the shock intensity and refuse to continue the experiment. Only a minute fraction would continue through to the highest intensity.

After conducting his experiments, however, Milgram was astounded to find that 60 percent of the subjects followed the orders of the "scientist" and administered the highest intensity of shock, even after the person in the chair pleaded to be freed and to stop the experiment. Milgram repeated his experiment several times with subjects of differing classes and nationalities but always found that between 60 and 85 percent were fully obedient. In his analysis of his experiments, Milgram found that the subjects justified their obedience by viewing themselves as mere machines following the scientist's orders, devoid of any responsibility for judging the moral content of their actions. This perspective, combined with the desire to gain praise from the authority figure, contributed to their willingness to proceed with the experiment long after they would have stopped in the absence of such an authority figure.

No matter what their explanation for their obedience, however, the fact remained that a sickening number of the subjects obeyed an authority figure even when it was evident that they were causing great pain and injury to another person. The message which we, as individuals, must realize is the power and influence that groups and authority figures possess over us, for it is when this power is abused that Hitlers rise and Holocausts occur. See Stanley Milgram, "Behavioral Study of Obedience," *Journal of Abnormal and Social Psychology* 67 (1963): 371–78.

For the persuasion to have effect, however, the spectators had to feel motivated to participate in the experiment, and what better motivation than the possibility of personally living an extraordinary experience, face to face with the supernatural? The experience was made to seem even more extraordinary because I constantly repeated that these phenomena didn't happen all the time, and didn't happen to just anyone: only the "chosen" few could live this wonderful experience. This is the shortage principle: a chance appears more attractive the more its availability appears to be limited.

Also, the fact that I had an unassuming and not a challenging attitude, and that I apologized various times in case the demonstration failed, helped to make me more likeable: without acknowledging it, the spectators were desiring that everything go well and were ready to act their part toward this end.

At this point, the spectators were ready to interpret anything happening in their houses (no matter how prosaic) as a proof of the reality of my psychic powers.[4] There was still one more very important persuasive factor that played a role as soon as the phone calls started arriving: the social confirmation principle. "If people are calling to say that their cat is behaving strangely, or that their watch is working again," some spectators may have reasoned, "maybe I too should call to say that the light went off for a few seconds!"

The illusion created by the phone calls that kept arriving at the TV station was that *all* the spectators tuned to that same channel were personally experiencing some spectacular demonstration of psychic phenomena, a fact which inevitably encouraged further phone calls, and could very well have stimulated headlines in the following day's newspapers had we not revealed the hoax. Actually, only a small percentage of the audience calling in was enough to quickly jam the switchboard of the TV station for a few hours.[5]

CONCLUSION

Considering the complexity of our world, it is natural that people making decisions do not take advantage of all the available data, but rely only on some isolated and representative item. This "economy" strategy, to proceed by short cuts, leads us inevitably to make inferences on the basis of incomplete data. As a consequence of this, wrong decisions can be made. As Cialdini wrote: "We need simple, reliable and effective rules of conduct. But if the tricks of the sharks undermine their functionality, we loose faith in these rules, we use them less and we find ourselves ill equipped in facing the burden of decisions that today's life places upon us. We can't surrender to this without fighting. The stakes are too high."[6]

NOTES

1. See James Randi, *The Truth about Uri Geller* (Amherst, N.Y.: Prometheus Books, 1983); Piero Angela, *Viaggio nel mondo del paranormale* (Journey in the World of the Paranormal) (Milano: Garzanti, 1978); David Marks and Richard Kamman, *The Psychology of the Psychic* (Amherst, N.Y.: Prometheus Books, 1980); and Martin Gardner, *Science: Good, Bad and Bogus* (Amherst, N.Y.: Prometheus Books, 1981).

2. Obviously, at the end of each show we revealed that it had all been a "joke" and that I did not possess any psychic power.

3. Robert B. Cialdini, *Influence: How and Why People Agree to Things* (New York: William Morrow and Co., 1984). Italian edition: *Le armi della persuasione* (Firenze: Giunti, 1990).

4. One of the most impressive phenomena, that of the stopped watches working again, has been studied by David Marks and Richard Kamman: ". . . we canvassed some jewelers for their opinions and ideas. They told us about half the watches and clocks that come in for repairs are only jammed with dust and gummy oil—such pieces are given the familiar 'cleaning and overhaul.' But some of the jewelers pointed out that, if a watch or clock is held in the hand for a few minutes, body heat could warm and thin the oil, thus freeing the mechanism. Of course, the mild bumps and shakings that accompany the handling of the watch

or clock would contribute, too." To test this hypothesis, Marks and Kamman asked seven jewelers to check how many customers' watches they could start by holding and handling procedures before opening the watch case. "One week later, they had started 60 out of 106 watches attempted, for a 57 percent success rate!" From *The Psychology of the Psychic*, pp. 107–108.

5. In my case, according to an Auditel survey, the show had been followed by approximately two million viewers. If, of these, only 10 percent (200,000 people) really took a watch and of these, at least 1 percent of the watches had started again. (It is a very prudent estimate, actually. At least five watches out of ten usually start working again after shaking them.) there would have been 20,000 spectators with a "fixed" watch. Of these, let's suppose that only one in ten places a call, and we have 2,000 people very excited calling and keeping the switchboard busy for a few hours. In my case, the phone calls stopped after one hour only because we had revealed very soon that it was all a joke.

6. Cialdini, *Influence*, p. 217.

PART 2

HISTORICAL
INVESTIGATIONS

CHAPTER THREE

EUSAPIA'S SAPIENT FOOT

A New Examination of the Feilding Report

by Massimo Polidoro and
Gian Marco Rinaldi

---

*E*usapia Palladino (1854–1918) is considered one of the most gifted mediums of all times. Born in the province of Bari, Italy, she was the daughter of peasants and had little or no formal education. As a young girl working as a domestic in a Naples household, she took part in a séance and, according to her account, was able to stimulate spontaneous manifestations. Her séances quickly attracted the attention of many learned men, including Prof. Cesare Lombroso and Prof. Charles Richet, who attended various séances with Eusapia and became convinced that she was the real thing. This allowed her to visit Paris, Warsaw, Cambridge, and Geneva, where she was tested by some of the leading figures of that day in psychical research. Although scientists were usually impressed by her, not all witnesses were satisfied that the possibility of cheating had been completely ruled out. When she was caught at cheating she would round on her investigators for failing to control her properly, pleading that she could not be held responsible for what she might do while in a trance!

In 1908, however, a new series of sittings took place in Naples under the auspices of the Society for Psychical Research and under the guidance of Everard Feilding, then honorary secretary of the SPR. The "Feilding Report," a complete examination of all the séances, was written by Feilding but endorsed by the other members of the committee as well.[1] The conclusion was reached that "some force was in play which was beyond the reach of ordinary control, and beyond the skill of the most skilled conjurer" (FR). The conditions of the séances were such, they added, that it was inadmissible to suppose that there were any accomplices. The only conclusion they could draw, and with "great intellectual reluctance," was "that there does actually exist some hitherto unascertained force liberated in her presence" (FR). The Feilding Report remained, as parapsychologist John Beloff has said, "one of the mainstays of the case for the paranormal and a stumbling-block for sceptics."[2]

Just recently, psychologist and conjuror Richard Wiseman has quite effectively demonstrated in the *Journal of the Society for Psychical Research* how the Feilding Report was badly flawed, and how the controls against fraud, as described by the investigators, were inadequate.[3] He has shown this by taking into consideration the hypothesis that an accomplice may actually have been present within Palladino's séance cabinet.[4]

Besides the question of whether an accomplice was really present or not at the 1908 Naples séances, what we think has clearly emerged from Wiseman's work is that the three investigators were simply no match for Eusapia. We would like to stress this point further by considering a different "normal" explanation for Palladino's phenomena as described in the Feilding Report (from now on referred to as the "Report"), one that has been discarded too quickly: namely, that of her ability to free her limbs via "substitution." Wiseman says: "It seems implausible that Palladino would, under these conditions, be able to *continually* perform such trickery" and concludes that "the 'substitution' hypothesis seems able to explain, at best, a relatively small number of reported phenomena."[5] However, a reexamination of the conditions and a few of the episodes described in the Report may suggest otherwise.

The Investigating Committee

It must be stressed that the SPR had already had an opportunity to examine Palladino in Cambridge thirteen years before, and they had reached the conclusion that systematic fraud had been used and that there was no adequate reason for concluding in favor of any supernormal agency having been at work during the course of the sittings.[6] However, in consideration of the attention that Eusapia continued to attract among distinguished scientists on the Continent, including Camille Flammarion, Marie Curie, Oliver Lodge, Charles Richet, and Enrico Morselli, the Society felt that her case could not be lightly dismissed and decided to reopen it.

Since it was clearly felt that the primary object of the investigation was to determine whether the phenomena were due to trickery or not, it was essential that the investigators be persons well versed in the methods of trickery. But were they really? In the Report, this is how the credentials of Feilding, Baggally, and Carrington are described:

Mr. Carrington has been for some time the investigator for the American Society for Psychical Research, and is the author of a book, *The Physical Phenomena of Spiritualism* . . . , in which is a detailed exposure of the tricks employed by fraudulent mediums, of which he has made a special study. For many years Mr. Carrington has been an amateur conjurer, and is able to reproduce almost any of the slate writing and other "tests" offered by the average "medium." In the course of his work for the American Society he has investigated many cases of poltergeists, physical phenomena, etc., etc., and in all the ten years of such work had never seen anything that he was unable to account for by trickery, which in many cases he could improve upon.

Mr. Baggally has similarly been for many years an investigator of the phenomena of spiritualism and has been specially interested in the physical phenomena. He, also, is an amateur conjurer of much experience. Notwithstanding the fact that he had investigated nearly all the mediums who have appeared upon the spiritualist horizon since the days of D. D. Home, he, like Mr. Carrington, had never yet met with what appeared to him a genuine example of any agency other than that of more or less easily discoverable trickery, and before the experiments with Eusapia, had come to an entirely negative conclusion as to the probability of any genuine physical phenomena.

Mr. Feilding, though not himself a conjurer, had had a reasonably extensive experience in the investigation of physical phenomena and the advantage of a fairly complete education at the hands of fraudulent mediums. While preserving an open mind as to the possibility of the existence of some hitherto unascertained force in nature whereby the manifestations testified to by so many observers of high standing were produced, the discovery of repeated fraud had produced in him an attitude of complete scepticism as regards the probability of his ever finding any examples of the exercise of such a force. (FR 319–20)

This certainly sounds impressive, but, from what one can ascertain by reading the Report, such "complete scepticism" and high levels of competence in the researchers for detecting trickery must have disappeared somewhere.

Let's examine, for example, an episode that occurred during the eighth séance (FR 499–500). Sometimes, but it was not a rule, Eusapia's feet were tied with cords: for this particular séance each foot had been tied with a separate cord to the legs of the experimenters' chairs, at the right and left sides of the table. Eusapia asked Feilding to feel the cord of her left leg, to see whether it was fastened. He checked the cords around both the left and right legs and found that they were still tied. Then Eusapia said that she was tired and needed some rest, so she put her head on the table, while the experimenters thought they had control of her hands. The lights were faint, but there wasn't complete darkness. After two minutes, the experimenters saw one cord thrown onto the table: one end was still fastened to the experimenter's chair, but Eusapia's left foot was free.

It was Baggally, "an expert knot-tier," who had tied the cord around Eusapia's ankles with four knots: they were so tight that when, at the end of the séance he had to unfasten the cord around the other ankle, it took him "about two minutes" (FR 504).

This episode should at least have given the experimenters a chance to admit that the knots were not all that difficult to untie surreptitiously, that the cord maybe wasn't the best suited for the purpose, that the hands of the medium weren't being carefully controlled, that the light was insufficient for observing her movements, and that all of them (there were, for this séance, four more observers) had been unable to prevent Eusapia from freeing herself when she wished to do so. Nothing of this kind ever passed through their minds. On the contrary, after this they listed the "untying of knots" as one of the "marvels" produced at the séances (FR 330, 340, and 557). They don't even refer to the episode in the "Notes" preceding the report of séance 8; and in the reports of following séances, only Feilding mentions it, lamenting the fact that "Eusapia's 'spirits' or 'fluidic force,' or whatever the agency might be which produced them" had to "intrude into a series of respectable phenomena one of such indubitably Davenportish associations as the untying of the cord" (FR 504). Not one of them accuses her of fraud.

The General Conditions of the Séances

The eleven séances described in the Report were held at the Hotel Victoria in Naples, in Feilding's room on the fifth floor.[7] They usually started at 10 P.M. and lasted about three hours. The experimenters (usually three, sometimes two, sometimes three plus some visiting observers) sat at the table with Eusapia, and the stenographer sat at another table. The fact that all the events observed during the séances were described to the stenographer and then published in detail in the Report has always been cause for admiration. The Report is unique, not in the sense of offering sound proof of supernormal activity, however, but in the fact that it offers a comprehensive description of Eusapia's methods of trickery, already generally known but never presented in such detail. If nothing else, it is a fascinating opportunity to admire Palladino's superb deceptions.

Two thin black cashmere curtains, supplied by Eusapia, hung across a corner of the room in which the spirit cabinet was located; inside, a small table and various toy music instruments, purchased for the occasion, were

Fig. 3.1. A view inside the spirit cabinet at the Hotel Victoria. On the top of the small table are a tambourine, a bell, a flute, and a toy piano; on the floor, a toy guitar is resting upside down. (Society for Psychical Research and Mary Evans Picture Library)

placed (see fig. 3.1). The depth from the angle of the walls to the middle of the curtains was 2 ft. 8 in. (80 cm). Immediately in front of the curtains, with the back of her chair touching them (see fig. 3.2), sat Eusapia. She had before her a custom-made, rectangular table; she sat at the narrow end and the experimenters sat on every other side.

These were Eusapia's usual conditions of work: the ones she dictated to the experimenters and the ones they allowed her. Even the curtains and the table were her own. The only new condition was the presence of the stenographer, to whom the experimenters continuously dictated their observations. This was a fantastic advantage for Eusapia, who could constantly be kept informed of the state of the controls moment by moment.[8]

Fig. 3.2. Eusapia Palladino in the room at the Hotel Victoria (Naples) where the séances described in the Feilding Report were held. Eusapia is resting on the light-weight custom-made table; behind her are the curtains of the "cabinet." (Society for Psychical Research and Mary Evans Picture Library)

The Lights

In describing how the Naples séances and those in Cambridge differed, the researchers note: "None of the present writers had the advantage of being present at these Cambridge sittings, which appear to have differed markedly in certain respects from those which form the subject of the present report. The chief points of difference lie in the condition of light and in the degree of control of her hands permitted by Eusapia" (FR 315–16). We'll examine later the degree of control of her hands; it is interesting now to see what exactly were the conditions of light "permitted by Eusapia."

Since illumination was very important in allowing Eusapia to present the effects as needed, she went so far as to dictate how this should be, and the experimenters, again, satisfied her requests. They prepared an elaborate system of electric lights to produce varying degrees of illumination. This allowed an ample choice of low-power lights: from dim light (the strongest prevailing light is described as a light "in which we were able to read small print" [FR 331]) to almost pitch black, and it was Eusapia who requested, during the séances, whether the lights be raised or lowered according to her needs. Here are descriptions of the various degrees of light:

1. a lamp covered by three thicknesses of thin brown tissue paper, arranged and hung from the ceiling at a distance of six feet (two meters) from the position of the medium's head.*

2. photographic light (a candle lamp) with red linen sides, standing on the stenographer's table, plus light coming from the next room, which was lit by an ordinary electric light, and the door was ajar about six inches.

3. light further lessened by closing the door more, so only the red lamp and a feeble light coming through the crack of the door remained: shapes were visible.

---

*It is unclear where the light is positioned in relation to the medium's head, though it would appear to have been above the medium.

4. Still less light, the door into the next room being further closed: shapes not visible.
5. Electric light turned right out. Only photographic lamp on stenographer's table not shaded.
6. Photographic lamp shaded so as to throw light only on stenographer's book.

From séance 3, however, a change was made in the lighting arrangements by the "fitting up of a group of four electric lamps hanging in the same position as the original lamp. By means of a commutator standing on the shorthand writer's table, the light could be successively reduced from the ordinary light of the room down to a rather faint glow" (FR 375).

It is important to stress the fact that Eusapia didn't usually want complete darkness, but a very particular amount of light, according to the phenomena she was going to produce or the controls to which she was subjected. If, for example, she was going to move an object, she needed enough light to allow the sitters to see the object move, but not enough that they could discern how the movement was accomplished.

Furthermore, such dim light conditions present various other advantages for a medium. The experimenters, for example, already have enough trouble trying to see what phenomena are happening, so their attention is obviously distracted from the controls, here mainly of a tactile kind, of hands and feet. Then, with some suggestions, it's easy to lead people to believe they are seeing things they aren't. Finally, it is very useful for a medium to continually see the experimenters, to know where they are and what they are doing and, in such a way, prevent any unpleasant surprise.

The Skirt

As can be seen from figure 3.2, Eusapia is wearing black clothing with a long full skirt. When she is seated, the skirt covers quite generously the sides and the front of the chair, hiding both Eusapia's feet and the ends of the table legs closest to her. Behind her, the skirt touches the curtains, which are also black. In near darkness these are the perfect conditions for allowing her to use her feet to raise the table or to bring one foot inside the cabinet behind her.

The Table

The table was custom-made and the one Eusapia used in most of her séances. It was 2 ft. 10.75 in. (87 cm) long by 1 ft. 7.25 in. (48 cm) broad and weighed only 10.5 lbs. (4.75 kg). Such a light table is very easy to raise: imagine Eusapia sitting at the narrow end of it, with her legs touching the inside legs of the table (separated from each other by 1 ft. 4.25 in. [41 cm], the broad measure minus the width of the legs of the table). By slightly opening her legs she could very easily seize the table and move it about or raise it a few inches from the ground.

THE PHENOMENA

The phenomena that occurred during the eleven séances (470 are described) belong to Eusapia's usual repertoire. First of all there were the movements and levitations of the séance table: "partial" levitations, where the table remained tilted at an angle on two legs, and "complete" levitations, where the table was lifted off all four legs simultaneously. Levitations of this kind lasted momentarily, "but occasionally for several seconds" (FR 347), and the table was raised, at the most, about a foot off the ground.

Then there were the phenomena inside the cabinet: noises came from it, objects moved about or were taken out, the appearances of indefinable objects from those curtains and movements of those objects. Also, a small stool, which stood about three feet from the medium, was occasionally moved and various touches were felt by the experimenters.

Note that all phenomena occurred within hand or foot distance of the medium.

THE METHODS USED BY EUSAPIA
TO PRODUCE THE PHENOMENA

It is well known from the many investigations to which Eusapia was subjected that she was not the kind of medium who used trick apparatus or conjuring machines. At most she could use a thread or hair for some PK demonstrations, but typically she only relied on her bare hands and feet to produce the phenomena described.

Let's examine, for example, the complete levitation of the table. Eusapia's main method of accomplishing such an effect was to tilt it sideways on two legs (usually the ones on her right side) by pressing on top of it; then, she inserted her left foot under the left table leg closer to her. This position is known as the "human clamp": by pressing with her left hand on the table, she could straighten it and raise it, horizontally, to different heights. If she had her left heel on top of the experimenter's foot sitting on her left, she could only raise her toes and the table could only "levitate" a few inches. However, if she could control the foot of the experimenter on her left by different means (for example, by touching his foot with her right foot, or by having his foot on top of her empty boot) she could very easily hold the table much higher.

Now, with this method in mind, read the following description of a complete levitation which occurred during séance 2. The conditions were as follows: Eusapia's hands were held flat on the top of the table, *partially* resting on the experimenters' hands; C. (Carrington) sits on her left, F. (Feilding) on her right:

10.58 P.M. The table tilts on the two right legs.

C. The medium's left hand is held in mine over the table, her left foot being pressed on my right, and my right knee being in contact with her left knee.

F. Her right hand was on my shoulder.

F. The table was then completely levitated, and both C. and she afterwards pressed on C.'s side of the table, which went up in spite of their pressure.

C. I pressed strongly.

11.00 P.M. Complete levitation of the table. (FR 364)

This "poverty" of means certainly posed a limit to the spectacularity of the phenomena, but it protected her from the risks of deliberate fraud. In fact, whenever she was caught using a free limb, she claimed she was in a trance and excused herself by saying that she acted involuntarily; furthermore, she blamed the experimenters for not being sufficiently alert with their controls. In similar cases the experimenters were more than willing to think her behavior was innocent. She could not have gotten away with this if she had decided to go into the materialization business and impersonate "John King," the "ghost" that Eusapia claimed she could materialize when in a trance. She couldn't have claimed involuntarity for a fake beard.

By using only hands and feet, her chances of success depended entirely on whether the experimenters' controls allowed her to use them or not. Her main trick, an art in which she certainly was a recognized master, was the ability to free herself from the experimenters' control hands and feet.

The Control of Hands and Feet

In discussing Eusapia's Cambridge sittings, the three researchers note that: "Dr. Hodgson had been invited over from America to attend these sittings, and his observations, with those of other sitters, ended in convincing all those who had any prolonged experience of the sittings that the substitution of hands and feet described by Prof. Richet as possible, and already detected by Dr. Reichmann, constantly occurred and could be observed if attention was directed to it" (FR 315). On what basis, then, are we asked to believe that the phenomena described in the Report are authentic? "The chief points of difference," the authors write, "lie in the condition of light and in the degree of control of her hands *permitted* by Eusapia" (FR 316, italics added). As for the lights, we have already seen how Eusapia could obtain the exact degree of illumination that she desired; let's now discuss the control of hand and feet that Eusapia "permitted."

Usually, as in the Neapolitan séances, the control was performed by the two experimenters sitting at the sides of the table, on the right and left of Eusapia. The one on the right controlled the right hand and foot, and parallel control was exerted by the one on the left. By "controlling" here is meant: to prevent the medium from using her hands or feet to perform the phenomena.

It would have been very easy for the experimenters to apply a really effective control: the hand, or the wrist, of the medium had to be kept tight, never letting it go; the ankle had to be held tightly between the legs and, with the other hand, the experimenter would have been free to check the knee and head of the medium. In this way, it would have been impossible for Eusapia to accomplish anything, even in pitch darkness. But this is far from the kind of control that was being used by Feilding and his associates. What happened here, as clearly emerges from the transcripts of the séances, is that it was not the experimenters who where controlling the medium, but, rather, the medium who controlled the experimenters.

From the stenographed transcription of the séances, here are some examples of how the experimenters performed their controls: "Both feet being on our feet" (FR 350); "Her right foot was on mine" (FR 352); "Her left foot was on my right foot. My right hand was held by the medium beneath the table in her lap about one foot from the table" (FR 352); "Her right hand was on my left hand" (FR 363); "Her left hand was over my right" (FR 363); and so on. As stated above, the medium held the experimenters' hands and feet still, not vice versa. These conditions were exactly what was needed for Eusapia to perform her "classic" number: the substitution of a limb.

The trick consisted, for example, in freeing one hand and using the other one to keep contact with the hands of both the experimenters: one hand of the medium partly on top of the hand of one experimenter and partly on the hand of the other; or the hand of an experimenter on the back of the hand of the medium, and this same hand on top of the hand of the other experimenter. She could also free both her hands by letting the experimenters hold on to each other's hands and letting them think they were each holding one of Eusapia's hands; however, this special trick doesn't seem to have been required for these séances.

Obviously the Feilding group was perfectly aware of Eusapia's ability with the substitution trick. It seems paradoxical that, being aware of it, they allowed their conditions to be so little restrictive as to make it easy for the medium to accomplish this same trick. Their conviction was that, being aware of the trick, they would be able to detect it if she used it (FR 357). This is a conviction that an experimenter should never have in such conditions. Every now and then, they tried to check if there had been a substitution (for example, by checking by the position of the fingers if it was really the right hand they were holding); but this, according to the transcripts, only happened occasionally. It must be stated that, on a few occasions, they found that a substitution had, in effect, been made, but they noticed it only by chance (for example, somebody had been able to discern, in near darkness, her free hand moving about) and only after the fact, not while it was happening. They had to admit that:

> [T]he skill with which the substitution was performed was remarkable. The tactile sensation of continuity of contact was unbroken. On neither occasion in Séance III., when the substitution was performed, was F. aware of it, though it was immediately seen by C., on whose side the hand was released; while in Séance XI., though visible to F. from the other side of the table, the release was not *felt* either by him or by Mrs. H., who was controlling on the side on which it happened. (FR 326)

Even easier was the substitution of a foot: when, as it often happened, each of the two experimenters felt a foot on top of his, it could easily have been only one foot, pressing with the heel on the shoe of one experimenter and with the toes on the shoe of the other. Only rarely, according to the transcripts, did one of the experimenters think to check with a hand under the table and feel whether the medium's knees and legs were both where they were supposed to be. The medium, then, after freeing one foot, slipped it out of the shoe (which remained at its place and could be mistaken for the foot) and could use it, as we shall see, to produce the phenomena.

THE SAPIENT FOOT

Eusapia's secret weapon was her left foot. With it, even during these séances, she accomplished her best demonstrations (see, for example, the final part of séance 6, and its very impressive phenomena).

The substitution of the foot was much easier to accomplish than that of the hand because it happened under the table, where the light was extremely dim, and furthermore, under cover of the large skirt. The structure of the table also helped in many ways. Sitting at the narrow end of the table not only allowed Eusapia to move it about by slightly opening her legs, but also, being so narrow it caused the two experimenters sitting on the sides to have the toes of their feet very close to each other: an ideal position that allowed Eusapia to keep contact with both the experimenters' feet with just one foot placed sideways.

The main advantage, however, rests in the fact that the three experimenters did not suspect that she could use a foot to produce the majority of the phenomena they were experiencing. Though they might think she could use her foot to raise the table, it never crossed their minds that she could also use it to move objects in the cabinet behind her, or produce bulges on the curtain behind her at the height of her head, or touch the experimenters on the face. Eusapia, by then, was fifty-four and quite heavy: she didn't look at all like a contortionist. Thus, it never dawned on the experimenters, as is evident many times from the Report, that Eusapia could have a hip so articulated that it allowed her such movements while she was sitting with her torso still. For example, when they see a bulge in the curtain (formed from the inside to the outside of the cabinet) they think of a thread, but they have to discard the hypothesis since there are no threads and the bulge is rounded, not pointed. Sometimes Eusapia allows them to touch or feel, through the curtain, that something produces the bulges; they then feel that there are fingers and nails on the fingers, and conclude without a doubt that it's a hand. Then, they immediately check for the medium's hands and, finding them both on the table, they surrender to the evidence of an inexplicable phenomena.

It also happens that Eusapia let her foot come slightly out of the curtains (in a very dim light, obviously), and the experimenters think they are watching some kind of monster which they describe as having a small head with a long neck. They never think to check where her feet are.

That Eusapia's secret weapon was her articulated hip is not conjecture; it is a proven fact. It is understandable that, given her age and size, this supposition could look ridiculous, but proof that Eusapia was still very active and agile came the year following the Naples séances, during the disastrous American tour. The three experimenters here were much more cunning than Feilding, Baggally, and Carrington. We shall soon discuss this. For now, it is interesting to note a forgotten, curious episode that preceded Feilding's experiments.

Warnings from "Gurney" and "Myers"

It happened a few months before the séances in Naples and is related by psychical researcher Alice Johnson. Those were the years when the leaders of the SPR, and in particular Johnson, were discovering the concept of "cross-correspondence."* One of the main "automatists" was Mrs. Holland. In some of the messages received by Mrs. Holland in 1905 there were references to Eusapia and the problems posed by the control of her phenomena. The "entities" communicating were usually those of Edmund Gurney and Frederic Myers, two founders of the Society for Psychical Research who sent to Johnson, through Mrs. Holland, suggestions on the subject. Here is a suggestion by "Gurney": "Her [Eusapia's] feet are very important—Next time can't Miss J [Johnson] sit with the sapient feet both touching hers—Let her fix her thoughts on the *feet* and prevent the least movement of them." (Eusapia was often also called Sapia, and Sapient Foot was quite a nice wordplay). And here is a suggestion by "Myers": "Ask her [Eusapia] to allow you to secure each foot in a slight card-board box—case or cover—She will refuse for the instep does most of the phenomena of raps and movement."9

---

*Cross-correspondence is the belief that spirits in the afterlife can communicate through mediums, and that communications through various mediums, in different times, can contain cross-references to one another. If this were true it could give more credibility to the messages, since it would be difficult (but not impossible) to organize mediums in order that they give messages that contain similar information and details.

Probably Mrs. Holland was writing such phrases because she had read some papers dealing with the discussions being held at the time on Eusapia's phenomena, or because she knew that Johnson was quite skeptical. It's certain that the leaders of the SPR, anxious to obtain messages from their dead founders, would take these into serious consideration.

The American Incidents

After the popular Naples séances, Carrington went back to America where he became an impresario and organized for Eusapia a 1909–1910 tour, for a very handsome cachet ($125 for a single séance, quite a lot of money in those days). It is widely known what happened during that tour, but it is worth reporting in full a couple of episodes, as described by the American witnesses. We'd like to point out that in the Report of the Neapolitan séances the phenomena repeatedly described are exactly the same as the ones Eusapia produced in the American séances, when the "sapience" of her left foot was discovered—the only difference being that, in Naples, not one of the experimenters ever suspected that the phenomena might be produced by a foot.

The first description is by Hugo Münsterberg, the famous psychologist and philosopher of German birth, who worked at Harvard University. It refers to a séance held on the night of December 18, 1909:

> One week before Christmas, at the midnight hour, I sat again at Madame Palladino's favorite left side and a well-known scientist on her right. We had her under strictest supervision. Her left hand grasped my hand, her right hand was held by her right neighbor, her left foot rested on my foot while her right was pressing the foot of her other neighbor. For an hour the regulation performance had gone on. But now we sat in the darkened room in the highest expectancy while Mr. Carrington begged John [King, Eusapia's spirit control] to touch my arm and then to lift the table in the cabinet behind her and John really came. He touched me distinctly on my hip and then on my arm and at last he pulled my sleeve at the elbow. I plainly felt the thumb and the fingers. It was most uncanny. And, finally, John was to lift the table in the cab-

inet. We held both her hands, we felt both her feet, and yet the table three feet behind her began to scratch the floor and we expected it to be lifted. But instead, there suddenly came a wild, yelling scream. It was such a scream as I have never heard before in my life, not even in Sarah Bernhardt's most thrilling scenes. It was a scream as if a dagger had stabbed Eusapia right through the heart.

What had happened? Neither she nor Mr. Carrington had the slightest idea that a man was lying flat on the floor and had succeeded in slipping noiselessly like a snail below the curtain into the cabinet. I had told him that I expected wires stretched out from her body and he looked out for them. What a surprise when he saw that she had simply freed her foot from her shoe and with an athletic backward movement of the leg was reaching out and fishing with her toes for the guitar and the table in the cabinet! And then lying on the floor he grasped her foot and caught her heel with firm hand, and she responded with the wild scream which indicated that she knew that at last she was trapped and her glory had shattered.

Her achievement was splendid. She had lifted her unshod foot to the height of my arm when she touched me under cover of the curtain, without changing in the least the position of her body. When her foot played thumb and fingers the game was also neat throughout. To be sure, I remember before she was to reach out for the table behind her, she suddenly felt need of touching my left hand too, and for that purpose she leaned heavily over the table at which we were sitting. She said that she must do it because her spiritual fluid had become too strong and the touch would relieve her. As a matter of course in leaning forward with the upper half of her body she became able to push her foot further backward and thus to reach the light table, which probably stood a few inches too far. And then came the scream and the doom.[10]

Notwithstanding the damning exposure, Carrington kept Eusapia in America and had her continue giving séances. In one of these, however, unknown to her, three professional magicians, W. S. Davis, J. L. Kellogg, and J. W. Sargent, together with J. L. Rinn, an amateur magician and friend of Houdini, participated and detected the exact methodology used by her to produce the phenomena. A report on these exposures was published in *Science*.[11] Rinn and a Columbia student, Warner C. Payne, had been hiding under the chairs of the experimenters during this séance held on April 24 at Columbia University. From this position they were able to witness the substitution of the foot: they saw the medium free her left leg by maneuvering her right foot so that her heel rested on Davis's toe and her toe on Kellogg's toe. What happened then is the usual repertoire of phenomena, identical to those observed in Naples:

> In a few moments, after some ejaculations in Italian from the medium, the table began to wobble from side to side; and a foot came from underneath the dress of the medium and placed the toe underneath the leg of the table on the left side of the medium, and, pressing upward, gave it a little chuck into the air. . . . A short time after the lights were lowered she swung her left foot free from her dress at the back and kicked the curtain of the cabinet quickly, which caused it to bulge out toward the sitters. This was done several times so daringly that under the chairs where I lay it seemed almost impossible that the people above the table could not have observed it.
>
> Later the medium placed her left leg back into the cabinet and pulled out from behind the curtain a small table with certain articles upon it, which was dashed to the floor in front of the cabinet on the left-hand side. It remained there in varying positions and was kicked by the medium a number of times. At one time the medium juggled the table that had been kicked out from behind the curtain on the end of her left toe in a very clever manner, so that it gave the appearance as if the table was floating in the air.[12]

It was the end of Eusapia's American tour and also of her career. Carrington did admit that sometimes the medium cheated, but he insisted that on other occasions she was completely genuine; he stood by his claim until the end of his long life in 1958.

Fig. 3.3. A portrait of Eusapia Palladino signed by her: her signature was the only thing she was able to write. (Mary Evans Picture Library)

THE TRUST IN THE MEDIUM'S INNOCENCE

Let's now go back to the Naples séances to understand what kind of attitude the experimenters had toward the medium on the occasions when they caught her trying to cheat. It is indicative of their real degree of "skepticism" that, even when they had the evidence for the fraud before their eyes, they still conceded her presumed good faith.

In séance 3 Eusapia was caught, having freed a hand by a substitution, and the control for the feet was also unsatisfactory. Notwithstanding this, in the introductory remarks to the séance, it is stated that "no delib-

erate conscious fraud was proved" (FR 378), and in a further note, per-
taining to this séance, but written at the end of the entire cycle, Feilding
writes:

> I have come, therefore, to feel it possible that, *so far as our own series of*
> *experiments is concerned*, the cases of hand-substitution practised were
> innocent in intent, though obtaining our previous consent, she other-
> wise frequently did,—touch the curtain or pull it over the table,—and
> did it, half automatically and without consulting us, though without
> any intention of producing a spurious phenomenon. It is necessary to
> say that never once, in the course of hundreds of phenomena, did we
> detect a single case of undoubted fraud, and it is my personal belief at
> present that though there were many phenomena which must be classed
> as non-evidential, there were in fact none which we should be justified
> in thinking to be probably spurious. (FR 397)

After séance 10, still in relation to the hand substitution, Feilding
writes:

> My own experience on this occasion, however, leads me to think it is
> not impossible that it is often, in the darkness, thought she had
> resorted to it when, in fact, she has not, and that her hands have,
> through weariness or carelessness, got into what may be called the "sub-
> stitution position," without its being taken practical advantage of. I
> noticed that I only had half her hand, and immediately felt for the
> other half, and found it on B.'s [Baggally's] left hand. I at once jumped
> to the conclusion that she must have produced the touches on B.'s back
> with her other hand. In accordance with my promise I told her my con-
> trol was not good. She agreed; but lifted my hand to feel her other
> hand, which I found was under B.'s right. (FR 535)

Eusapia was really lucky in dealing with such experimenters: she
could boldly cheat, and in the event that she was caught at it, not only was
the episode attributed to innocent distraction, but she was at once
informed that the control was not good, so that she could immediately
reestablish it. A phrase in the previous passage definitely needs to be

underlined: "in accordance with my promise." It will appear odd, but the fair play of these gentlemen stretched to the point of promising the medium that, "if ever we actually caught her tricking, at once to tell her" (FR 437). Eusapia, then, enjoyed the incredible advantage of being able to proceed coolly with her moves, because if no one spoke she knew that no one had noticed anything.

On another occasion, discussing an accurately performed hand substitution at séance 11, their comment is: "It seems difficult to suppose that her intent was fraudulent, as she must have known that in the light which prevailed a trick would have been detected" (FR 541). To sum up: if the trick is not detected, everything's good for the medium; if, however, the trick is detected, everything's still good for her, because the conditions are such that "a trick would have been detected," and so her intent could not have been fraudulent!

An Episode from Séance 9

An incident which occurred during séance 9 at 11:06 P.M. well represents the degree of acquiescence and subjection of the experimenters toward the medium.

Baggally and Carrington were sitting at the sides of the table, B. at the left and C. at the right of the medium; Feilding was sitting in front of her. At 11:06 Feilding, dissatisfied with the foot "controls," seeks to verify their actual position and puts his hand under the table. Eusapia prevents this: she wakes up from her "semi-trance," in which it is said she was at the moment, and gets very angry (FR 514). A long discussion, or better a *sceneggiata*,* follows which lasts about forty minutes before the séance can be started again! This is a further confirmation that it was the medium, not the experimenters, who directed the séance.

About this incident and what happened in the minutes preceding and following it, there are various observations which can be made to better show the reliability (or lack thereof) of the experimenters.

---

*A type of popular theater-drama in Naples.

The Timetable

The sitting started at 10:12 P.M. At 10:27 strange phenomena happen which would require the use of a foot on the part of the medium, in particular for the repeated movement of the small stool placed on the ground at the medium's left (it is interesting to note that the stool was always placed at her left, the side where she preferred to do her footwork). From that moment until the incident of 11:06 (forty minutes), not one of the three experimenters performs any real verification of the position of her feet. These are the conditions of "control" of her feet as transcribed from the stenographer's notes on the Report (B. stands for Baggally, C. for Carrington):

10:27 P.M. B. Her left foot on my right foot.

C. Her right foot pressing against my left foot, her right knee in contact with my left knee.

10:30: B. Her left knee is against my right knee. Her left foot against my right foot.

C. Her right knee pressing against my left knee; her right foot pressing against my left foot.

10:33: B. Her left foot is resting on my right foot.

C. I can feel her right knee against my left. Her right foot is in contact with mine.

10.34: B. Her left foot distinctly held on my right foot.

C. My left knee in contact with her right knee. Her right foot pressing against my left foot.

10:37:   B. My right knee pressing against her left knee, and my right foot under her left foot.

          C. The control of feet as before.

10:40:   B. I distinctly felt her left leg against my right leg.

          C. Control exactly the same as before.

10:41:   [No mention of controls, although there had been a phenomenon]

10:42:   [No mention of controls]

10:44:   B. I can feel her left foot against my right foot, and her left knee against my right knee.

          C. [No mention of controls]

10:47:   B. [No mention of controls]

          C. My left knee and foot in contact with hers.

10:47:   B. Same control of feet.

          C. Control of feet as before.

10:48:   B. Same control.

          C. Same control here.

10:57:   B. Her left leg against my right leg.

          C. [No mention of foot]

11:00:   B. Synchronizing with these tilts [of the table] she presses her left foot slightly [on mine]. Owing to the position of her left leg against my right leg she was not able to touch the table leg with it.

           C. Her right foot clearly on my left foot.

And here we are at the incident of 11:06 P.M. The previous phrases were extrapolated from the Report (FR 511–13) where, of course, the hand control and phenomena were reported too. For all this time the light was pretty dim. In reading the preceding controls, it appears that Eusapia could very easily have freed her left foot and kept contact with both experimenters with her right foot and leg. Considering what happened at 11:06, the experimenters could have suspected that the controls from the preceding forty minutes were not good and that all the phenomena had to be discarded as nonevidential. It goes without saying that the experimenters do not discard those phenomena.

The Cords

That same night, as in the previous séance, the medium's feet were tied with cords. They were not immobilized, since there was about four feet of cord between each foot and the chair to which it was fastened. The geometry of the disposition of the chairs and the exact distance in inches are not given so it is not easy to establish how many of the phenomena (like the movement of the stool) could have been performed even with the foot fastened to the rope, and how many would require that foot to be free. We'd say, however, that there were phenomena which could only, or more competently, be performed with a free foot.

That Eusapia had unfastened her foot from the cord (as she also did in séance 8: see page 62) appears evident from the fact that, as soon as one experimenter tried to check the control of the feet, she burst into a prolonged temper tantrum. During this time—with the light still dim—she could have retied the cord as though she had never unfastened it. The experimenters don't check immediately whether Eusapia's feet are fastened or not. It's only at 11:40, more than half an hour later, that Eusapia allows the light to be raised and lets her feet be checked. Even later, the experimenters do not suggest that she had freed herself.

The Stenographer

The person who checked the cord at 11:40 P.M. was not one of the experimenters, but the stenographer. He hadn't participated in the controls in any way and had no experience at all in sitting with mediums; he was just a stenographer, hired in Naples for this specific task. Furthermore, he was always engaged in writing down what was being dictated to him and couldn't have participated in the experiments.

It was Baggally (the expert knot-maker) who tied Eusapia's feet at the beginning of the séance, helped by Feilding; it should have been they who checked if everything was still the same as when they started. Considering that for thirty-four minutes, since the séance had been interrupted, they had been idle (they did not have to check the hands, and so on), there is no reason why it was not they who checked on the cord. Actually, one can easily imagine, even if it is not said, that Eusapia prevented them.

The Temper Tantrum

What seems surprising—or, rather, what is not surprising at all, considering the attitude of trust in the innocence of the medium by the three experimenters—is that faced with such an incident, neither Feilding, Baggally, nor Carrington think that there had been some hanky-panky and that the exaggerated reaction of the medium had only been a ruse to hide it. This is evident from their notes preceding and following the séance. In the preceding remarks, two pages long, the sole reference to the incident comes only after the statement that the phenomena up to that moment had been quite noteworthy:

... [I]t seems probable that some further and more startling manifestations might have followed, had it not been for the unfortunate "misunderstanding" that took place at 11:06 P.M. and to which further reference is made in C.'s and F.'s notes. The discussion which arose in consequence lasted nearly three-quarters of an hour. (FR 506)

Carrington is held responsible for the "misunderstanding," as he himself admits in his final notes: "This séance started most propitiously, and it was possibly owing to what was perhaps a blunder on my part that we did not get many more startling phenomena than we did" (FR 523).

It was Carrington, then, who had committed a blunder in trying to check the controls and putting a hand under the table! He apologizes, saying that he had forgotten that the medium's feet were tied and that there was no reason then to doubt. In other words, had he remembered that her feet were tied he would have not tried to check. Still trying to apologize, he explains that one of the reasons for his actions was to keep the promise already discussed above: "We had agreed to tell the medium at once as soon as any laxness of the control became apparent" (FR 523).

Baggally doesn't even mention the incident in his notes. He only states that when the stool was moving: "I was sure I had a good control of her left leg. My right foot was not only against her left, but the whole length of my right leg was between hers and the stool" (FR 524). He never suspects for a second that what he was checking could have been her right leg, not her left.

Feilding, who appears to admit (opposed to Carrington, who doesn't) that Carrington had found something irregular in the position of the feet when he tried to check, believes that this is the only incident of its kind in the whole set of séances, and doesn't suggest that the phenomena preceding it should be discarded. He also appears to believe in Eusapia's story about the sensitivity of her left foot and of her hands:

I have complained to her more than once that she ought to allow her hands to be fully enclosed [in the hands of the experimenters]. She said that during a séance she became very hyperaesthetic and nervous, and that the touch of certain people's hands, especially if these are at all moist or hot, is so acutely unpleasant to her that she cannot endure her hands being held inside them. She said that this sensation had no connection with her liking for people otherwise, and that there were certain persons to whom she was greatly attached in her normal condition who were profoundly antipathetic to her as neighbours during a séance, and vice versa. As regards her feet, especially her left foot, she said she was still more sensitive. Her left foot, she told me, had once been run over by the wheel of a cab, and she cannot stand pressure on the instep, while both her feet have a tendency to go to sleep, so that she gets a sensation of pins and needles in them, and has to press violently every now and then with them so as to restore sensation. (FR 521–22)

For being run over by a cab, her left foot seemed to work just fine, as the American records show.

The Language Question

Feilding gives another interesting detail in his notes when he says that Eusapia wanted to know what the others were saying and be thus informed about their suspicions. Here is how Feilding relates the incident of 11:06 P.M.

During this séance, however, C. did notice a change, and forgetting that, owing to the fastening, she had only a certain range of action, he stooped down to feel, and found that Eusapia had crossed her feet. He told me in English that the foot control was not good. Eusapia, who detests English, and is always annoyed when she does not know what is being said, yet has a flair for the meaning of things so remarkable as to amount almost to the dignity of telepathic perception, was furious. She worked herself up into a passion and covered us with rich Neapolitan reproaches for our suspicion and inexperience of her phenomena. The storm raged for about an hour, and when at length calm was, to a certain extent, restored, and we all expressed unfeigned astonishment at the activity of the stool, which performed a pas seul outside the cabinet, she said sarcastically: "You have spoiled all the better phenomena, and now you are amazed at a straw (*paglia*) like that." (FR 522)

Elsewhere it is said that, after the incident, the medium said: "Better phenomena are spoilt for the evening" (FR 514). Obviously she needed such threats to keep the experimenters quiet; if they thwarted Eusapia's wishes the phenomena would disappear.

How much the experimenters were anxious not to irritate her, and how much Eusapia was in charge of the game, can be seen from a trivial episode from the night of séance 6. The medium arrived late at the hotel, blaming her cab driver. Then, along with Feilding, she went up the five floors to the séance room. It took twenty-five minutes to reach the fifth floor because she kept stopping on the stairs to chat with Feilding—he thought she was telling him about a theft that she had once suffered. She spoke in strict Neapolitan dialect, which he did not understand, so he was not able to tell her that she was being paid to keep the séance, not to chat. We would have really loved to be flies on the wall and hear what Eusapia actually said to Feilding in Neapolitan dialect in those twenty-five minutes.

PSYCHOLOGICAL ASPECTS

There are various psychological aspects to be considered, to have a better idea of the conditions in which the Feilding group operated. We have already discussed the submission of the experimenters to the medium, and their wish never to irritate her. This, of course, had an influence on the kind of control they were "allowed" to apply: "The degree of control permitted by her varied very much, and appeared to depend upon her mood" (FR 323).

Eusapia, however, used various other psychological ruses. For example, a much longer treatise would be needed to discuss her use of sexual calls: "as a rule she is apparently overwhelmed by sleep, throws herself often into the arms of her neighbours" (FR 324); "sometimes she encircled the leg of one of the controllers tightly between her own or rested both her legs across his knees" (FR 327); "Medium asks us to put our hands on her legs" (FR 352); "my right hand was then also grasping her thigh" (FR 364). It is clear that such behavior could be used to her advantage in many ways.

Her use of misdirection is also interesting; Eusapia, for example, would frequently hold an experimenter's hand high, toward the curtain, and while attention was on the hand she could kick the curtain below, thus producing movements and bulges in it: "Medium holds my right hand towards the left curtain with hers and makes two slow movements which are reciprocated by movements of the curtain" (FR 353).

Here is a description of an attempt at misdirection to cover a feet substitution, which was detected by the skillful experimenters at Columbia University; the one talking is W. S. Davis:

> We were next favored with responsive raps,—doubling up her hands she beat the air with her fists in a jerky, spasmodic way when we heard the light noises on the wood. The exhibition above board did not occupy our entire attention. Every one in the party was interested in the theory of using a foot as a lever to raise the table. As she beat the air with her clenched fist, she correspondingly slid her feet away until we felt the pressure on the toe end of our feet only, whereas there had previously been pressure on the insteps. Kellog [sic] and I both suspected that she had succeeded in removing one foot and was making the other do duty for two.[13]

The two magicians hiding under the table later confirmed that this was exactly what had taken place.

Finally, Eusapia tried hard to appear cooperative and ready to do her best to make the experimenters happy; she would, for example, ask for better light only to have her "control," "John King," refuse it: "In the early stages of trance the directions for diminuation of the light are usually given through tilts or levitations (sometimes apparently without contact) of the table. Eusapia herself frequently opposes these directions, but as a rule the table continues, by repeated series of five tilts, often of great violence, to demand a reduction of light to which she ultimately gives way" (FR 325). "John tilts five times for less light. Medium is annoyed and says 'No.'" The tilts continued to ask for less light and eventually she yielded (FR 467).

Throughout the report, there are many instances where she appears to cooperate but still gets her way: "Eusapia was in a nervous, anxious mood, perpetually interrupting to ask if the control was satisfactory, and perpetually rendering it as difficult as possible for us to make it so" (FR 325–26).

WHAT THEY COULD HAVE DONE

Since the purpose here has been to point out the various pitfalls of one of the most famous psychic investigations, and thus to stress the need for future investigations to be carried out and reported in such a way as to minimize retrospective counterexplanations, we would now like to offer a few suggestions as to what the experimenters might have done to prevent being tricked (or, at least, to be conscious of what happened).

First of all, as we have seen, Feilding, Carrington, and Baggally go to great lengths to ensure that every request of Eusapia's is satisfied. Since the main reason for a new SPR investigation was "merely to attempt to determine whether the phenomena were due to trickery or not" (FR 319), it would have been wise to attempt testing her under "controlled conditions" sometimes. They do not do this since, as they explain: "our time in Naples was limited" and "we preferred to adopt conditions to which the medium was used and in which therefore it was probable that the effects would be produced, rather than impose others which might possibly impede the production of what we had gone to study" (FR 322).

To let Eusapia act under the conditions she was used to was not a bad idea: this is the best way to see how "usual conditions" and "test conditions" that would prevent fraud differ. However, after a few of these tests, where phenomena were produced under the usual conditions, new tests with stricter controls should have been tried. If nothing happened under these conditions, what conclusion would have to be drawn?

Luckily, somebody did attempt exactly this kind of test on Eusapia: it was the same committee of Columbia University who hid two persons under the experimenters' chairs to observe Eusapia's foot substitution. Their plan was to allow Eusapia to go through her act in the first part of the séance, so that they could see exactly what she did. After thirty minutes, however, at a given signal, the experimenters (two magicians) sitting on her sides tightened the controls. Eusapia's hands and feet were completely controlled, and they would not allow her to shift or get free. She cursed and shrieked, of course, but during this period of tight control nothing else happened. Then again, at the agreed signal, the controls were loosened for thirty minutes and manifestations were again produced by the skillful use of a free hand or foot. In the end they tightened controls and again nothing happened. In this way they established a kind of conditional relationship: whenever the controls were loosened, phenomena occurred. When they were tightened, there were no manifestations.[14]

In Naples the experimenters did not follow this kind of strategy: "We felt," they explained, "that if, in a reasonable number of experiments, persons specially versed in conjuring tricks and already forewarned concerning, and familiar with, the particular tricks to be expected, were unable to discover them, it would not be presumptuous to claim as a probable consequence that some other agency must be involved" (FR 322). Quite a wrong conclusion, as we have seen. Even at the Columbia University sittings, the two professional magicians sitting at Eusapia's sides were not at all sure whether she had substituted her feet or not: "Kellog [sic] and I both *suspected* that she had succeeded in removing one foot and was making the other do duty for two" (italics added).[15] However, they were not really sure until, after the séance, the two persons hiding under the chairs confirmed that she had actually been able to substitute her foot in that way.

Eusapia complained that her limbs were too sensitive to be held too tightly, and we know how careful the Feilding group was not to hurt her sensitivity. However, just once, they could have tried a couple of very simple controls: (1) move the séance table five feet away from the curtains at the back; and (2) rotate the table so that Eusapia sat at the center of the longer side. If anything still happened inside the cabinet, or if the table still levitated on all four legs in such conditions, *then* something interesting would really have been observed. To be honest, they did try this second control during séance 7, but after almost an hour, during which there were only partial levitations of the table, mainly tilts toward the medium, Eusapia said that "she did not like the table that way" (FR 471) and it was again turned back to the usual position for good.

They could have also asked her to dress in white clothes, which would have allowed the experimenters to better see her movements; also, she could have been asked to dress in trousers instead of ample skirts; or to sit on a creaking chair (notice that the chair on which she sits in figure 3.2 is different from the other chair shown in the same picture. Did Eusapia also bring her "tested/silent" chair, along with her table and curtains?). Ironically, many other suggestions of this kind were proposed by Count Perovsky-Petrovo-Solovo in the same *Proceedings* issue which contained the Feilding Report.

The only new test they try is to put "stocks"* on the legs of the table to prevent the medium's feet from levitating the table. However, they then discover that she can still move the table with her hands. With the experimenters now aware of this, she has to present different phenomena, but this time she is caught at a substitution. Not to worry, however, since the experimenters, as usual, decide that "no deliberate conscious fraud was proved" (FR 378).

CONCLUSIONS

We don't know whether Eusapia Palladino was a genuine medium or not, but we observe that: (1) her best demonstrations were those performed with no real controls and before people with little knowledge of tricks; (2) whenever she was observed by a competent reseacher she was invariably caught using tricks. It has often been claimed that the best experiments done on Eusapia are those by the Feilding group; from what we have seen, however, we can consider the Feilding committee a group of highly incompetent researchers. On the basis of these observations, we strongly suspect that Eusapia Palladino was only a very good magician, who depended on her highly polished and rehearsed methods of deception for her living, and who probably didn't need an accomplice for any of the

---

*A container in which two legs of the table can be inserted to prevent a medium from lifting the table with his or her feet.

470 phenomena described in the Report. The gullibility of her experimenters was enough.[16]

NOTES

Reprinted with the permission of the editors from the *Journal of the Society for Psychical Research* 62, no. 850 (January 1998). Copyright 1998 by the Society for Psychical Research.

1. Everard Feilding, W. W. Baggally, and H. Carrington, "Report on a Series of Sittings with Eusapia Palladino," *Proceedings of the Society for Psychical Research (SPR)* 23, pt. 59 (1909): 309–569. Reprinted in Everard Feilding, *Sittings with Eusapia Palladino & Others* (London: University Books, 1963). Subsequent citations of this report will be referenced parenthetically as FR. Page numbers are from *Proceedings of the Society for Psychical Research*.

2. John Beloff, *Parapsychology: A Concise History* (London: Athlone Press, 1993), p. 120.

3. Richard Wiseman, "The Feilding Report: A Reconsideration," *Journal of the Society for Psychical Research* 58 (1992): 129–52.

4. This idea has stimulated an interesting debate in the pages of *Journal of the Society for Psychical Research*, with Wiseman's critics (Barrington 1992; Fontana 1992 and 1993; Martinez-Taboas and Francia 1993) trying to disprove his hypothesis and Wiseman (1993 a, b, c, and d) responding point by point to each criticism.

5. Wiseman, "The Feilding Report," p. 134.

6. R. Hodgson, "The Value of Supernormal Phenomena in the Case of Eusapia Palladino," *Journal of the Society for Psychical Research* 7 (1895): 36–79.

7. The exact location of the Hotel Victoria (Vittoria, in Italian) has recently been found by us. It was in Via Partenope 8, along the beach. From an old *Touring Club Guide* (1960), it also appears that the hotel was second-rate (at least in 1960) and had sixty rooms (twenty-one with bathrooms); the price for a room was between 800 and 1300 lire (without bathroom).

Further research, conducted with the help of Dr. Massimo Finizio, living in Naples, has shown that in recent years the hotel had reduced the number of rooms and had finally been closed. In its place there is now a branch of the Banca Popolare di Novara. The bank, however, occupies only the first floor. The other floors have been converted into private apartments. Since considerable renovation work has been done on the building over the years (also, a sixth floor has been added), and since it has been impossible to find any living member of the original hotel staff, it appears very difficult now to have firsthand information on the hotel, Feilding's room, or its doors.

8. The experimenters dictated in English, but it can be assumed that Eusapia, having already been tested in various parts of Europe for many years, often with English-speaking researchers, was able to understand at least the meaning of the simple and typical phrases that were continually repeated by the experimenters to define the controls. That this is the case, and that Eusapia wanted things to be also said in Italian (Feilding, at least, appears to have had some knowledge of the language), is confirmed by Feilding, who notes that Eusapia "detests English, and is always annoyed when she does not know what is being said, yet has a *flair* for the meaning of things so remarkable as to amount almost to the dignity of telepathic perception . . ." (FR 522).

9. Alice Johnson, "On the Automatic Writing of Mrs. Holland," *Proceedings of the Society for Psychical Research* 55 (1908): 276–77.

10. Hugo Münsterberg, "Report on a Sitting with Eusapia Palladino," *Metropolitan Magazine* (February 1910), quoted in C. E. M. Hansel, *The Search for Psychic Powers* (Amherst, N.Y.: Prometheus Books, 1989), pp. 240–41.

11. D. S. Miller, "Report on an Investigation of the Phenomena Connected with Eusapia Palladino," *Science* 77 (1910).

12. Miller, "Report," quoted in Hansel, *The Search for Psychic Powers*," p. 242.

13. Quoted in Harry Houdini, *A Magician among the Spirits* (New York: Harper & Brothers, 1924; reprint, New York: Arno Press, 1972), pp. 56–57.

14. J. F. Rinn, *Sixty Years of Psychical Research* (New York: Truth Seeker Company, 1950).

15. Davis, quoted in Houdini, *Magician*, p. 56.

16. When this work originally appeared in the *Journal of the Society for Psychical Research* it created quite a stir among its readers and contributors. Here is a selection of the articles and countercriticism to our work that was published in the *Journal*: M. R. Barrington, "Palladino, and Those Who Know How She Did It," *Journal of the Society for Psychical Research* 63 (1998): 56; D. Fontana, "Poli-

doro and Rinaldi: No Match for Palladino and the Feilding Report," *Journal of the Society for Psychical Research* 63 (1998): 12–25; M. Keen, "Palladino and Her Critics," *Journal of the Society for Psychical Research* 63 (1998): 56–57; and A. Martínez-Taboas, "Some Critical Comments on the Thesis of 'Eusapia's Sapient Foot,'" *Journal of the Society for Psychical Research* 63 (1998): 26–33.

CHAPTER FOUR

THE CASE
OF
ANNA EVA FAY
The Medium Who Baffled
Sir William Crookes

*B*etween 1870 and 1874 William Crookes—the discoverer of tallium, inventor of the radiometer, developer of the Crookes tube, pioneer investigator of radiation effects, Fellow of the Royal Society, and later knighted—conducted a series of experiments with some of the most remarkable mediums of the age. D. D. Home, possibly the greatest medium of all, was studied by Crookes and declared genuine, as were Florence Cook, a young woman who specialized in the materialization of a ghost named "Katie King"; Kate Fox, one of the originators of Spiritualism and later a self-confessed fraud; Mary Rosina Showers, another young materializing medium; and Anna Eva Fay, a vaudeville entertainer.

There are some very strong doubts about these investigations; for example, it has been claimed that the married Crookes had a love affair with Florence, and that the experiments were just a ruse for their meetings.[1] However, Crookes's supposed complicity with the medium, or his inability to conduct reliable, scientific tests in Spiritualism, are still

Fig. 4.1. A portrait of
William Crookes.
(Mary Evans Picture Library)

debated today. There exists, however, at least one episode that shows without a doubt Crookes's failure to detect open trickery when confronted with it. This happened when Crookes met Anna Eva Fay, an interesting personality, now largely forgotten, who deserves to be remembered.

THE "INDESCRIBABLE PHENOMENON"

Anna (sometimes referred to as Annie) Eva Heathman was born in Southington, Ohio, in the 1850s (she preferred to keep the exact date to herself). She left home quite young and became interested in theosophy and mysticism. At one time she said that she became Mme. Helena Petrovna Blavatsky's* pupil, living with her and helping her in her work. When she left, along with a handsome shawl presented to her by Mme. Blavatsky, Annie had to earn her own living and decided to go on stage as a mind-reader, a specialty she presented until her last performance in Milwaukee in 1924.

*Mme. Blavatsky was one of the co-founders of the Theosophical Society.

Fig. 4.2. William Crookes and the spirit of "Katie King"
(or is it medium Florence Cook in disguise?). (Mary Evans Picture Library)

Her first public performance as a psychic entertainer took place in a schoolhouse in New Portage, Ohio. When she married her first husband, Henry Cummings Melville Fay, a self-proclaimed medium, they decided to work on stage as a couple and presented an intriguing number.

Annie sat on a stool in an open-front cabinet. A few volunteers, supervised by Melville Fay, tied her to the stool. One tied her left wrist at the center of a long strip of cloth with many knots, one on top of another; a second volunteer followed suit with her right wrist. She held her hands behind her back as they bound the two strips together and knotted the cloth to a harness ring that was securely embedded in an upright post at the rear of the cabinet. Another piece of tape was tied at the back of the medium's neck, and the ends were fastened to a staple higher on the same post. One end of a long rope was lashed around her ankles; the other was held by a spectator throughout the performance that followed.

Annie appeared to go into a trance, and Melville Fay placed a hoop in her lap and closed the curtain at the front of the cabinet. A second later he threw open the drape: the hoop now encircled Annie's neck. Removing the hoop, he placed a guitar on his wife's lap, closed the curtain, and strumming sounds were heard. As soon as he opened the drape, the music stopped and the guitar fell to the floor. The same thing happened with other musical instruments; other phenomena followed: nails were hammered into a block of wood and paper dolls were snipped from a piece of paper. Finally, a knife was placed in Annie's lap. Though the curtain was closed for only a few seconds, the spirits seemingly had time to sever her bonds. She stood up and came forward to take numerous bows.[2]

The Fays billed their demonstration as "The Indescribable Phenomenon," never quite openly claiming spirit intervention. Actually, theirs was a typical magic performance, introduced first by Laura Ellis, and following in the steps of many similar performances, like the Davenports' "Spirit Cabinet" (see page 108), which combined escapology and spiritualistic themes. A perfect rendition of the "Indescribable Phenomenon" is still performed today by mentalists Glenn Falkenstein and Frances Willard. Annie was bold enough to feature tricks and illusions along with her main act: a "Spirit Dancing Handkerchief," a "Rapping Hand," and a "Levitation" were included for years on her program.

At the time, few in America considered the Fays' performance a real example of Spiritualism. Emma Hardinge, a medium and historian of Spiritualism, in her book *Modern American Spiritualism* (1870), stated that Melville Fay's deceptions had been "openly exposed by the Spiritualists themselves"; John W. Truesdell, a skeptic of the time, agreed that Fay was a rascal. It seems clear that Annie's claims were adjusted to her audience: when dealing with Spiritualists, she claimed mediumistic powers, and when performing on the music-hall stage she let the audience be the judge, an attitude adopted by other mentalists of the time, like the Piddingtons.

SCIENTISTS AND MAGICIANS

When the Fays reached London in June 1874, the advertisements for their performances at the Queen's Concert Rooms, Hanover Square, mentioned "entertainments comprising light and dark séances every day," "mysterious manifestations," and a "series of bewildering effects";[3] however, there is no suggestion that they had any relation to Spiritualism. Nevertheless, Annie found herself hailed as a physical medium. Immediately she started receiving the attention of various psychical researchers; F. W. H. Myers, for example, later to be one of the leading founders of the Society for Psychical Research, expressed interest in an "extensive investigation of Mrs. Fay's mediumship."[4] William Crookes, however, stated clearly that he wanted to be the first to examine her. In an interesting comment made by Myers in a letter to his collegue Henry Sidgwick,* the former says, after mentioning Crookes, that "the lion will not let himself be robbed of his cub—nor the cub of her lion," suggesting that Crookes was trying to make Eva his personal protégée and that Eva was not averse to acting in such a role.[5]

It was about this time that John Nevil Maskelyne and George Alfred Cooke, two well-known British magicians who possessed their own theatre at Egyptian Hall and had already exposed the tricks used by the Dav-

---

*Cofounder of the Society for Psychical Research.

Fig. 4.3. A portrait of
Anna Eva Fay.
(Mary Evans
Picture Library)

enport brothers, added to their show "An Indescribable Séance," with Cooke tied in the same way as the American and duplicating her feats.

It was possibly to counteract this exposure by saying that Anna Eva Fay, a vaudeville performer who found herself the center of a body of eminent literary and scientific men and treated as a "medium" whom it was necessary to "investigate," succumbed to temptation and accepted her new role. If the psychical researchers were determined on her being a medium, then she would cash in on it while she could, thus restoring her reputation and promoting public interest in her performances.

The most important by far of all the experiments conducted on Annie's "mediumship" were Crookes's "electrical tests," held at his own home February 1875.[6]

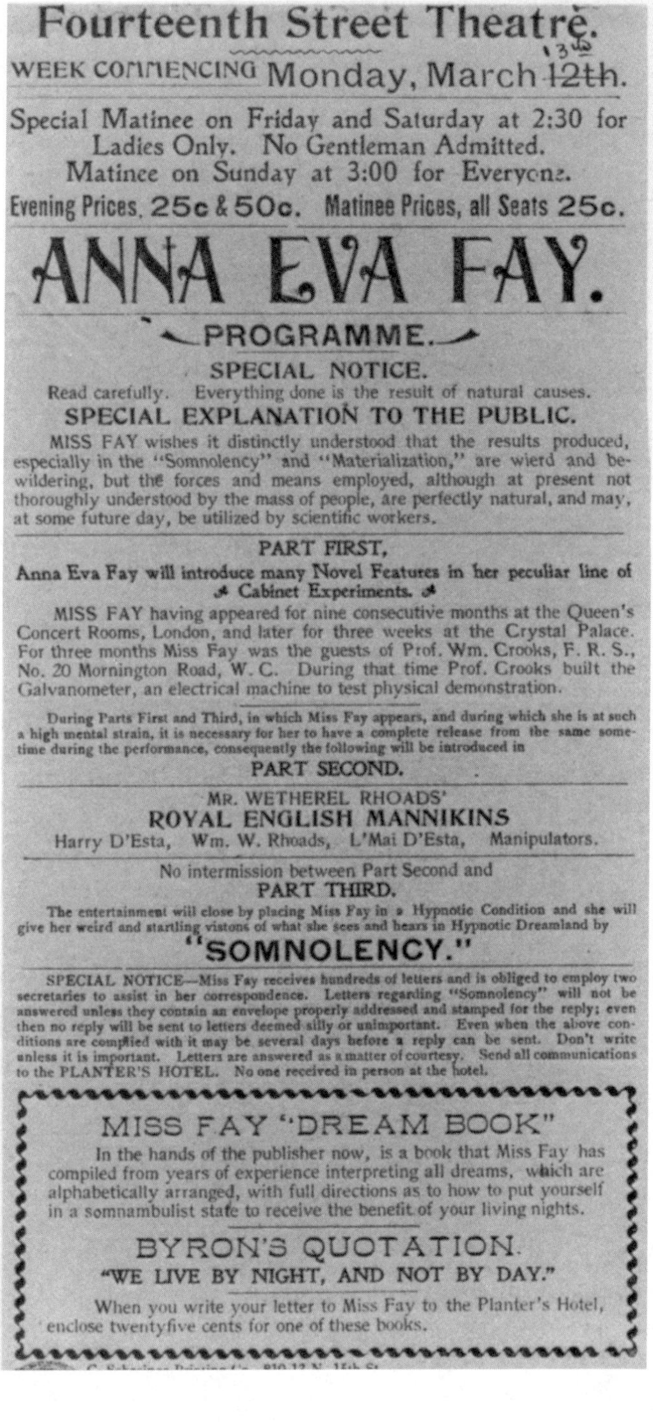

Fourteenth Street Theatre.

WEEK COMMENCING Monday, March 12th.

Special Matinee on Friday and Saturday at 2:30 for Ladies Only. No Gentleman Admitted. Matinee on Sunday at 3:00 for Everyone.

Evening Prices. 25c & 50c.   Matinee Prices, all Seats 25c.

ANNA EVA FAY.

~PROGRAMME.~

SPECIAL NOTICE.

Read carefully.   Everything done is the result of natural causes.

SPECIAL EXPLANATION TO THE PUBLIC.

MISS FAY wishes it distinctly understood that the results produced, especially in the "Somnolency" and "Materialization," are wierd and bewildering, but the forces and means employed, although at present not thoroughly understood by the mass of people, are perfectly natural, and may, at some future day, be utilized by scientific workers.

PART FIRST,

Anna Eva Fay will introduce many Novel Features in her peculiar line of ♪ Cabinet Experiments. ♪

MISS FAY having appeared for nine consecutive months at the Queen's Concert Rooms, London, and later for three weeks at the Crystal Palace. For three months Miss Fay was the guests of Prof. Wm. Crooks, F. R. S., No. 20 Mornington Road, W. C. During that time Prof. Crooks built the Galvanometer, an electrical machine to test physical demonstration.

During Parts First and Third, in which Miss Fay appears, and during which she is at such a high mental strain, it is necessary for her to have a complete release from the same sometime during the performance, consequently the following will be introduced in

PART SECOND.

MR. WETHEREL RHOADS'

ROYAL ENGLISH MANNIKINS

Harry D'Esta,   Wm. W. Rhoads,   L'Mai D'Esta,   Manipulators.

No intermission between Part Second and

PART THIRD.

The entertainment will close by placing Miss Fay in a Hypnotic Condition and she will give her weird and startling visions of what she sees and hears in Hypnotic Dreamland by

"SOMNOLENCY."

SPECIAL NOTICE—Miss Fay receives hundreds of letters and is obliged to employ two secretaries to assist in her correspondence. Letters regarding "Somnolency" will not be answered unless they contain an envelope properly addressed and stamped for the reply; even then no reply will be sent to letters deemed silly or unimportant. Even when the above conditions are complied with it may be several days before a reply can be sent. Don't write unless it is important. Letters are answered as a matter of courtesy. Send all communications to the PLANTER'S HOTEL. No one received in person at the hotel.

MISS FAY "DREAM BOOK"

In the hands of the publisher now, is a book that Miss Fay has compiled from years of experience interpreting all dreams, which are alphabetically arranged, with full directions as to how to put yourself in a somnambulist state to receive the benefit of your living nights.

BYRON'S QUOTATION.

"WE LIVE BY NIGHT, AND NOT BY DAY."

When you write your letter to Miss Fay to the Planter's Hotel, enclose twentyfive cents for one of these books.

Fig. 4.4. A playbill headlining Anna Eva Fay. (Mary Evans Picture Library)

For these séances, Cromwell F. Varley, another Fellow of the Royal Society, provided an electrical control circuit, a slightly modifed version of the one used by Crookes with medium Florence Cook. To make sure that the medium, seated in a curtained cabinet, could not slip her bonds, Crookes asked her to clench both handles of a battery. If she let go either handle, the current would be interrupted and send the meter to 0. Fay managed, somehow, to present her manifestations though the contact remained unbroken.

At a later séance, two of the guests were more skeptical than their host. When they inspected the electrical control system before the session began, they discovered that a damp handkerchief stretched between the handles would keep the circuit open. At the suggestion of one of these men, Crookes nailed the handles so far apart that a handkerchief could not span them. Apparently no one considered the possibility that a longer strip of cloth or some other type of resistor might be used.

Success at these experiments fueled Annie's tour of the English provinces; however, when she opened at Birmingham in May, she was again described as the "Indescribable Phenomenon" and her show was billed as an entertainment.[7] Apparently, at the end of her tour, her manager, dissatisfied with the fact that the scientists' investigations did not put any money in his pockets, wrote to John Nevil Maskelyne, one of Britain's greatest magicians, suggesting a public exposure of his ex-client. For a substantial sum of money, he offered to reveal how the Crookes experiments had been faked. Maskelyne declined the offer, so the impresario wrote again, presenting him to Miss Lottie Fowler, another pretty mystic, who could do the Fay tricks and went on tour with the same routine when Annie left England.

EXPOSURES AND CONFESSION

Exposures of Annie's performance appeared now and then on the press. On April 12, 1876, Washington Irving Bishop, an ex-member of Fay's American troupe and later to become one of the greatest mentalists of all times himself, revealed to the *New York Daily Graphic* how her tricks were accomplished. Unruffled, she continued her work with her usual success and reinserted her mind-reading act into her program. Pads were distributed and members of the audience were invited by her husband to write questions, sign their names, tear off the sheets, and hold the pieces of paper folded in their hands. Later, Annie, blindfolded, divined correctly the content of the sheets of paper and answered the questions written on them. She called this portion of the show "Somnolency," adapted from "Somnomancy," the name Samri S. Baldwin, "The White Mahatma," had given to the similar act which he had invented.

In 1906 H. A. Parkyn, editor of the magazine *Suggestion*, contributed a long article on the trick methods used by Miss Fay in her billet-reading tests, describing the preparation of the pads and the use of confederates among the audience. This "exposure" was hardly necessary, since it was at this time that she was stating in her program that credulous and foolish persons should not be influenced by her performance, since she was "not a spiritualistic medium" and there was nothing "either supernatural or miraculous" about her performance.

In spite of the disavowals of any supernatural power, further exposures occurred in February 1907, when Prof. W. S. Barnickel described some of her methods, and in January 1911, when Albini, the magician, exposed her "Somnolency" act; still, the public filled theatres where she was featured.

Her son, John T. Fay, married Anna Norman, one of the assistants in Eva's show, then left home and set up on his own with his wife, calling themselves "The Fays." When John died in 1908, his widow set up her own show and billed herself as "Mrs. Eva Fay, The High Priestess of Mysticism." Obviously, Annie resented her using a stage name so similar to her own, but never took legal action to stop her.

In 1912 Annie visited Europe again and when she reached London, where she performed at the Coliseum, the Spiritualists were still ready to marvel at her supernatural powers. One of them, J. Hewat McKenzie, claimed he had been able to discover Eva's secret: her manifestations were done by a small pair of materialized hands and arms, somewhat like those of a monkey, which protruded from her chest. He knew because he had been able to "smell the odour from the emanation of the psycho-plastic matter" during a performance. This same man would later claim he knew how Houdini performed his escapes: by "dematerializing his body," of course.[8]

During her visit, psychic researcher and magician Eric J. Dingwall, who described her as "extremely prepossessing with a perfect complexion and sparkling blue eyes," was successful in getting her proposed and elected as the first Honorary Lady Associate of the Magic Circle.[9]

For another eleven years she continued to attract capacity crowds wherever she performed. Due to an accidental injury, she played her final engagement in Milwaukee in 1924. In July of that year she received a visit from Harry Houdini.

Houdini considered her "one of the cleverest mediums in history" and noticed her "straw diamond white" hair and penetrating eyes, from which "great big streaks of intelligence would flash in and out." "It is small wonder," he observed, "that with her personality she could have mystified the great mental giants of the ages,—not our age, but of the ages."[10]

They talked for hours and she revealed to him all her secrets. "She spoke freely of her methods," Houdini noted. "Never at any time did she pretend to believe in spiritualism."[11] She told him how she had tricked Crookes at the electric test: she had simply gripped one handle of the battery beneath her knee, keeping the circuit unbroken but leaving one hand free to do as she wished.

A year later she announced her plan to leave the ten houses on her Melrose Heights property to destitute actors and actresses, but she died on May 20, 1927, before working out the final details of her project.

Anna Eva Fay's revelation to Houdini of the way she had gulled Crookes was confirmed years later when psychical researcher Colin Brookes-Smith found one of the galvanometers used by Crookes at the Science Museum in London. The machine was repaired and brought to working order. Brookes-Smith reports that "there was no difficulty at all in sliding one wrist and forearm along over one handle and grasping the other handle, thereby keeping the circuit closed through the forearm, and then releasing the other hand without producing any large movement of

Fig. 4.5. Houdini poses with Anna Eva Fay in 1924.
(McManus-Young Collection, Library of Congress,
Rare Books and Special Collection Division, LC-USZ62-96050)

the galvanometer spot." In a second test, he "tucked both electrodes successively right down into my socks and let go so that my hands were free
without producing any large galvanometer spot excursions." In this way,
not only did he confirm Eva's revelation but also "Houdini's 1924 foot-
note explanation that in 1874 Florence (Cook) could have detached one
of the electrodes consisting of a gold sovereign and saline soaked blot-
ting-paper pad from one wrist and held it under her knee."[12]

There is no doubt now that trickery actually took place during
Crookes's tests, exactly as described by Anna Eva Fay; what still needs to
be cleared up is whether he was a complete fool (unlikely) or a willing
accomplice. In any case, one thing can't be denied: the great William
Crookes had a special interest in attractive, young mediums needing a
scientific pedigree and was willing to test them all, even if they were out-
right fakes like Eva Fay, in his own house, right under his wife's nose.

NOTES

Reprinted with permission of the editors from the *Skeptical Inquirer* 24, no. 1 (January/February 2000). Copyright 2000 by the Committee for the Scientific Investigation of Claims of the Paranormal.

1. T. H. Hall, *The Medium and the Scientist* (1962; reprint, Amherst, N.Y.: Prometheus Books, 1984).

2. M. Christopher, *Mediums, Mystics & The Occult* (New York: Thomas Y. Crowell Co., 1975), p. 170.

3. Ibid., p. 161.

4. Ibid.

5. Eric J. Dingwall, *The Critics' Dilemma* (Crowhurst, Sussex: privately printed, 1966), p. 36.

6. William Crookes, "A Scientific Examination of Mrs. Fay's Mediumship," *Spiritualist* (March 12, 1875).

7. Dingwall, *Critics' Dilemma*, p. 41.

8. Arthur Conan Doyle, *The Edge of the Unknown* (1930; reprint, New York: Barnes & Noble, 1992), p. 28.

9. Dingwall, *Critics' Dilemma*, p. 51.

10. Quoted in K. Silverman, *Houdini!!! The Career of Ehrich Weiss* (New York: HarperCollins, 1996), p. 308.

11. Ibid., pp. 308–309.

12. Colin Brookes-Smith, "Cromwell Varley's Electrical Tests," *Journal of the Society for Psychical Research* 723, no. 43 (March 1965): 178.

CHAPTER FIVE

HOUDINI
AND
CONAN DOYLE
The Story of a Strange Friendship

With the release, in October 1997, of the film *Fairy Tale: A True Story*, devoted to the famous case of the Cottingley fairies, a new generation of cinema-goers has had a glimpse (though only in a fictional way) into the strange relationship that linked, more than seventy years ago, two most singular characters.[1] They were Harry Houdini—master magician, escape artist, and mystifier extraordinaire—and Sir Arthur Conan Doyle—author and creator of Sherlock Holmes.

They were both profoundly interested in the subject of spiritualism; however, their views differed completely. Houdini was a skeptic, an exposer of psychic frauds; Doyle was a believer, the St. Paul of spiritualism. How these two persons became affectionate friends and then bitter enemies is a fascinating tale.

A COMMON INTEREST

It began in early 1920, when Houdini, touring the British Isles, sent Sir Arthur one of his books, *The Unmasking of Robert-Houdin*. In it, he made reference to the Davenport Brothers, two American medium-magicians who became very famous in various parts of the world, during the middle of the nineteenth century. Their specialty was the presentation of the "Spirit cabinet," a wooden cabinet in which they sat and were securely tied with meters of rope. No sooner had the cabinet doors been closed than rappings were heard, a bell and a tambourine would play, and hands would appear at the openings of the doors. Examination of the mediums at the conclusion of the séance, or at any time during its progress, revealed the mediums tied as before.

The question was: were they genuine mediums or clever magicians who somehow managed to free themselves from the bonds and produce the manifestations themselves? Houdini had had a chance, in 1910, to speak at length with Ira Davenport, the only surviving brother, and felt privileged to learn directly from him the clever secret of their act. They were forerunners of the escape act that later made Houdini famous, and Ira admitted to him that they had always used trickery; however, for publicity reasons, they let their audiences decide for themselves as to the true source of their sensational demonstrations.

In thanking Houdini for the book, Sir Arthur wrote that he didn't put much faith in this kind of revelation: "As to Spiritualist 'confessions,' they are all nonsense. Every famous medium is said to have 'confessed,' and it is an old trick of the opposition." He also showed that he believed in one of the oldest ruses used by fake mediums and psychics to convince onlookers of the reality of their powers; namely, that failure is proof of genuine paranormal powers (see chapter 1). He wrote, in fact: "I can only learn, so far as 'exposures' goes, that there were occasions when they could not undo the knots, but as there are intermittent periods in all real mediumship, that is not against them. It is the man who could always guarantee spirit action whom I should suspect most."[2]

In various subsequent letters, Sir Arthur reverts to the Davenports repeatedly, writing: "I've been reading the Davenport book you gave me" (41). And, after Houdini sent him a picture of himself with Ira, he wrote: ". . . you said that Ira Davenport did his phenomena by normal means. But if he did (which I really don't believe) then he is manifestly not only a liar but a blasphemer, as he went round with Mr. Ferguson, a clergyman, and mixed it all up with religion. And yet you are photographed as a friend with one whom under those circumstances, one would not touch with a muck-rake. Now, how can one reconcile that? It interests me as a problem" (42).

Houdini, anxious to cultivate a friendship with Doyle, replied somewhat ambiguously: "I can make the positive assertion that the Davenport Brothers never were exposed," meaning that no one had discovered their tricks (45). Doyle, however, preferred to interpret this as a confirmation of his beliefs: they were never exposed because there was nothing to expose: "Unless I hear to the contrary I will take it that I may use your authoritative statement as the occasion serves" (83).

In a further letter, Doyle went straight to the point: "I had meant to ask you, in my last, and I will do so now, whether you, with your unique experience, consider that the Davenport phenomena were clever physical tricks, or whether their claim to occult power was a true one" (84). Houdini, again, was noncommittal: "Regarding the Davenport Brothers, I am afraid that I cannot say that all their work was accomplished by the spirits" (84). Doyle found the reply satisfying and so their friendship started.

SKEPTIC AND BELIEVER MEET

At about this time, Houdini's most profound interest in the world of spirits developed. However, he presented himself to Doyle as a longtime student of spiritualism: "I have gone out of my way for years to unearth mediums, so that I could really find a truthful representative—and regret to say that, so far, I have never witnessed a séance which had the ring of sincerity" (84). And, in another letter: "During my tour in Australia, I met a man who was supposed to have laid low Mrs. Piper; I was in Berlin,

Fig. 5.1. Houdini and Conan Doyle pose in front of a restaurant in London.
(Mary Evans Picture Library)

Germany, at the trial of Miss Rothe, the flower medium; I know of the methods of the Bangs Sisters, the famous Chicago mediums; I was in court when Anna O'Delia Diss De Bar, who was mixed up with the lawyer Luther Marsh, was sentenced . . ." (113).

He also proposed himself to Doyle as a disciple: "You will note that I am still a sceptic, but a seeker after the Truth. I am willing to believe, if I can find a Medium who, as you suggest, will not resort to 'manipulation' when the Power does not 'arrive' . . ." (85).

On April 14, they finally met at Windlesham, Doyle's country house in Crowborough, Sussex. Houdini wrote in his diary: "Met Lady Doyle and the three children. Had lunch with them. They believe implicitly in Spiritualism. Sir Arthur told me he had spoken six times to his son. No possible chance for trickery. Lady Doyle also believes and has had tests that are beyond belief. Told them all to me" (67).

Houdini asked Doyle's help to find a true medium: "I am very, very anxious to have a séance with any medium with whom you could gain me an audience. I promise to go there with my mind absolutely clear, and willing to believe. I will put no obstruction of any nature whatsoever in the medium's way, and will assist in all ways in my power to obtain results" (88). Doyle consented and arranged a number of sittings for him in London and elsewhere.

SITTING WITH EVA C.

The most famous séances in which Houdini participated during this period were those with French medium "Eva C." These séances were held in London, at the rooms of the Society for Pyschical Research, and Houdini was invited to participate in several of them. Eva C. (aka Eva Carrière, although her real name was Marthe Béraud) specialized in the production of "ectoplasm," apparently emanating from her mouth and other orifices of her body. In order to study her case, and verify whether these phenomena were produced normally or not, the SPR invited Eva over to England.

Several of the sittings attended by Houdini were complete blanks: nothing happened. He tells this to Sir Arthur in a letter dated June 19, 1920: "Baggally and Dingwall [two SPR investigators] inform me that she has really mystified them, with her manifestations, and I am rather keen to be present, and am going again Monday night" (56). That night was, at last, rich of phenomena, as Houdini relates in this letter:

My Dear Sir Arthur,

Well, we had success at the séance last night, as far as productions were concerned, but I am not prepared to say that they were supernormal.

I assure you I did not control the medium, so the suggestions were not mine. They made Mlle. Eva drink a cup of coffee and eat some cake (I presume to fill her up with some food stuff), and after she had been sewn into the tights, and a net over her face, she "manifested,"

1st. Some froth-like substance, inside of net. It was about 5 inches long; she said it was "elevating," but none of us four watchers saw it "elevate."

Committee, Messrs. Feilding, Baggally, Dingwall and myself.

2nd. A white plaster-looking affair over her right eye.

3rd. Something that looked like a small face, say 4 inches in cir- cumference. Was terra-cotta colored, and Dingwall, who held her hands, had the best look at the "object."

4th. Some substance, froth-like, "exuding from her nose." Baggally and Feilding say it protruded from her nose, but Dingwall and I are positive that it was inside of net and was not extending from her nose; I had the best view from two different places. I deliberately took advan- tage to see just what it was.

It was a surprise effect indeed!

5th. Medium asked permission to remove something in her mouth; showed her hands empty, and took out what appeared to be a rubberish substance, which she disengaged and showed us plainly; we held the electric torch; all saw it plainly, when presto! it vanished.

The séance started at 7.30 and lasted till past midnight.

We went over the notes, Mr. Feilding did, and no doubt you will get a full report. I found it highly interesting. (56–57)

After receiving this letter, Sir Arthur wrote to Houdini: "This is very interesting. I am glad you got some results. It is certainly on the lowest and most mechanical plane of the spiritual world, or borderline world, but at least it is beyond our present knowledge" (58–59).

Houdini, however, did not reveal immediately to Conan Doyle his further thoughts on the séance. In private he noted: "I was not in any way convinced by the demonstrations."[3] A few years later, in *A Magician Among the Spirits*, he explained that he had detected the various tricks employed. He believed, for example, that the disappearance of the rubberish substance had been accomplished by sleight of hand: "I know positively that the move she made is almost identical with the manner in which I manipulate my experiment." (He was referring to the "Hindu needle trick.")[4] In conclusion, he felt that Eva and her assistant, Mme. Bisson, were subtle tricksters: "I have no hesitation in saying that I think the two simply took advantage of the credulity and good nature of the various men with whom they had to deal."[5]

GLIMPSES OF DOYLE'S CREDULITY

At this time Doyle became engaged in the story of the fairy photographs. He wrote to Houdini: "I have something far more precious: two photos, one of a goblin, the other of four fairies in a Yorkshire wood. A fake! you will say. No, sir, I think not. However, all inquiry will be made. These I am not allowed to send. The fairies are about eight inches high. In one there is a single goblin dancing. In the other four beautiful, luminous creatures. Yes, it is a revelation" (96).

It is interesting to note that Houdini had no comment to make on this subject in any of his letters; perhaps he could not bring himself to discuss it seriously.

Meanwhile, Sir Arthur was becoming more and more convinced that Houdini himself had some kind of supernatural powers. "I have heard of your remarkable feat in Bristol," he wrote. "My dear chap, why go around the world seeking a demonstration of the occult when you are giving one all the time? Mrs. Guppy [a well-known medium] could dematerialize, and so could many folks in Holy Writ, and I do honestly believe that you can also,—in which case I again ask you why do you want demonstrations of the occult? My reason tells me that you have this wonderful power, for there is no alternative, tho' I have no doubt that, up to a point, your strength and skill avail you. . . . I am amused by your investigating with the S.P.R. Do they never think of investigating *you*?" (99).

In April of 1922, Sir Arthur went to the United States for a series of lectures on spiritualism. They created a sensation, and the lecture halls where Doyle appeared were always filled to capacity. His opening lecture at Carnegie Hall had to be repeated seven times to satisfy all those interested. Houdini attended one of the lectures but did not discuss it with Doyle. Instead, the two men met about a month later, on May 10, when Sir Arthur and his wife went to New York to have lunch at Houdini's house.

Houdini showed his huge collection of books on magic and related arts to Sir Arthur, who was duly impressed but noticed the lack of any works on spiritualism, that is, in favor of it. In a memorandum, Houdini noted later that day: "There is no doubt that both Sir Arthur and Lady Doyle believe absolutely in Spiritualism, and sincerely so. They related a number of incidents which they accepted without proof. They stopped for lunch and we enjoyed the visit very much. Lady Doyle passed a comment that this was the most home-like home that she had ever seen. After luncheon we called a car and took them to the Ambassador Hotel" (139).

While in the car, Houdini showed Doyle a very childish trick, the apparent removal of the first joint of his thumb. Doyle's reaction to this was quite exemplary of his naiveté: "Just a line to say how much we enjoyed our short visit yesterday. I think what interested me most was the little 'trick' which you showed us in the cab. You certainly have very wonderful powers, whether inborn or acquired" (139).

The Fatal Séance

Doyle's lecture tour in the United States was quite hectic and he wrote to Houdini: "Until Thursday is over I shall be in turmoil. Then, when I can breathe, I hope to see you—your normal self, not in a tank or hanging by one toe from a skyscraper" (133).

In early June, Houdini invited Doyle to attend the Society of American Magicians' annual banquet in New York: "You will meet some notable people and, incidentally, this is quite an affair to our organization, as some of the city officials and big business men will be there. . . . I know that you will be interested in witnessing the magicians' performance from a looker-on viewpoint" (101–102).

To this, however, Sir Arthur replied: "I fear that the bogus spiritual phenomena must prevent me from attending the banquet, which you have so graciously proffered. I look upon this subject as sacred, and I think that God's gift to man has been intercepted and delayed by the constant pretence that all phenomena are really tricks, which I know they are not. I should be in a false position, for I must either be silent and seem to acquiesce, or else protest, which a guest should not do" (102). Houdini assured him "as a gentleman that there will be nothing performed or said which will offend anyone" (102). Finally, Doyle agreed to attend: "Of course we will come. All thanks. But I feel towards faked phenomena as your father would have felt towards a faked Pentecost" (103).

It was at this annual banquet of the Society of American Magicians that Sir Arthur showed some of the film later to be incorporated into the movie adapted from his book *The Lost World*.[6]

Later in the month, Doyle and his family took a well-deserved rest in Atlantic City. It was a wonderful chance to spend some time with the Houdinis. "The children would teach you to swim!" wrote Sir Arthur, "and the change would do you good" (155). Houdini liked the idea and replied at once: "Mrs. Houdini joins me in thanking you for the invitation to come to Atlantic City, and if you will be there next Saturday or Sunday, Mrs. Houdini and I would like to spend the week-end with you. . . . Most important of all, if the kiddies want to teach me to swim I will be there,

Fig. 5.2. Houdini and Conan Doyle on a beach in Atlantic City.
(Mary Evans Picture Library)

and in return will show them how to do one or two things that will make it very interesting" (155).

The weekend was June 17–18, 1922, and the hotel at which the Houdinis and Doyles stayed was the Ambassador. On Saturday they spent their time playing with the children in the hotel swimming pool. The next day, Bess and Harry Houdini were sunning themselves on the beach when Doyle showed up. He had come to suggest that Lady Doyle should give Houdini a private sitting, at which she should endeavor to obtain for him a message from his beloved mother, through the instrumentality of her own mediumship and by means of automatic writing. However, he asked if Mrs. Houdini wouldn't mind waiting outside: "You understand, Mrs. Houdini, that this will be a test to see whether we can make any Spirit come through for Houdini, and conditions may prove better if no other force is present."[7] This is how Houdini recalls what happened next:

> I walked with Sir Arthur to the Doyles' suite. Sir Arthur drew down the shades so as to exclude the bright light. We three, Lady Doyle, Sir Arthur and I, sat around the table on which were a number of pencils and a writing pad, placing our hands on the surface of the table.
>
> Sir Arthur started the séance with a devout prayer. I had made up my mind that I would be as religious as it was within my power to be and not at any time did I scoff at the ceremony. I excluded all earthly thoughts and gave my whole soul to the séance.
>
> I was *willing* to believe, even *wanted* to believe. It was weird to me and with a beating heart I waited, hoping that I might feel once more the presence of my beloved Mother. . . .
>
> Presently Lady Doyle was "seized by a Spirit." Her hands shook and beat the table, her voice trembled and she called to the Spirits to give her a message. Sir Arthur tried to quiet her, asked her to restrain herself, but her hand thumped on the table, her whole body shook and at last, making a cross at the head of the page, she started writing. And as she finished each page, Sir Arthur tore the sheet off and handed it to me. I sat serene through it all, hoping and wishing that I might feel my mother's presence.[8]

The first sheet began: "Oh, my darling, thank God, at last I'm through.—I've tried so often—now I am happy. Why, of course, I want to talk to my boy—my own beloved boy—Friends, thank you, with all my heart for this" (161). It continued in the same vein for fifteen pages. After the séance was over, Houdini asked about trying automatic writing at his own home, took a pencil, and wrote the name "Powell." Doyle was shocked, for a friend of his by that name, the editor of the *Financial Times* of London, had died about a week previously. For Doyle it was further proof that Houdini himself was a medium: "Truly Saul is among the Prophets."

When Houdini and Doyle parted that evening, they had already formed two very different opinions about what had happened. According to Doyle, Houdini left "deeply moved" and when they met two days later in New York, remarked to Sir Arthur: "I have been walking on air ever since."

Houdini's account, however, was much different. There were various details which could not be reconciled with what he knew about his mother. "Although my sainted mother had been in America for almost fifty years," he wrote, "she could not speak, read, nor write English," and Lady Doyle's message was in perfect English. Also, her message began with the sign of a cross and the wife of a rabbi would hardly have communicated such a symbol. Furthermore, Houdini had been thinking all during the séance about familiar things that he had always discussed with his mother, and he had expected to see some reference to them in the message. There was none, as there was no reference to the fact that the day before the séance, June 17, was her birthday.

For the moment, Houdini did not reveal to Doyle his doubts about the séance; however he protested Doyle's casting him as a medium. Regarding the "Powell" incident, in fact, Houdini explained that he was referring to a magician friend, Frederick Eugene Powell, with whom at the time he was having a great deal of correspondence.

"No, the Powell explanation won't do," was Sir Arthur's immediate reply. "Not only is he the man who would wish to get to me, but in the evening Mrs. M., the lady medium, got 'there is a man here; he wants to say that he is sorry he had to speak so abruptly this afternoon.' The message was then broken by your mother's renewed message, and so we got no name. But it confirms me in the belief that it was Powell. However, you will no doubt test your own powers further" (167).

Before returning to England, Doyle accepted an invitation from Houdini: "Mrs. Houdini and I are going to celebrate our twenty-eighth marriage anniversary June 22nd. Would you care to join us in a little box party?" (106). They went to see Raymond Hitchcock starring at the Carroll Theater in *Pinwheel*, "a hodge-podge of good-natured stuff" (106). During the performance, Hitchcock called the attention of the audience to the presence of the two distinguished guests. Then he asked Houdini to do a little stunt. Urged by Sir Arthur and by the whole audience yelling his name, Houdini went onstage and performed the "Hindu needle trick," in which he apparently swallowed a quantity of needles and some thread, and then brought up the needles threaded. "Seldom," wrote one reviewer the next day, "has there been heard such applause as that with which Houdini was greeted at the conclusion of the mystery. He finally made his way to his seat, but, with the audience speculating on the mystery, the *Pinwheel* performance was curtailed and the show swung into its closing number. Such an incident is unique, for . . . [there is] no mention, in the memory of the theatrical historian, of the feat of an artist not only stopping but curtailing a show in which he was not programmed to have a part" (108).

Doyle finally left America with Houdini's telegram in his pocket: "Bon Voyage. May the Decree of Fate send you back here soon for another pleasant visit" (108).

END OF A FRIENDSHIP

The decline of Houdini and Conan Doyle's friendship started when Houdini published an article in the *New York Sun*, in October 1922, in which he emphatically stated that he had "never seen or heard anything that could convince me that there is a possibility of communication with the loved ones who have gone beyond." Sir Arthur, evidently hurt by the obvious implication that Lady Doyle's séance too had been fake, replied: "I felt rather sore about it. You have all the right in the world to hold your own opinion, but when you say that you have had no evidence of survival, you say what I cannot reconcile with what I saw with my own eyes." He concluded: "I don't propose to discuss this subject any more with you, for I consider that you have had your proofs and that the responsibility of accepting or rejecting is with you" (168).

Houdini, never one to shy away from a challenge, replied: "You write that you are very 'sore.' I trust that it is not with me, because you, having been truthful and manly all your life, naturally must admire the same traits in other human beings" (168). He then went on to explain all of his doubts concerning the séance and trusted Doyle would "not harbor any ill feeling." "I know," he stated, "you treat this as a religion, but personally I cannot do so for, up to the present time, and with all my experiences, I have never seen or heard anything that could really convert me" (169).

Their private quarrel soon became a public battle.

Early in 1923, Houdini became a member of the *Scientific American* committee to investigate mediums, a fact that left Conan Doyle puzzled: ". . . you can't sit on an impartial Committee. . . . It becomes biased at once" (188). Later he expressed his opinion publicly: "The Commission is, in my opinion, a farce, and has already killed itself. Can people not understand that 'psychic' means 'of the spirit,' and that it concerns not only the invisible spirit or the spirit of the medium, but equally those of every one of the Investigators?"

In April, Doyle returned to the United States to continue his lecture tour and met Houdini in Denver. They had long discussions about spiritualism and some recent psychic investigations. Doyle had witnessed a demonstration by the Zancigs, a couple of vaudeville mind-readers, and was convinced they were real telepaths. Houdini, however, knew them personally; they were acknowledged magicians and members of the Society of American Magicians, but none of this moved Doyle. "Sir Arthur said that he was capable of detecting trickery," wrote Houdini in his notes, "and we had a discussion in which I said that I did not think he could. He looked amazed at me, and I said, 'Why, Sir Arthur, I have been trained in mystery all my life and every once in a while I see something I cannot account for.'"

Doyle was interviewed for the local Denver newspaper. The reporter told him that Houdini was offering five thousand dollars for any medium's feat he could not duplicate, and Doyle said that he would give the same amount of money if Houdini could "show me my mother." Immediately, Doyle apologized to Houdini, saying he had been misquoted.

It was Houdini's turn next to be misquoted, by a Los Angeles newspaper. After reading the interview, in which Houdini typically stated his views on spiritualism, Doyle wrote to him: "I have had to handle you a little roughly in the *Oakland Tribune*, because they send me a long screed under quotation marks, so it is surely accurate. It is so full of errors that I don't know where to begin . . . I hate sparring with a friend in public, but what can I do when you say things which are not correct, and which I have to contradict or else they go by default?" (199–200). In a subsequent letter, Doyle further explained: "I am very sorry this breach has come, as we have felt very friendly towards Mrs. Houdini and yourself, but 'friendly is as friendly does,' and this is not friendly, but on the contrary it is outrageous to make such statements with no atom of truth in them" (200–201).

The breach grew wider still; in another letter, Doyle remarked: "Our relations are certainly curious and are likely to become more so, for so long as you attack what I *know* from experience to be true, I have no alternative but to attack you in return. How long a private friendship can survive such an ordeal I do not know, but at least I did not create the situation" (201).

The last letter which passed between them was written in February 1924 by Doyle. In reply to some request by Houdini for information, Sir Arthur wrote: "You probably want these extracts in order to twist them in some way against me or my cause" (203). Some time later, Houdini sent a short note inquiring whether Doyle wanted to receive a copy of his new book, *A Magician Among the Spirits*, but got no answer.

Their friendship was over, but their quarrels would continue.

THE LAST QUARREL

In the summer of 1924, the biggest stir in psychical research was caused by a powerful, attractive medium named "Margery" (Mina Crandon). She had entered the *Scientific American* competition and was considered to be the likeliest winner of the prize. That is, until Houdini sat with her. He was immediately able to discern her true methods and promptly revealed them to the world.

Sir Arthur, who had met Margery and endorsed her powers, considered Houdini's revelations trash. Doyle wrote a newspaper article based on the correspondence of Dr. Crandon, Margery's husband, which told the story of the investigation. The article was meant to discredit Houdini: "It should be the end of him as a Psychic Researcher," he wrote Crandon, "if he could ever have been called one."[9]

When the article was published, Houdini announced that he would "contemplate legal action" against Sir Arthur for slander. "There is not a word of truth in his charges against me," he told a newspaper. "Sir Arthur has been sadly misinformed. Anyhow, I fail to see how he, being 3,500 miles away, qualifies as a judge." He attributed the sharpness of Doyle's attack to his being "a bit senile . . . and therefore easily bamboozled," and to a desire for revenge, since Houdini had "often expressed the belief that Lady Doyle was not a valid medium."[10] Doyle replied to Houdini's statements by diagnosing an "abnormal frame of mind" that he called "Houdinitis," one of whose symptoms was the belief "that manual dexterity bears some relation to brain capacity."[11]

What had started as a beautiful friendship, nourished by mutual respect and admiration, ended in sharp words and threats of legal actions. However, when Houdini died on October 31, 1926, Doyle put his ill feelings aside and expressed fondness and shock: "I greatly admired him, and cannot understand how the end came for one so youthful. We were great friends. . . . We agreed upon everything excepting spiritualism."[12] In a letter to Beatrice Houdini, Doyle wrote: "Any man who wins the love and respect of a good woman must himself be a fine and honest man," and went on to describe Houdini as "a loving husband, a good friend, a man full of sweet impulses" (211).

HOUDINI THE "MEDIUM"

"Who was the greatest medium-baiter of modern times? Undoubtedly Houdini. Who was the greatest medium of modern times? There are some who would be inclined to give the same answer."[13]

This is the incipit of "The Riddle of Houdini," an essay by Sir Arthur Conan Doyle, published in the July 1927 issue of *Strand* magazine, and later included in Doyle's last book, *The Edge of the Unknown* (1930). The essay opened describing Houdini's many merits: "Let me say, in the first instance, that in a long life which has touched every side of humanity, Houdini is far and away the most curious and intriguing character whom I have ever encountered. I have met better men, and I have certainly met very many worse ones, but I have never met a man who had such strange contrasts in his nature, and whose actions and motives it was more diffi-cult to foresee or to reconcile" (*Edge* 11).

Doyle admired Houdini's "essential masculine quality of courage. . . . Nobody has ever done, and nobody in all human probability will ever do, such reckless feats of daring." He also praised Houdini's "cheery urbanity" in everyday life: "One could not wish a better companion so long as one was with him, though he might do and say the most unexpected things when one was absent" (*Edge* 12).

Aside from these and other virtues, Doyle noted that "a prevailing feature of his character was a vanity which was so obvious and childish that it became more amusing than offensive. . . . This enormous vanity was combined with a passion for publicity which knew no bounds, and which must at all costs be gratified" (*Edge* 13).

The main feature of the essay, however, was the exposition of Doyle's theory that Houdini was a real medium. He claimed that no tricks could explain Houdini's feats, such as his escapes from jails: "It takes some credulity, I think, to say that this was, in the ordinary sense of the word, a trick" (*Edge* 24–25).

"I contend," stated Doyle, "that Houdini's performance was on an utterly different plane, and that it is an outrage against common sense to think otherwise" (*Edge* 26–27). According to Doyle, Houdini possessed strong psychic powers that enabled him to dematerialize from his confinement and then rematerialize outside of it.

The fact that Houdini had always told him that he had no psychic powers whatsoever and that he only used trickery, a fact that Bess had repeated to him after her husband's death, did not convince Doyle. In fact, these denials further induced him to believe that his theory was correct: "Is it not perfectly evident that if he did not deny them his occupation would have been gone for ever? What would his brother-magicians have to say to a man who admitted that half his tricks were done by what they would regard as illicit powers? It would be 'exit Houdini'" (*Edge* 31).

This was one of Doyle's last works. In one of his last letters, to B. M. L. Ernst, Houdini's lawyer, Sir Arthur wrote: "I write this in bed, as I have broken down badly, and have developed Angina Pectoris. So there is just a chance that I may talk it all over with Houdini himself before long" (*Edge* 13). On July 7, 1930, four years after the death of Houdini the archskeptic, Sir Arthur Conan Doyle, the extreme believer, died.

NOTES

Reprinted with permission of the editors from the *Skeptical Inquirer* 22, no. 2 (March/April 1998). Copyright 1998 by the Committee for the Scientific Investigation of Claims of the Paranormal.

After writing this article and considering the kind reaction of readers, I decided that the friendship between Houdini and Doyle deserved to be told in detail. I thus set about writing a book which was finally published in 2001 by Prometheus Books, titled: *Final Séance: The Strange Friendship Between Houdini and Conan Doyle.*

1. For an account of the Cottingley fairies, see Robert Sheaffer, "Do Fairies Exist?" *Skeptical Inquirer* 2, no. 1 (1977): 45–52; also James Randi, *Flim-Flam!* (Amherst, N.Y.: Prometheus Books, 1982).

2. B. M. L. Ernst and Hereward Carrington, *Houdini and Conan Doyle: The Story of a Strange Friendship* (New York: Albert and Charles Boni, 1932), p. 40. All quotations from letters between Houdini and Conan Doyle have been

taken from this source. Numbers which appear in parentheses in the body of this chapter refer to page numbers from this work.

3. Kenneth Silverman, *Houdini!!! The Career of Ehrich Weiss* (New York: HarperCollins, 1996), p. 258.

4. Harry Houdini, *A Magician Among the Spirits* (1924; reprint, New York: Arno Press, 1972), p. 170.

5. Ibid., p. 172.

6. Edward Summer, "Conan Doyle's Revenge," *Skeptical Briefs* 5, no. 4 (1995): 1–2.

7. Houdini, *Magician*, p. 151.

8. Ibid., pp. 151–52.

9. Silverman, *Houdini*, p. 351.

10. Ibid., p. 352.

11. Ibid.

12. *New York Times*, November 2, 1926.

13. Arthur Conan Doyle, *The Edge of the Unknown* (1930; reprint, New York: Barnes & Noble, 1992), p. 11.

CHAPTER SIX

HOUDINI
VERSUS
MARGERY

*When the Magician Met
the Blond Witch of Lime Street*

---

*I*n the century-long history of serious psychic research, the "Margery"
episode is probably one of the most interesting. No other medium
since Daniel Dunglas Home, not even Eusapia Palladino, attracted as
much interest and controversy as Mina Stinson, also known as Margery,
the "Blond Witch of Lime Street." Like Home, Stinson (her birth name)
didn't ask for money for her demonstrations but, unlike her predecessor,
she refused even donations or jewels. No ignorant peasant coming from a
country town like Eusapia, she was instead the wife of a respected and
wealthy Boston physician, Dr. Le Roy Goddard Crandon. By all accounts
Stinson was brilliant and quick-witted, and, in her early thirties, with
blue-eyes and long, brown hair, a very attractive woman. Margery was the
last famous case of physical mediumship to be presented as proof of the
reality of the powers of mind over matter, or psychokinesis, until the
arrival fifty years later of Uri Geller. With her ended the era of the great
mediums that began with Daniel Home.

LIFE AT LIME STREET

The events that interest us began in the spring of 1923, at number 10 Lime Street, a four-story brick house in the stylish neighborhood of Beacon Hill in Boston. Margery's husband, Dr. Le Roy Goddard Crandon, was a dour and aristocratic man with many hobbies and interests beyond medicine, ranging from a passion for the sea to the study of the writings of Abraham Lincoln. It was inevitable that this nimble mind would turn to a subject that interested everybody in the 1920s—psychic research. His interest was sparked by a meeting he had with Sir Oliver Lodge (1851–1940), a physicist of great renown who, after the death of his son Raymond during the war, had announced he believed in human survival after death and in the possibility of communicating with the dead. Lodge had suggested a book to Crandon, *The Psychic Structures at the Goligher Circle* by Dr. William J. Crawford. After reading the story of Kathleen Goligher and her family, strange thoughts crept into the doctor's mind. Was it really possible, wondered Crandon, that the "psychic cantilevers" that Crawford talked about existed? And if so, how could these "pseudopods" have the strength to lift even a table? Crandon decided to try to find out for himself, and in a few weeks had a table built to the exact specifications of the one that had been used in the Goligher case. On May 27 Crandon sat around the table with his wife and a few friends on the top floor of the house in Lime Street. The chamber was darkened and, following Crandon's instructions, the sitters joined hands and waited. Suddenly the table moved slightly. Then it moved again and tilted up on two legs. Someone suggested they try to find out which one of them might be the medium, so one at a time each sitter left the room. Since the table continued to rock and stopped only when Mina, the doctor's wife, departed, there was no doubt: she was the medium.

MINA THE MEDIUM

Mina Stinson (1888–1941) had previously been married to the owner of a small grocery store, Earl P. Rand, and had always been a vivacious, active woman. As a teenager she played in various professional bands and orchestras; she worked as a secretary, loved sports, and was active in various social-action church groups. The marriage with Crandon required that she give up her dynamic lifestyle, which in those days was not considered suitable for a physician's wife. The new experience of the séance of May 27 provided a pleasant change from the confined life of leisure of a wealthy woman. For the whole summer the Crandons held private séances in their home. The doctor became more and more excited each time he discovered his wife had a new "power." Her abilities seemed limitless and he only had to read about some new mystery and "Psyche"—as he had begun to fondly call her—would duplicate it at the next séance. Raps and flashes of light were among the earliest phenomena to appear in the darkness of her séances and, along with more traditional effects like the movement of the table, Mina appeared to be able to stop a watch simply by concentrating on it, or to produce dollar bills and live pigeons, things that seemed to be taken directly from the repertoire of a magician. Soon there was a new turn. Mina had conducted her séances awake and fully conscious of what was happening around her, but her husband suggested that she try to fall into a trance. The request met with immediate success and various "entities" started to communicate through the medium. One of these began to appear more frequently and came to dominate. Dr. Crandon and the others agreed that this visitor had to be Walter, Mina's brother. Walter Stinson had died twelve years earlier, at the age of twenty-eight, crushed by a railroad boxcar and he became Mina's spirit control for eighteen years. Walter's voice, not surprisingly, was the same as Mina's, only a little more hoarse. His language was scurrilous and he had a ready wit and irritable manners, a personality quite foreign to the kind and polite lady medium. In August of 1923 Dr. Crandon wrote an enthusiastic letter to Conan Doyle, telling him about his wife's wonderful abilities. Before he even met her, Doyle immediately declared that he was convinced the phenomena was genuine. Deeply impressed, Conan Doyle told J. Malcolm Bird, the secretary of the *Scientific American* committee for the investigation of spiritualism, about her.

SCIENTIFIC AMERICAN INVESTIGATES

In November 1923, Bird paid a visit to the Crandons and met an undoubtedly interesting couple: a somber doctor and a spirited and fascinating woman. Mina's charm clearly affected him, so much so that many would later question the reliability of his observations. Bird had elicited a similar response when he commented with particular kindness on the demonstrations of a medium about whom others had serious doubts. On that occasion, Walter Franklin Prince, reviewing Bird's book *My Psychic Adventures*, wrote: "Mr. Bird, if he wishes to achieve the authority in psychical research which I invoke for him, must hereafter avoid falling in love with the medium."[1]

Before leaving Boston, Bird invited Mina to enter the contest announced by *Scientific American*. She agreed and said that if she won, the prize would go to psychic research. She even insisted on paying all the expenses that might arise from the investigation, including those of the committee's stay in Boston. The only condition that she imposed was that the committee should come to her instead of her going to them. The Crandons would lend their house to the investigators. An article about the medium, written by Bird, appeared in the July 1924 issue of *Scientific American*. To protect Mina's privacy, Bird rebaptized her "Margery"; "Walter" was called "Chester," and Dr. Crandon "F. H." The readers of *Scientific American* learned that at last a potential winner of the prize had arrived: "With 'Margery,'" Bird wrote, ". . . the initial probability of genuineness are much greater than in any previous case which the Committee has handled."[2] The committee then moved to Boston; Bird, Hereward Carrington (a famous psychic investigator), and occasionally the other members of the committee gladly agreed to be guests of the Crandons during the investigation. William McDougall, a psychologist at Harvard who lived in Boston, remained at his own home, while Prince, chief research officer of the American Society for Psychical Research (ASPR), preferred to stay at a hotel. Harry Houdini, the only member of the committee who was not informed about the investigation, had to rely on the newspapers to find out what was happening, and what he read piqued his skeptical interest, to say the least: "Margery, the Boston Medium, Passes All Psychic Tests"; "Scientists Find No Trickery in a Score of Séances"; "Versatile Spook Puzzles Investigators by Variety of His Demonstrations." The surprise was even greater when, opening the July issue of *Scientific American*, Houdini learned that the investigators of Margery's claims were his colleagues on the committee. Houdini was furious: why hadn't he been informed? Bird explained to Houdini in a letter: "Our original idea was not to bother you with it unless, and until it got to a stage where there seemed serious prospects that it was either genuine, or a type of fraud which our other Committeemen could not deal with. . . . Mr. Munn feels that the case has taken a turn which makes it desirable for us to discuss it with you."[3]

Houdini arrived at the New York offices and asked Bird directly: "Do you believe that this medium is genuine?" "Why, yes," answered Bird, "she is genuine. She does resort to trickery at times, but I believe she is fifty or sixty per cent genuine." "Then you mean that this medium will be entitled to get the *Scientific American* prize?" Houdini responded. "Most decidedly," Bird confessed. Houdini pulled no punches:

> Mr. Bird, you have nothing to lose but your position and very likely you can readily get another if you are wrong, but if I am wrong it will mean the loss of reputation and as I have been selected to be one of the Committee I do not think it will be fair for you to give this medium the award unless I am permitted to go up to Boston and investigate her claims, and from what you tell me I am certain that this medium is either the most wonderful in the world or else a very clever deceiver. If she is a fraudulent medium I will guarantee to expose her and if she is genuine I will come back and be one of her most strenuous supporters.[4]

THE WIZARD AND THE WITCH

Houdini and Orson D. Munn (editor of the *Scientific American*) arrived in Boston on July 22 and took rooms at the Copley Plaza Hotel. Houdini was shocked at hearing that Bird and famed psychic researcher Hereward

Carrington had accepted the Crandons' hospitality. How unbiased could their judgment be if they were guests of the party that they were asked to investigate? But the accommodations, as later became known, were not the only blandishment offered to the members of the committee. Carrington, for example, had borrowed some money from Dr. Crandon, and Bird had even received a blank check for his expenses. An even more dangerous influence, however, threatened the integrity of the investigators: the attractions of Mina, who wore only a filmy dressing gown and silk stockings during the séances. She obviously enchanted Bird and only many years later was it known that she and Carrington had likely slept together. "It is not possible to stop at one's house [sic]," Houdini explained, "break bread with *him* frequently, then investigate *him* and render an impartial verdict" (*Houdini Exposes the Tricks Used by Boston Medium "Margery,"* p. 5).

On July 23, 1924, Houdini participated for the first time in a séance with the medium. A feat that had baffled the members of the committee involved the use of a wooden box with an electric switch that, when pressed, would ring a bell placed inside the box. In the previous sittings the box had been put on the floor between Margery's feet, and the bell had rung even while the medium's hands and feet were supposedly being held. For control there was a member of the committee on the left and her husband presumably doing the same on the right. With the medium so "immobilized," the sitters reasoned the one responsible for the phenomena could only be Walter the spirit guide. When Houdini arrived he sat on the medium's left and the box was placed between his feet. His hand held that of the medium while his ankle would control her leg. Houdini picks up the story from there: "All that day I had worn a silk rubber bandage around that leg just below the knee. By night the part of the leg below the bandage had become swollen and painfully tender, thus giving me a much keener sense of feeling and making it easier to notice the slightest sliding of Mrs. Crandon's ankle or flexing her muscles" (p. 6). The precaution appeared to be crucial when, after pulling her skirts well up above her knees, Margery asked for darkness. In fact, continued Houdini in his account of the séance:

I could distinctly feel her ankle slowly and spasmodically sliding as it pressed against mine while she gained space to raise her foot off the floor and touch the top of the box. To the ordinary sense of touch the contact would seem the same while this was being done. At times she would say: "Just press hard against my ankle so you can see that my ankle is there," and as she pressed I could feel her gain another half inch. When she had finally maneuvered her foot around to a point where she could get at the top of the box the bell ringing began and I positively felt the tendons of her leg flex and tighten as she repeatedly touched the ringing apparatus [see fig. 6.1]. (p. 7)

When the bell stopped ringing, Houdini felt the leg of the medium slowly sliding back to its original position on the floor. Bird sat at her right with one hand free to "explore" and the other on top of those of both the medium and Dr. Crandon. Suddenly, Walter asked for an illuminated plaque to be placed on the lid of the box that held the bell. Bird got up to get it and at that moment Walter called for control. Margery placed her free hand in Houdini's and immediately the cabinet was violently thrown backward. The medium then gave Houdini her right foot and said: "You have now both hands and both feet." Then Walter called out: "The megaphone is in the air. Have Houdini tell me where to throw it." "Toward me," replied the magician, and it instantly fell at his feet. Notwithstanding the clever work of misdirection created by the medium, Houdini understood what had really happened in the darkness. When Bird had left the room to search for the luminous plaque, Margery was left with her right hand and foot free. This had allowed her to tilt the corner of the cabinet enough to get her free foot under it; then, picking up the megaphone she placed it on her head, dunce-cap fashion. (See figs. 6.2 and 6.3.) She was then able to throw the cabinet using her right foot, which she would later give to Houdini. While it would appear that Margery was under complete control by Houdini, simply jerking her head would cause the megaphone to fall at his feet. After the séance, Houdini commented: "This is the slickest ruse I have ever detected" (p. 8). Houdini had seen through deceptions after just one séance, while the other members of the committee hadn't, even after thirty.

6.1

6.2

6.3

Figs. 6.1–6.3. Three drawings from Houdini's pamphlet: Malcolm Bird leaves his place, freeing Margery's right hand. She can now put the megaphone on her head and slide the cabinet using her feet. (Massimo Polidoro Collection)

Bird resented this air of superiority and was close to Dr. Crandon in his dislike of the man. Crandon, as well as Bird, had also shown racial hate for Houdini, when, in a letter to Sir Arthur Conan Doyle, he expressed his regret that "this low-minded Jew has any claim on the word American."[5]

THE SECOND SÉANCE

The following night, Margery agreed to hold the séance in the hotel suite in which Dr. Comstock stayed. This time the group sat around a table, with Houdini to the left of the medium. Walter ordered everyone to move back from the table so that he might gather the necessary force to lift it. "This," commented Houdini, "was simply another ruse on the medium's part, for when all the rest moved back she moved back also and this gave her room enough to bend her head and push the table up and over."[6] (See figs. 6.4 and 6.5.) Houdini confirmed his theory when, letting go of Munn's hand, he began groping around under the table until he felt the medium's head. The magician whispered to Munn that he could denounce and expose her at once but the editor proposed to wait and the séance continued.

It was then time for the bell-box. Again it was placed between Houdini's feet, again Margery put her ankle against the magician's, and again in the darkness, Houdini, who had rolled up his trouser leg like the night before, felt her stretching her foot to ring the bell. The buckle of Houdini's garter, however, caught the medium's stocking, preventing her from reaching the box. "You have garters on, haven't you?" she asked. "Yes," replied Houdini. "Well, the buckle hurts me." After taking the garter off, Houdini felt the woman's leg stretching again and the bell ringing each time her muscles extended. The séance over, the Crandons left the room and the committee discussed what had happened. Houdini told the others about his discovery and gave a practical demonstration. The committee, however, decided to wait until they were back in New York before issuing a press release. Meanwhile, it was necessary that the Crandons be left in the dark about Houdini's discoveries. Munn and Houdini left for New

6.4   6.5

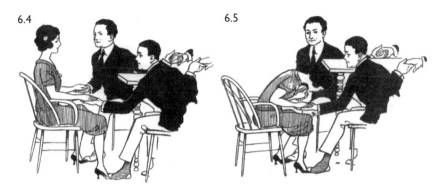

Figs. 6.4–6.5. Houdini's explanation of how Margery was able to levitate a table by using her head. From Harry Houdini, *Houdini Exposes the Tricks Used by the Boston Medium "Margery"* (1924). (Massimo Polidoro Collection)

York and Bird remained as a guest with the Crandons for three more days. Later it became known that he told Mina and her husband what Houdini had discovered and what the committee intended to do. From that moment on Margery would be on guard. Arriving in New York, Munn spiked an article by Bird for *Scientific American*, already in print, in which he praised Margery's abilities. He couldn't stop newspapers from reporting Bird's declarations. Some headlines that appeared in the newspapers of the day read: "Boston Medium Baffles Experts"; "Baffles Scientists With Revelations, Psychic Power of Margery Established"; "Experts Vainly Seek Trickery in Spiritualist Demonstration"; and one that had the magician boiling with rage: "Houdini the Magician Stumped."

HOUDINI'S MISSTEP

When the committee met a month later, there clearly was open war between Houdini, who wanted to expose the medium once and for all, and Margery, who wanted to make Houdini look foolish. It was then that Houdini made his worst move, introducing in the experimental setting a ridiculous constraint to control the medium. It was a big wooden box inside which the medium would sit, leaving only her head and hands sticking out. The main problem with such an extreme form of control is that it gave the medium the opportunity to complain that the cabinet prevented the materialization of the "pseudopods" needed to perform the phenomena and gave her an alibi for a possible absence of the same. There was also another drawback: if the cabinet wasn't really as fraud-proof as Houdini believed it to be, and Margery could find a way to do tricks, it could become proof of a true paranormal demonstration. If the fraud were later discovered, Houdini would appear incompetent.

On August 25, in the apartment of Dr. Comstock, Margery was "boxed" and the lights turned out. The box with the bell, placed on a table in front of the cabinet, rang but, when the lights were turned on, the lid on the cabinet appeared to have been forced open. Houdini suggested that, with the lid open, Margery could have rung the bell by projecting her head forward. The medium denied any responsibility, claiming that Walter had forced open the cabinet-box. The cabinet had proved its uselessness but Houdini wanted to try again. He had the lid sealed with steel strips and locks and prepared for the next night. That evening began with the dramatic entrance of Bird, who demanded to know why he had been left out of the séances. Houdini answered coldly, "I object to Mr. Bird being in the séance room because he has betrayed the Committee and hindered their work. He has not kept to himself things told him in strictest confidence as he should as Secretary to the Committee."[7] Bird at first denied it, but then admitted that a worried Margery had convinced him to tell her the facts. He then resigned from the committee and left.

There and then Prince was elected as the new secretary. The séance began with Margery confined in the cabinet-box and Houdini and Prince at her sides holding her hands. Houdini particularly insisted that Prince never let go of the medium's hand until the séance was over. This provoked Margery to ask Houdini what he had on his mind. "Do you really want to know?" asked Houdini. "Yes," said the medium. "Well I will tell you. In case you have smuggled anything into the cabinet-box you cannot now conceal it as both your hands are secured and as far as they are concerned you are helpless." "Do you want to search me?" she asked. "No, never mind, let it go," said Houdini. "I am not a physician." Soon after,

Fig. 6.6. Margie in Box: Margery inside the box,
with Houdini holding her left hand. (Mary Evans Picture Library)

Walter appeared in the circle saying: "Houdini, you are very clever indeed
but it won't work. I suppose it was an accident those things were left in the
cabinet?" "What was left in the cabinet?" asked the magician. "Pure accident was it? You were not here but your assistant was." Walter went on and
then stated that a ruler would be found in the cabinet-box under a pillow
at the medium's feet and accused Houdini of having had his assistant put

Fig. 6.7. The cover of Houdini's 1924 pamphlet on Margery, *Houdini Exposes the Tricks Used by the Boston Medium "Margery."* (Massimo Polidoro Collection)

it there to throw suspicion on his sister. Then he finished with a violent outburst in which he exclaimed: "Houdini, you God damned son of a bitch, get the hell out of here and never come back. If you don't I will!"[8]

A search of the cabinet revealed the presence of a collapsible carpenter rule. But the question remained: who put it there? Houdini claimed that it was Margery. By sticking the rule through the neck opening, the magician explained, she could easily have rung the bell. Also, the medium had suggested that the arm holes in the sides of the cabinet be boarded up, which would allow her to move her hands freely inside the cabinet. Margery rejected the accusations and accused Houdini, suggesting that his assistant, Jim Collins, had hidden the ruler to discredit her. However, Collins was interrogated that same night, in Houdini's absence, and took an oath that he did not place any ruler inside the cabinet, that he had never seen that ruler, and that his ruler was in his pocket. According to writer William Lindsay Gresham, Collins had hid the ruler: "I chucked it in the box myself. The Boss told me to do it. 'E wanted to fix her good."[9] Milbourne Christopher, magician and magic historian, expressed doubt about this incident: "The source of this story, though not given by Gresham, was Fred Keating, a magician who had been a guest of the Crandons in their house on Lime Street at the time Carrington was investigating the medium. Keating, however, was not unbiased. Several days before Gresham spoke to him, Keating had seen an unpublished manuscript in this author's collection in which Houdini, while praising Keating as a magician, had commented in unflattering terms on Keating's abilities as an investigator of psychic phenomena. In this writer's opinion, the story of Collins's admission is sheer fiction."[10] The incident remains doubtful to this day. It could have been revealing if, at the time, a laboratory could have examined the ruler for fingerprints or other useful traces. Evidently the *Scientific American* committee was not that scientific after all.

The Last Séance

A last séance was planned for August 27. That afternoon Munn, Prince, Dr. Crandon, Mina, and Houdini dined together outside Boston. The medium, upon hearing that Houdini was about to denounce her from the stage at Keith's Theatre in Boston, protested that she didn't want her twelve-year-old son to read that his mother was a fraud.

"Then don't be a fraud," Houdini told her.

To which she said that, if he misrepresented the facts, some of her friends would come up on stage and give him a good beating. Houdini replied that he was not going to misrepresent her.

Dr. Comstock had invented a device to immobilize the medium for the committee's last séance. It was a low box into which Margery and one investigator, sitting one in front of the other, would put their feet. A board, connected to the box, would be locked on top of the knees, preventing withdrawal of the feet. The sides of the box remained open, allowing any possible "psychic structure" to operate. Her hands were held by the investigator and the box with the bell was placed outside the control-box. Then the séance began. While waiting for something to happen, Dr. Crandon remarked: "Some day, Houdini, you will see the light and if it were to occur this evening, I would gladly give ten thousand dollars to charity." "It may happen," replied Houdini, "but I doubt it." "Yes sir," Dr. Crandon repeated, "if you were converted this evening I would willingly give $10,000 to some charity."[11] It was an uneventful séance; that is, nothing happened. Houdini was not converted and Dr. Crandon kept his $10,000, which Houdini had interpreted as an attempted bribe. Dr. Comstock's device, obviously better than the one used by Houdini, had shown that when the medium was immobilized and controlled by an investigator (rather than by her husband) the phenomena disappeared, as usually happens in such cases: when controls are at 0 percent, phenomena are at 100 percent; when controls are at 100 percent, phenomena are at 0 percent. Margery didn't win the *Scientific American* prize. In the eyes of the public, however, the doubt cast over her honesty by the committee investigation was not enough to destroy her. Malcolm Bird resigned from

Scientific American after Houdini anounced on a radio program: "I publicly denounce here Malcolm Bird as being an accomplice of Margery!" After resigning, Bird spent his time promoting Margery.

DIFFERENT OPINIONS

Houdini, convinced that he had indisputably debunked Margery, wrote in one of his pamphlets: "I charge Mrs. Crandon with practicing her feats daily like a professional conjuror. Also that because of her training as a secretary, her long experience as a professional musician, and her athletic build she is not simple and guileless but a shrewd, cunning woman, resourceful in the extreme, and taking advantage of every opportunity to produce a 'manifestation.'"[12]

Carrington, the first to defend her, charged Houdini with being interested only in publicity and declared: "The reason I didn't go to Boston when he [Houdini] held his sittings with 'Margery' was that I knew he distrusted me and I knew that anything he could not explain he would bring to my presence there."[13] Finally, it comes as no surprise that one of the most strenuous defenders of the medium was Conan Doyle: "[T]his self-sacrificing couple bore with exemplary patience all the irritations arising from the incursions of these fractious and unreasonable people, while even the gross insult which was inflicted upon them by one member of the committee did not prevent them from continuing the sittings. Personally, I think that they erred upon the side of virtue, and that from the moment Houdini uttered the word 'fraud' the committee should have been compelled either to disown him or cease their visits."[14]

According to Conan Doyle, the only honest and trustworthy members of the committee were Carrington and Bird. Regarding Bird, Conan Doyle said that he had a "better brain than Houdini's" because after fifty séances "he was completely convinced of the genuinity of the phenomena."[15] In the past, Conan Doyle had expressed his opinion on how to form an "impartial" committee: "What I wanted was five good clear-headed men who would stick to it without prejudice at all—like the

Dialectical Society of London, who unanimously endorsed the phenomena."[16] Conan Doyle's curious definition of the term "open mind" connected it with the phrase "believe in the phenomena and endorse it." Houdini didn't have an "open mind" as Conan Doyle intended it and he also expressed his surprise that a committee consisting of gentlemen should have permitted an attack on the reputation of a lady, and allowed a man "with entirely different standards to make this outrageous attack." The official report of the committee took six months to be completed.

Committee members had been sworn to reveal nothing about the sittings until the publication of the report, while Bird and Dr. Crandon, not restricted by such a burden, kept on telling journalists what Houdini considered to be "black lies."

While Houdini's irritation and the public curiosity for the committee verdict mounted, a preliminary report was published in October in *Scientific American*. It only reported the singular members' views, but at least freed them from their vow of confidentiality. Houdini then published at his own cost a pamphlet entitled *Houdini Exposes the Tricks Used by the Boston Medium "Margery"* and started a tour where he completely exposed Margery's act.

MARGERY'S SUSPICIOUS-LOOKING ECTOPLASM

In 1924, while the discussions continued, Margery had begun to produce ectoplasm during her séances. Like another famous medium, Eva C., her substance also was said to pour out from her bodily orifices. This is a supposition, of course, since she, like Eva, used to perform in the dark. Meanwhile, Margery's fame had spread to Europe and she was particularly well known in England. Conan Doyle, who had already met the Crandons, had expressed the wish to participate in new sittings with the medium, but the meetings never took place and the newspapers reported: "Margery Fears Fog May Block London Séances." The American Society for Psychical Research was also interested in the case, and if the medium wouldn't come to the society, the society would go to the medium. This happened through English researcher Eric J. Dingwall, who was duly impressed when, during a séance in the red light of an electric torch turned on and off by Dr. Crandon following the orders of Walter, things that looked like materialized hands rested on Margery's lap. Excited, he wrote to psychic researcher Von Shrenck-Notzing: "It is the most beautiful case of teleplasm and telekinesis with which I am acquainted. One is able to handle the teleplasm freely. The materialized hands are connected by an umbilical cord to the medium; they seize objects and displace them. The teleplastic masses are visible and tangible upon the table, in good red light. I hold the hands of the medium, I know where her fingers are and I see them in good light. The control is irreproachable."[17]

His enthusiasm, however, died quickly and Dingwall began to have doubts. He realized that he had never been able to actually see the ectoplasm pouring out of the medium's body. The faint light was not as good as he had earlier described, and the hands were partially or completely formed and were static rather than moving. Dingwall remembered that when he was allowed to hold the materialized substance, "the medium at once began to turn in her chair and the mass was pulled out of my hand. It seemed simply an elastic bag and crumpled up as it was pulled away. I tried to follow it when it fell into the medium's lap, but she resisted strenuously, throwing her left leg on to the table and forcing my hand away from it with her own. Another crucial test had failed completely."[18]

The substance was clearly lifeless. At one point, as the materializing ectoplasm was spotlighted, Margery actually put her hand down with Dingwall's hand still controlling it, and threw the mass upon the table. But what was this substance made from? The pictures taken by Dingwall show a very doubtful ectoplasm. The mass had the appearance of animal tissue and an examination of the enlargements of the photographs displayed certain ring markings that "strongly resembled the cartilaginous rings found in the mammalia trachea. This discovery led to the theory that the 'hands' had been faked from some animal lung material, the tissue cut and joined, and that part of the trachea had been used for the same purpose."[19] Further examinations of the pictures by biologists at Harvard led to the same conclusion—the ectoplasm "undoubtedly was composed of the lung tissue of some animal."[20] Besides going to any butcher and obtaining the material, Dr. Crandon wouldn't have had any difficulty in obtaining the needed substances since he worked at a Boston hospital. In his report, Dingwall preferred not to draw any conclusion, but suggested that the medium could hide the faked ectoplasm in her bodily cavities and could expel it afterward by way of muscular contraction. In the meantime, the *Scientific American* committee had at last issued its official verdict on Febraury 11, 1925.

"We have observed phenomena," the report stated, "the method of production of which we cannot in every case claim to have discovered. But we have observed no phenomena of which we can assert that they could not have been produced by normal means."

Hardly what Houdini would have liked. In any case, this meant that Margery didn't win the prize.

THE HARVARD INVESTIGATION

Though refused entrance to any more séances with Margery, Houdini had been able to infiltrate a journalist friend, Stewart Griscom, who kept him updated on the latest developments. This allowed the magician to continuosly update his stage exposé, to the amazement of Margery's followers. Houdini's attacks received support from an investigation conducted in the late spring of 1925 by a group of psychologists from Harvard University.

In the results, published in the *Atlantic Monthly* (November 1925), it was revealed that Margery had been observed performing various kinds of subterfuges.

She took off a luminous band placed on her ankle to track her movement and with her free foot managed to "float" a luminous disk; the Harvard group also established she had been able to use her right foot to ring a bell and to touch sitters. Finally, Margery fell into a trap. One experimenter sitting at one side offered to free her hand: she immediately accepted and used it to take some fake ectoplasm out of her lap and put it on the table.

SUSPICIONS AND MORE SUSPICIONS

One investigator after another remained unsatisfied by Margery's séances, and after Dingwall and the Harvard group it was time for Joseph Banks Rhine, professor at Duke University who in 1935 would start the study of parapsychology in a scientific laboratory. Invited by the ever-enthusiastic Bird, Rhine arrived in Lime Street on July 1, 1926, and the Crandons greeted him with their usual hospitality. From the start, Rhine and his wife knew that it would be impossible to test the facts as they would have liked to. For example, they couldn't examine the ectoplasm with the lights turned on and Rhine was prevented by Crandon from examining the various instruments that filled the séance room and that were supposed to document and measure this or that phenomena. Still, the professor was able to notice that the ropes of a device that was sup-posed to hold the medium had been removed, allowing complete freedom of movement. When Rhine saw Margery's foot kicking a megaphone during a séance to give the impression that it was levitating, the crudity of the deception was clear.

If he had been able to detect all these things in one séance, wondered Rhine, why didn't Bird, with three years of experience, have any suspi-cions? Could he be a confederate of the medium? Bird denied the accu-sations, saying that they were Rhine's "personal opinions," but the pro-fessor wondered what could have led men like Bird or Carrington to play the medium's game, and observed: "It is evidently of very great advantage to a medium, especially if fraudulent, to be personally attractive; it aids in the 'fly-catching business.' Our report would be incomplete without mention of the fact that this 'business' reached the point of actual kissing and embracing at our sitting, in the case of one of the medium's more ardent admirers. Could this man be expected to detect trickery in her?"[21]

This could partially explain the motives of Bird and colleagues, but what about Dr. Crandon? If he was a confederate too he certainly couldn't be motivated by the desire of a love affair with the medium since she already was his wife. Rhine offered the following motive: "[Crandon] gradually found out she was deceiving him, but had already begun to enjoy the notoriety it gave him, the groups of admiring society it brought to his home to hear him lecture and to be entertained, the interest and fame aroused in this country and Europe, etc. This was especially appreciated by him in view of decided loss of position and prestige suffered in recent years."[22]

The publication of Rhine's report in the *Journal of Abnormal Social Psychology* (the ASPR, whose new chief research officer was now Bird, had refused it because of its skeptical nature) caused the inevitable protests by Margery's supporters. Sir Arthur Conan Doyle bought space in the Boston newspapers and inserted an ungentlemanly, black-bordered notice stating simply: "J. B. Rhine Is an Ass."

MALCOLM BIRD SINGS

What happened to Bird? After 1931 his name disappears from the list of contributors of the ASPR. He vanished and nothing was ever heard of him. Hypotheses about his fate ranged from personal jealousy inside the society to his accepting a tempting job offer, but only recently, with the discovery of some unpublished documents, new facts regarding the relationship between Bird and Margery were made public. Prince, in whose files the documents were found, hinted in 1933 in an article he wrote for *Scientific American*: "About two years ago . . . he [Bird] sent in to his employers a long paper claiming the discovery of an act of fraud and reconstructing his view of the case to admit a factor of fraud from the beginning. This paper has not been printed and very few of the believers in Europe or America know of its existence."[23] Here are some extracts from this report/confession by Bird to the Board of Trustees of the ASPR (May 1930):

> [S]ince May 1924 when I first concluded that the case was one of valid mediumship, my observations have never been directed in any large sense toward the detection of fraud, and even less toward its demonstration. As I went along with my séances, here and there I made, as a

matter of routine, observations that some particular episode was
normal in its causation. All that the present report aims to do is to
acquaint the Board with the date upon which is based in my own mind,
the statement which I have made whenever occasion has arisen to make
it: that the Margery phenomena are not one hundred per cent supernormal. It is not now possible for me to state positively whether the
episode occurred in July or in August, 1924. . . . The occasion was one
of Houdini's visits to Boston for the purpose of sitting. . . . She sought
a private interview with me and tried to get me to agree, in the event
that phenomena did not occur, that I would ring the bell-box myself, or
produce something else that might pass as activity by Walter. This proposal was clearly the result of Margery's wrought-up state of mind.
Nevertheless it seems to me of paramount importance, in that it shows
her, fully conscious and fully normal, in a situation where she thought
she might have to choose between fraud and a blank séance; and she
was willing to choose fraud.[24]

Margery's Misstep

Around 1926 Margery added a new effect to her repertoire; maybe it was
one too many, as we shall see. Walter claimed that his ethereal body was
such an exact replica of the one he had had while alive, that to prove his
presence, he could even create a fingerprint of his thumb in wax. Mina
paid a visit to her dentist, Dr. Frederick Caldwell, to ask for a suggestion
in carrying out the experiment. The doctor suggested the use of dental
wax, which would make a detailed print. He softened a piece of wax in
boiling water and pressed his thumbs in it to show the practicality of his
proposal. Mina took Caldwell's sample and asked for a few more pieces of
wax. That evening at a séance she tried the experiment. She put some wax
in a small basin and after the séance two prints were found. Margery
claimed they were those of Walter. Dr. Crandon insisted on having an
expert of his acquaintance authenticate the prints. This shadowy figure,
most probably a confederate, was named John Fife and claimed to be
chief of police at Charlestown Navy Yard and a recognized expert on fin-

gerprints. W. F. Prince, who, after the *Scientific American* investigations, had continued to collect a file of private information regarding personal investigations on Margery's case, found that the Boston Police Department had never heard of Fife. Crandon, however, claimed that the man had found thumbprints on Walter's razor that perfectly matched those left in the wax by the "spirit." The success of this novelty led Dr. Crandon to employ, at his own expense, a Margery supporter, E. E. Dudley, to catalog every fingerprint left by Walter during the séances. Around 1931 Dudley began, on his own initiative, to collect the fingerprints of every person who attended a sitting with Margery. This way he could disprove the claims of those who said that the prints did not belong to Walter, but to a living confederate. Dudley was ending his weekly visits to collect the fingerprints of those who had participated in séances from 1923 to 1924 when he examined the prints of Dr. Caldwell, Crandon's dentist. Once at home, he compared the prints with those of Walter and made a bewildering discovery. He carefully reexamined both sets of prints to be sure, but there was no mistake: the thumbprints that Margery claimed had belonged to Walter were identical to Dr. Caldwell's! Dudley counted no less than twenty-four absolute correspondences. Clearly, the medium had used the wax samples on which Dr. Caldwell had shown Mina the procedure and had obtained imprint molds. It was easy in the dark to press the molds in the wax and obtain the effect that an entity foreign to the circle of sitters was the author. Dudley informed the ASPR about his discovery but W. H. Button, then president of the ASPR, replied that he wasn't interested in publishing the news. The image of the society was by then too connected with that of the medium, since they had often defended her and hidden unpleasant information about her. Prince, who had left the ASPR for this reason and had founded the Boston Society for Psychical Research (BSPR), had had enough. He accepted the Dudley revelation and an article was published in the society's *Journal* (vol. 18, October 1932). The scandal that followed had disastrous consequences. It was no mere case of somebody claiming to see the medium use her foot to move a table; this time the proof of fraud was damning and definite.

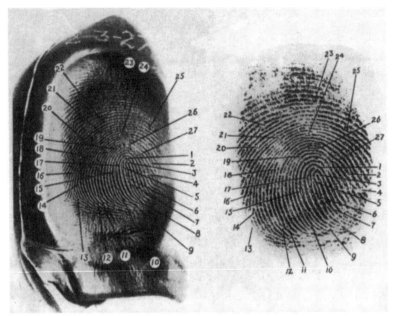

Fig. 6.8. A thumbprint from the spirit of "Walter," Margery's dead brother, matches perfectly that of the Crandons' dentist: a definitive proof of fraud. (Mary Evans Picture Library)

A WOMAN IN DECLINE

Margery's supporters left her one after another, and the woman, older and heavier, began to look for consolation in alcohol. The séances, meanwhile, continued, and Crandon tried for some time to keep alive the interest in his "Psyche" by resorting to any stratagem he could think of. At one of these sittings, for example, Margery tried to repeat the famous experiment of linking two wooden rings, attempted fifty years before by Professor Zollner with medium Henry Slade. "Success!" rejoiced Dr. Crandon. Margery had been able to link two rings made of different woods. At last there was definitive proof, something solid that defied physics, matter through matter. Since it is not difficult to finish the wood along the split in such a way to render it invisible to the eye, it was claimed that only x-rays could establish the truth. The rings were then sent to Sir Oliver Lodge in England for independent testing. When Lodge opened the parcel sent by the Crandons, however, he found that one of the rings had fallen to pieces, probably during the trip. What could have been the only solid existing proof of the reality of the supernatural, the "Rosetta Stone" of spiritualism, hadn't even been well packed. In 1939 Dr. Crandon died and Mina, an inveterate alcoholic, went into a deep depression. At one of her last séances she even tried to jump off the roof of the house. In the Prince files at the ASPR there is still a collection of unpublished documents and reports, written by the Harvard scientists and by various psychic researchers, from which emerges an interesting theory to explain the Margery séances.[25]

The séances were a sort of marital charade. Margery's intended audience was not Houdini, the *Scientific American* group, or the other investigators, but her husband whom she helped to delude to save their collapsing marriage. They were too different from one another, and Crandon got quickly bored by her after marriage; however, he also had a strong fear of death. In trying to keep him by her side, Margery hit on the idea of manifesting spirits for him and it worked. He now felt like a new Galileo for the half million followers of Margery, and always demanded new phenomena. He came to force his wife to perform new demonstrations with "downright brutality."

The opinion of the various experts was that Margery would have liked to give up séances and confess to fraud, except she knew it would end her marriage. Houdini's spy, Griscom, even revealed to the magician that once, when he was alone with the medium, she disclosed to him her admiration for Houdini for not being taken in by her, and for not being afraid "to say where he stands." "I respect Houdini," she said to Griscom, "more than any of the bunch. He has both feet on the ground all the time."[26]

Margery's story ends with a tale that sounds folkloric but suits the mysterious character that the medium built for herself. Sitting beside Margery's bed in the last days of her life, psychic researcher Nandon Fodor suggested to her that she would depart happier if she dictated a confession to him and revealed the methods she had used to obtain her phenomena. Mina muttered something unintelligible. Fodor asked her to repeat it. "Sure," she said, "I said you could go to hell. All you 'psychic researchers' can go to hell." Then, with something very like the old familiar twinkle of merriment in her eyes, she looked at him and chuckled softly: "Why don't you guess?" she said, and chuckled again. "You'll be guessing . . . for the rest of your lives."[27]

NOTES

Reprinted with permission of the editors from *Skeptic* 5, no. 3 (1997). Copyright 1997 by the Skeptics Society.

1. Walter Franklin Prince, "Review of *My Psychic Adventure*," *Journal of the ASPR* 18 (1923).

2. J. Malcolm Bird, "Our Next Psychic," *Scientific American* (July 1924): 29.

3. Harry Houdini, *Houdini Exposes the Tricks Used by Boston Medium "Margery"* (New York: Adams Press, 1924), p. 4.

4. Ibid., p. 5.

5. Kenneth Silverman, *Houdini!!! The Career of Ehrich Weiss* (New York: HarperCollins, 1996), p. 325.

6. Houdini, *Houdini Exposes*, p. 9.

7. Ibid., p. 15.

8. Ibid., p. 18.

9. William L. Gresham, *Houdini: The Man Who Walked through Walls* (New York: Macfadden Books, 1961), p. 219.

10. Milbourne Christopher, *Houdini: The Untold Story* (New York: Thomas Y. Crowell, 1969), p. 198.

11. Houdini, *Houdini Exposes*, pp. 21–22.

12. Ibid., p. 23.

13. *Boston Herald*, January 26, 1925.

14. Arthur Conan Doyle, *The Edge of the Unknown* (1930; reprint, New York: Barnes & Noble, 1992).

15. Ibid., p. 18.

16. Arthur Conan Doyle, in *Progressive Thinker* (April 18, 1925).

17. Eric J. Dingwall, "Report on a Series of Sittings with the Medium Margery," *Proceedings of the SPR* 36 (1928).

18. Ibid.

19. Ibid.

20. T. R. Tietze, *Margery* (New York: Harper & Row, 1973).

21. Joseph B. Rhine and L. E. Rhine, "One Evening's Observations on the Margery Mediumship," *Journal of Abnormal Psychology* (1927).

22. Ibid.

23. Walter F. Prince, "The Case Against Margery," *Scientific American* (May 1933).

24. Tietze, *Margery*, p. 137.

25. Silverman, *Houdini*, pp. 380–81.

26. Ibid., p. 383.

27. Tietze, *Margery*, pp. 184–85.

CHAPTER SEVEN

HOUDINI'S
LAST MIRACLE
Submerged!

*H*arry Houdini, the greatest magician that ever lived, died on October 31, 1926, at the young age of fifty-two. Before his end came, however, he would still astound the world with one last impressive feat.

By 1926, his campaign against fake mediums had been in full force for a few years, and in May of that year his attention was caught by a new wonder imported to the United States by psychic researcher Hereward Carrington, once Houdini's friend, turned "enemy" during the investigation of Boston medium "Margery." Carrington, in fact, along with Malcolm Bird, had been the only member of the *Scientific American* committee, of which Houdini was also a member, who had declared from the start the genuineness of Margery's mediumship (see chapter 6), and had worked as a sort of impresario in America for such mediums as Eusapia Palladino (see chapter 3) and Nino Pecoraro.

Carrington's new "attraction" was a self-styled Egyptian fakir, twenty-six-year-old Rahman Bey, who professed to a supernormal power whereby he could suspend animation in his own body. He had opened at Selwyn Theater, in New York, performing various physical feats: he stopped his pulse, forced hatpins through his cheek, had a block of sandstone placed on his chest and pounded with a sledgehammer, and did various other tests. All the while, Carrington lectured the audience, like a perfect master of ceremonies, on yogis and Hindu powers of meditation and supreme control over body functions. In his most astonishing test, Bey permitted himself to be shut in an airtight coffin for ten minutes or more, whereafter he would emerge alive and bowing. This, he explained, was possible thanks to his self-imposed "cataleptic trance."

Houdini, who went to the show and easily recognized many sideshow tricks which he had already explained in his *Miracle Mongers and Their Methods*,[1] thought that Bey's scientific-sounding explanations were just a "lot of bunk." Furthermore, after noticing Houdini in the audience, Carrington swiftly changed the tone of the presentation, claiming that Bey did not operate through supernatural, but only natural means. "That alone," noted Houdini afterward, "spiked my guns."[2]

In July, Bey presented a new version of his coffin stunt: he announced that he would stay submerged in the Hudson River, sealed in a bronze casket, for an hour. As soon as the coffin touched the water, however, the emergency bell inside the casket started to ring. It took the workmen about fifteen minutes to open the lid, but Bey claimed he did not remember having touched the bell, since he was in a trance. Nonetheless, he could boast that he had survived for about twenty minutes in the sealed coffin.

At once Houdini determined that he had to expose Bey for what he really was: a trickster. He issued his challenge and, through the *Evening World*, announced: "I guarantee to remain in any coffin that the fakir does for the same length of time he does, without going into any cataleptic trance."[3] A few days later, as if to raise the bet, Bey again tried his stunt: this time, however, he was submerged in the water of the Hotel Dalton swimming pool where, unbelievably, he stayed for an hour.

Houdini now had to keep his promise and duplicate the fakir's stunt. He had a bronze casket made by the Boyertown Burial Casket Company, the same firm which had supplied the bronze casket for Rahman Bey, and

Fig. 7.1. A poster from 1926 headlining what was going to be Houdini's new invention. His death on October 31, 1926, prevented him from presenting the illusion more than once. (James Randi Educational Foundation)

made arrangements with the Hotel Shelton, in New York, to use its swimming pool for the test. The challenge seemed lost from the start: Bey was twenty-six years old; Houdini was twice his age. He also was much heavier and more tired than a few years before, when he had been accustomed to staying underwater and holding his breath, even in icy waters. In any case, if there was someone in the world who had a chance of staying inside a casket for more than an hour and then coming out alive, he was certainly the greatest escape artist who ever lived.

The casket could hold 26,428 cubic inches of air less the space occupied by the body and by a telephone and batteries that Houdini installed. Before the official test, and to avoid surprises, Houdini decided to secretly try the stunt at home and see what happened. For the trial tests he used a glass top rather than the metal one, so that he could be observed by his doctor.

The first trial took place July 31, with Houdini's assistants and the doctor attending. Once the top had been shut, Houdini remained motionless. After forty-five minutes he started to perspire. He heard the doctor say: "I would not do that for $500." As time passed breathing became harder; each time he inhaled he had to "pump with all my might for air." This convinced him that panic shortened the lives of those who were trapped for long periods in mineshafts or vaults. "With my years of training," he noted afterward, "I can remain apparently motionless without an effort. I kept my eyes open for fear I would go to sleep."[4] When he could not take it any longer he signaled for the lid to be opened: an hour and ten minutes had passed. He was dripping wet from head to toe, but he had not felt too uncomfortable. This made him suspect that some air must have seeped inside.

For the next secret test, on August 4 at about noon, he made the lid airtight. This time the casket was submerged in a large container filled with water. The coffin felt moist and cold; the water seemed to chill the box. However, he felt more comfortable than at the first test. After fifty minutes he began taking longer breaths and started feeling very irritable: "I was annoyed by movements, annoyed by one of my assistants swaying over my head, even twisting of the key."[5] Despite his nerves, he managed to stay sealed for an hour and ten minutes, like he had on the previous try. Now he felt ready for the real challenge.

The date chosen for the test was August 5. Houdini invited journalists from all over the United States and many of his friends, like Walter Lippmann and Adolph Ochs, publisher of the *Times*; Joe Rinn acted as timekeeper, Joe Dunninger, the up-and-coming greatest mentalist was there, as well as Carrington. The invitation read: "HOUDINI's experiment of attempting to remain submerged one hour in an airtight metal coffin."

Houdini had prepared himself by eating very light: "had a fruit salad and a half a cup of coffee." He felt somewhat nervous, "but that I attribute to the excitement of the test, not through any fear."[6] In the three weeks of his training, he "reduced about twelve pounds."

Finally, stripped to brown trunks and white shirt, Houdini made his entrance in the pool room. He noticed worriedly that the overcrowded pool area felt overly warm and thought that the air was rarified. Before entering the new galvanized iron box (a better-looking—and larger—model than the one used during his trials), Houdini was tested by physicians, who found him normal. However, they stated that a human being could survive inside a sealed box of that kind for only three to four minutes: soon, in fact, all the oxygen would be consumed and the casket would be filled with carbon dioxide. "If I die," remarked Houdini before the lid was soldered, "it will be the will of God and my own foolishness. I am going to prove that the copybook maxims are wrong when they say that a man can live but three minutes without air—and I shall not pretend to be in a cataleptic state either."

The coffin was finally sealed and lowered into the pool. It took about 700 pounds of iron and eight swimmers standing on top of the casket to keep it level and beneath the waterline. Houdini felt disturbed by the strong heat he felt inside the box, and became more irritable than he had been during the tests. The man standing on the coffin seemed to be shaking it, and one even lost his balance and fell. The casket shot up above the surface and was quickly pushed down. "What's the big idea?" Houdini shouted through the phone to his assistant, Jim Collins. "What struck me?" He had visualized the box breaking in two and thought he was going to drown before he could be taken out of it. The effort of talking, however, left him gasping for air.

When the hour was reached, Collins phoned him with the news. Houdini, though breathing heavily now, wanted to try to stay a bit more. He reached for his handkerchief, which was wet, and pressed it to his lips, and feeling better he kept it there to lessen his strain.

"When Collins, my assistant phoned me that I had been in the coffin for one hour and twelve minutes," he noted later, "I was going to stay three more minutes, but watching my lungs rise and fall, thought I could stand the strain for another fifteen minutes."

He felt water trickling inside the box, and realized that the casket was slightly leaking.

"After one hour and twenty-eight minutes," he continued in his notes written after the experience, "I commenced to see yellow lights and carefully watched myself not to go to sleep. I kept my eyes wide open; moved on the broad of my back, so as to take all the weight off my lungs, my left arm being across my chest. I lay on my right side, my left buttock against the coffin, so that I could keep the telephone receiver to my ear without holding it, and told Collins to get me up at an hour and a half, thinking if I did go to sleep, he would get me up within that time."

When finally the casket was taken out of water, Houdini felt a physical elation and a curious irritation. When the air-vent caps were unscrewed, he thrust up an arm. A doctor took his pulse: it had been eighty-four at the time of entry; now it was one hundred forty-two. The lid was ripped open enough to let Houdini climb out. He was again dripping wet and, according to Carrington, looked "deathly white."

Once at home he recorded all the details of his experiment and later sent them to Dr. W. J. McConnell, a physiologist with the U.S. Bureau of Mines, feeling that his tests might be helpful to miners trapped in collapsed shafts. "When I was dictating this, I still had that metallic taste in my stomach and mouth; felt rather weak in the knees; had no headache, but just seemed listless." But he had beaten the fakir at his own game!

"There is no doubt in my mind," he added, "that had this test been where fresh air could have gotten into the galvanized iron coffin as I was

Houdini Outdoes Fakirs

Houdini—The World's Most Famous Handcuff King, Proves That There Is No Trickery in Remaining in a Sealed Coffin for One and a Half Hours. Claims Cataleptic State Unnecessary.

FOR quite a few months a Hindu fakir, Rahman Bey, has been demonstrating his powers of producing uncanny effects. He would entered a cataleptic state, would have himself buried in a coffin for from ten minutes to half an hour or thereabouts, and then would receive the attention of scientific men who would write up the "phenomenal feats." Harry Houdini, known throughout the world, demonstrated to a body of scientists and physicians that he could duplicate, and in fact do even more than the Hindu fakir without entering the cataleptic state, and thus proved that no man is super-human. Houdini remained in a sealed coffin for one hour, thirty-one minutes and thirty seconds, surpassing the stunt of the Hindu mystic.

THE photo above shows Harry Houdini stepping out of the casket at the close of the experiment. The one at the left shows the size and arrangement in the casket, and the one below is a picture taken in the Hotel Shelton pool with the casket submerged.

Scientifically this experiment is of great value. It demonstrates that miners could remain underground in a closed area or that men could survive in a submarine much longer than was at first supposed, if they will keep their wits about them. During one hour approximately twenty-nine cubic feet of air is breathed. Approximately one and a half cubic feet of oxygen is absorbed, and one and a quarter cubic feet of carbon dioxide is excreted. Pulse on opening casket was too high to count and about 90 seconds later dropped to 142. No objectionable stuffy odor was noticeable. When the covers of the coffin were removed, the air rushed in violently, showing that the carbon dioxide did not replace the oxygen absorbed. In sand pit burials there is a sufficient amount of air penetrating between the grains of sand to permit of life over many hours.

DR. HEREWOOD CARRINGTON wrote about Rahman Bey in the following terms in a newspaper article. "All medical authorities agree that it is impossible for a human being to live more than three to five minutes in a sealed coffin." Yet Houdini entered a sealed coffin at the Hotel Shelton pool and he remained therein for one hour, thirty-one minutes and thirty seconds, thus proving to Dr. Carrington that he is not an authority on medical subjects. Houdini disclaimed the exercise of any super-natural power and stated that every normal human being could get in the same coffin and stay there as long as he did, if the individual took care to breathe lightly and did not exert himself. Two editors of SCIENCE AND INVENTION Magazine carefully examined the casket before Houdini entered the same, and can attest to the fact that there was absolutely no deception practiced. No oxygen in any sealed containers entered the coffin. No air could get in. Houdini stripped, donned a bathing suit, and entered the casket, after which the cover was soldered in place. The caps were screwed on and then the entire casket was sunk into the pool. Weights were applied and men stood on the cover to prevent the casket from floating. Communication was had with Houdini by means of a telephone and a signal bell. The editors placed a thermometer in the casket. It read 99.2 at maximum.

Fig. 7.2. An article from *Science and Invention* magazine covers Houdini's underwater burial stunt at the Hotel Shelton. (James Randi Educational Foundation)

put in same," and not in the hotel where the air was warm and foul, "I could have readily stayed fifteen or thirty minutes longer."

"Am having a coffin made with a glass top," he concluded his notes for Dr. McConnell, "and as soon as it is ready will let you know. I know you are doing a worthwhile work and as my body and brain are trained for this particular line, I am at your service. Don't be afraid to ask any question, I will be glad to let you know."

Some magicians, and even Joseph Rinn, thought that Houdini must have used some hidden supply of oxygen. Houdini was annoyed at these suspicions: "There is a rumor going around," he wrote to a friend, "that there is a gimmick to the thing. I pledge my word of honor there isn't a thing to it excepting to lie down and keep quiet. I trained for three weeks in water to get my lungs accustomed to battle without air, and after one hour, did have to struggle and believe only due to the training was I able to stay so long. Rest assured there is no gimmick, no trick at all—simply lying on your back and breathing shallow breaths is all you do. Did it twice in a coffin with a glass top to test myself. There is no doubt in my mind that anyone can do it" (p. 2).

Carrington wrote a few years later: "Houdini remained submerged in a metal coffin for about an hour and a half; but when he emerged he was deathly white, running with perspiration and with a pulse of 142. I was present at this experimental burial, as at many others, and know whereof I speak. It is my opinion that Houdini appreciably shortened his life by this endurance burial."

NOTES

1. Houdini's *Miracle Mongers and Their Methods* was reprinted in 1982 by Prometheus Books and contains a foreword by James Randi.

2. The only person to attempt the stunt, twenty years later in 1955, was James Randi. He had a box built that was around the same size as Houdini's and was submerged in a pool in London for the TV show *Today*. He was able to stay submerged for one hour and three minutes. Three years later, in 1958, he repeated the test in the same Shelton pool used by Houdini for his experiment.

To commemorate the event, Randi was even able to find two of the assistants who, in 1925, had helped Houdini in his demonstration. This time Randi stayed under water for an hour and forty-four minutes, thus beating Houdini's record by thirteen minutes.

   3. Quoted in Kenneth Silverman, *Houdini!!! The Career of Ehrich Weiss* (New York: HarperCollins, 1996), p. 398.

   4. Letter of Harry Houdini to W. J. McConnell, New York, August 5, 1926, Library of Congress, Rare Book and Special Collections Division.

   5. Ibid.

   6. Ibid.

CHAPTER EIGHT

INVESTIGATING SPIRIT MOLDS

by Massimo Polidoro

and Luigi Garlaschelli

*S*ince the early days of spiritualism, when mediums began producing noticeable physical phenomena, paraffin-wax molds supposedly modeled around materialized "spirit hands" during séances were one of the best proofs presented as evidence of the paranormal.

Some of these molds, in fact, seemed to possess the characteristics of "permanent paranormal objects." (Presumably these objects could only be made using paranormal abilities. In other words, the very existence of these objects would be tangible, persistent proof that paranormal powers exist.) The empty paraffin molds found at the conclusion of séances, it was thought, could still be intact only because the hands around which the wax solidified had dematerialized.

Molds have not always possessed these characteristics, and even the celebrated D. D. Home warned against fraudulent mediums who produced these phenomena by casting molds of their own hands or smuggling already prepared ones into the séance room. After a period in which the interest in these phenomena faded away, they made a comeback in the 1920s with Polish medium Franek Kluski and others, and the general public was made better aware of their existence thanks also to articles in popular magazines such as *Scientific American.*

Some of the plaster casts of these molds are still preserved at the Institut Metapsichique International (IMI) in Paris, a fact which in part explains why the interest in the phenomenon periodically resurfaces.

In consideration of a recent debate over these paraffin-wax molds, we should like to offer our own experience on the subject.[1]

POSSIBLE NATURAL EXPLANATIONS

As has already been pointed out by others, various possible natural explanations accounting for the phenomena (besides "spirit intervention") have been proposed.[2]

Dr. Robin Tillyard, for example, suggested the following method: a tourniquet is fastened to one arm, and the hand is allowed to swell; after this, the swollen hand is immersed in the paraffin and in cold water. The tourniquet is then removed and the arm is lifted upward, in order to allow the blood to flow, until the swelling has gone down. The hand, having recovered its original size, will allow the paraffin glove to slip off easily (especially if the hand had previously been smeared with glycerol).[3]

A different procedure for casting spirit molds using normal means requires only one rubber glove perfectly imitating the hand's features. The supporters of this method agree that it is possible to reproduce hands of different size and shape, and that the glove might be easily hidden on the medium's body. To obtain such a glove, which shows the fingerprints and other distinctive lines, one should first impress a real hand on dental wax—avoiding plaster—which allows a much sharper outline of the skin marks. This imprinting should at once be used as a mold for making a rubber glove showing all the typical marks of a real hand.

This method, however, has flaws. It is generally recognized that paraffin molds are "first generation" imprints; following this technique they would be "third generation" imprints: first a negative in dental wax, then the rubber glove from this mold and finally the mold of paraffin over the glove. The end result would probably show some surface defects accumulated along the way.

Tests of this hypothesis, carried out by Gustave Geley with thin rubber gloves inflated or filled with water and then suspended in a basin containing paraffin, produced imprints, but they showed the typical, sausage-shaped fingers of gloves, clearly revealing that they were made with an inflated rubber glove.[4] This test by Geley doesn't rule out the possibility of obtaining convincing spirit molds by using gloves made with elastic but thicker materials, carefully crafted and not overly filled with water or air. However, in any case, the entire procedure appears uselessly complicated.

Some examples of how certain books encouraging the belief in spiritualism claim the impossibility of obtaining molds by natural means are given in these extracts:

> The moulds were shown to Gabrielli, a professional modeller, who stated that they could never have been forged with an ordinary process, as a human hand would have broken a paraffin glove when slipping out of it. A real hand coming out of a paraffin glove just one millimeter in thickness, like the gloves obtained at the IMI, is not possible; nor would it have been possible with a thicker glove, in that the palm of a hand is much larger than the wrist. The hand therefore would have had to break the glove to be able to slip it off the wrist. Contrariwise, the paraffin gloves are not damaged or broken at all. The only acceptable explanation was that the hand must have materialized into the glove itself. . . .
>
> By no means could one have made only one paraffin mould of the two hands of a living person clasped in such a way. . . .
>
> This double-handed mould is perhaps the clearest evidence for the impossibility of a normal removal of the genuine mould obtained from the paraffin.[5]

In reading these observations and comparing them with all the possible solutions suggested by both skeptics and believers in spiritualism, it turns out that only one solution gives a convincing rational explanation for the molds created by Kluski. And it is simply the production of wax molds directly from one's hand, as also pointed out by Coleman.[6]

OUR EXPERIMENTATION

We then decided to try and make some molds of our hands to test how difficult this really was. Strictly following Geley's instructions, we prepared two basins, each ten inches in diameter. One was filled with hot water (approximately five liters at 55° C), into which we poured a layer of molten paraffin (approximately one kg, previously melted in a pan with boiling water on a kitchen stove), and the other with cold water (five liters), which we later used to solidify the paraffin. We immersed our hands first in the basin filled with paraffin and then in the one containing water.

We gave our hands different shapes: an open hand, a fist, two V-shaped fingers, a finger pointing out (which, according to Geley, should have been considered "perhaps the clearest evidence for the impossibility of a normal removal of the genuine mold obtained from the paraffin"),[7] and two hands clasped. We remind the reader what supporters of spiritualism have claimed regarding this shape: "By no means could one have made only one paraffin mold of the two hands of a living person clasped in such a way."

In all of these cases, we were able, rather easily, to make some fairly thin molds (a few millimeters thick) just by immersing the hands a couple of times in the basin with the paraffin. But our most significant result was that in every instance we managed to remove our hands from the solidified paraffin glove without breaking it. In fact, it will be noticed from some of the pictures that the wrist in some of the molds we obtained is noticeably narrower than the width of the hand. This outcome is attainable simply by removing the hand very carefully.

Pictures in some books on spiritualism illustrate models that reproduce parts of the human body that look like sculptures. These illustrations are followed by statements like: "These shapes could not be removed

Fig. 8.1. First, the hand is dipped in a pot of hot water where melted paraffin floats. The water can be very hot. (Massimo Polidoro Collection)

Fig. 8.2. From left: Massimo Polidoro, Franco Ramaccini (standing), and Luigi Garlaschelli, prepare to reproduce "spirit molds." (Massimo Polidoro Collection)

from a mold without being broken," leading one to believe that this is the case. Actually, it is not the plaster cast that has to be removed from the thin wax mold—which really would be impossible to do without breaking it. One almost forgets that what has to be removed is a living hand, possibly the best-suited object to slip out of a mold without damaging it. In fact, a real hand is even more effective than any other artifices dreamed up to substitute for it. First, paraffin doesn't stick to the skin, only to quite long hair. Nonetheless, if one moves the fingers very slowly, one realizes that every small bit one pulls out gradually allows the rest of the hand to be removed. It's almost the same as pulling off a tight glove.

Later, when we poured some plaster into a few molds, it turned out that we made copies just like Kluski's, which are kept at the IMI.[8] The hands we obtained have all the hand's typical lines and also a few hairs stuck here and there. To convert a mold into a plaster cast, one has only to pour liquid plaster slowly into the mold. When the plaster is dry, the

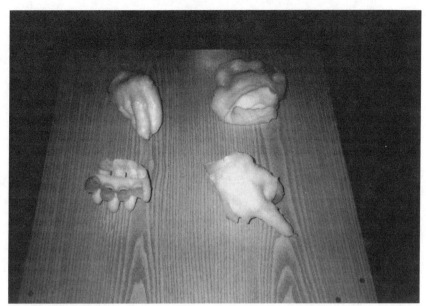

Fig. 8.3. A collection of paraffin casts in various shapes.
(Massimo Polidoro Collection)

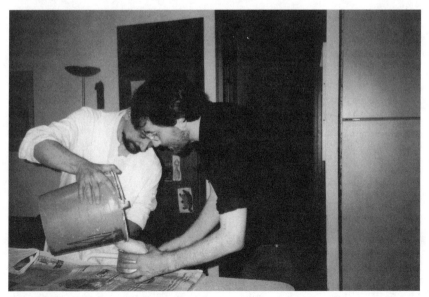

Fig. 8.4. The plaster is carefully poured into the casts.
(Massimo Polidoro Collection)

outer paraffin glove can be removed, either by scraping it off with the fingers or by melting it in hot water; we preferred to melt it by placing it on a plate inside an oven at 70° to 80° C.

The skin's wrinkledness in our molds appeared further enhanced: they looked like hands of a person older than the original model. This phenomenon may be caused by either greater evidence of superficial features when these are the only information available on the hand—color, movement, etc. being absent—or by the paraffin shrinking while it is cooled.

With regard to copies from hands smaller than those of the medium—or clearly different—it is well known that previously prepared gloves have repeatedly been found hidden among the medium's and/or other accomplices' clothes.[9] It would not be difficult to conclude, though, that particularly complex molds could have been shaped with extreme care, before a séance took place, by the medium himself or his accomplices and, during the séance, jumbled up with other molds forged at the moment of performing the spiritualist occurrence.

CONCLUSIONS

Our experiment, which everyone can try at home (plaster and paraffin are usually available in artists' shops), seems to suggest the following conclusions:

1. The claim of the impossibility of removing a hand from a thin paraffin mold without breaking it has once again been disproved.
2. The claim of the impossibility of removing a hand from an odd-shaped mold (clasped fingers, a fist hand, V-shaped fingers) has also been refuted.
3. The hypothesis claiming the impossibility of removing a hand from a mold which is narrower at the wrist has been disproved.

In closing, what we think the overall experience suggests is that, in the field of the paranormal, the simplest hypothesis will often explain a phenomenon most completely.

POSTSCRIPT

After this article, as also happened with the Palladino one (see chapter 3), the readers of the *Journal of the Society for Psychical Research* felt that our criticism was unjustified and an even larger debate started.[10]

Parapsychologist Alexander Imich, in particular, appeared to be quite skeptical of our experimentation; he writes: "The authors try to convince us that it is possible to withdraw a hand from a paraffin wax mold of a fist without breaking the mold. I shall analyze their statement and prove that it is not correct." In his letter Imich contends that it is not possible to do what we said we did: "To withdraw the hand from a mold of a fist, without destroying the mold, latex not paraffin has to be used."[11]

To this we replied with the following letter, published in the same issue of the *JSPR*:

> Dr. Imich seems to believe that we did not obtain our molds in the way described; he states that we must have been using latex instead of paraffin. We can assure him and the readers that we performed the experiment exactly as described using only paraffin. We didn't have to bend the layer of paraffin "by 110 degrees" to remove a fist, since human fingers do not need to be straightened to perform such a task.
>
> Furthermore, it was not the wrist section of the mold that "had to be enlarged to permit the exit of the hand," it was the hand that was squeezed out from it, much as one would do when removing a too-tight bracelet from one's hand: the diameter of the bracelet remains the same, it is the hand that changes shape. It is correct, then, that "flexibility" is needed in this kind of endeavor, but from the hand and fingers, not the paraffin. Also, the melting point of paraffin is 55° C; we did melt the paraffin beforehand, and not directly in the hot water container, for the simple reason that hot water above 50° can burn the skin.
>
> We obtained various forms in our trials but sent pictures of only a few samples: the hand with one finger pointing out and the hand with V-shaped fingers are quite self-explanatory, but we can easily provide captions for those needing them: "A hand with V-shaped fingers" (fig. 8.6); "A hand with one finger pointing out" (fig. 8.5); "Two hands with

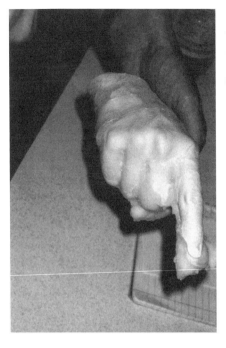

Fig. 8.5. A plaster cast where the paraffin has been almost completely removed. (Massimo Polidoro Collection)

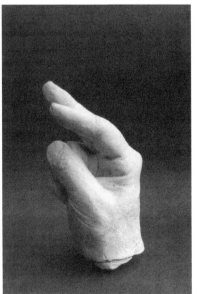

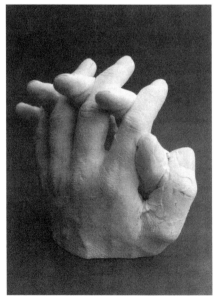

Figs. 8.6–8.7. Plaster casts with fingers in different shapes. (Massimo Polidoro Collection)

interlaced fingers" (fig. 8.7). We can also specify that the hand in fig. 8.6 belongs to Dr. Garlaschelli; the hand in fig. 8.5 to Dr. Polidoro and the hands in fig. 8.7 to a colleague of ours, Mr. Franco Ramaccini.

As for Kluski's "molds of hands smaller than human," we fail to understand what this has to do with our experiment. We wanted to demonstrate that so-called "Spirit molds" can easily be obtained without requiring any paranormal explanation: we did use adult hands in our experiment, but we might equally have used the hands of a child or of a midget, and Kluski may very well have done so too—or does Dr. Imich think that children and midgets are not "human"?

Dr. Imich can easily dispel his doubts about our work simply by trying the experiment himself, and we are quite ready to perform it in front of any public, should this be needed.

NOTES

Reprinted with permission of the editors from the *Journal of the Society for Psychical Research* 62, no. 848 (July 1997). Copyright 1997 by the Society for Psychical Research.

1. This debate was carried out between M. R. Barrington and M. H. Coleman in the pages of *JSPR* in 1994–1995. See vol. 59, pp. 340–46 and 347–51; and vol. 60, pp. 98–103, 104–106, 183–85, 348–50, and 350–51.
2. See M. H. Coleman, "Wax Moulds of 'Spirit' Limbs," *JSPR* 59 (1994): 340–46, and "Correspondence," *JSPR* 60 (1995): 183–85.
3. Robin J. Tillyard, *British Journal of Psychical Research* 1 (1926–28): 340.
4. Gustave Geley, "Materialized Hands," *Scientific American* (November 1923).
5. P. Giovetti, *I misteri intorno a noi* (Mysteries Around Us) (Milano: Rizzoli, 1988), my translation; Ugo Dettori, ed., *L'uomo e l'ignoto* (Man and the Unknown) (Milano: Armenia Editore, 1981), my translation; and Geley, "Materialized Hands."
6. Coleman, "Correspondence," pp. 183–85.

7. Geley, "Materialized Hands."

8. It is interesting to note that one of the theses of Kluski's advocates supporting the authenticity of the phenomenon assumes that the molds the medium obtained during the séances were so tight at the wrist that it was impossible for a hand to come out. Although this statement, as demonstrated, is not true, of all the molds kept at the Institut Metapsychique International almost none have this characteristic. The majority of the molds either end before the narrow part of the hand or include only the external, visible half of them, but never the internal half. The discovery of this fact was just what induced us to try to reproduce the phenomenon of the spirit molds.

9. See Coleman, "Wax Moulds"; and my *Viaggio tra gli spiriti* (Journey Among the Spirits) (Camago: Va.: Sugarco, 1995).

10. See D. Fontana, "Spirit Moulds: Observations on Kluski and His Critics," *JSPR* 63, no. 853 (1998): 43–45, and "Letter," *JSPR* 63, no. 856 (1999): 243–44; M. R. Barrington, "Letter," *JSPR* 63, no. 854 (1999): 127; Alexander Imich, "Letter," *JSPR* 63, no. 856 (1999): 243; and M. Coleman, "Letter," *JSPR* 64, no. 858 (2000): 55–57.

11. Alexander Imich, "Letter," *JSPR* 62, no. 852 (July 1998): 468–69. Our response was printed on pp. 469–70.

CHAPTER NINE

THE CHEMISTRY OF "SUPERNATURAL" SUBSTANCES

by Luigi Garlaschelli

As I wrote in the introduction to this book, my good friend
Luigi Garlaschelli is, among other things, one of the leading
experts in the investigation of claims related to the supernatural. He has investigated the Shroud of Turin, the liquefying blood of St. Januarius, the milk-drinking Hindu
statues, the weeping Madonnas, the mummified relics of
various saints, and many other apparent miracles. He is
now compiling a book on all such investigations. Meanwhile, however, to give you an idea of another field of study
we have developed at CICAP I have asked Luigi to tell you
the story of a less-famous liquefying blood. This was one of
the very rare occasions in which we were allowed to actually touch and physically examine a true relic.

MP

*T*he study of miracles, that is, paranormal phenomena of a religious or cultist nature, has proven to be even more elusive than the examination of paranormal events of the secular realm. This is, of course, the result of protection by the religious authority, who may feel either that the event needs no examination and should be accepted on faith, or that the investigation can only be performed by members of the religion or cult who already believe in the divine nature of the miracle.

Cooperation between secular and religious authorities in the investigation of miracles, such as was realized in the study of the Shroud of Turin, is the exception rather than the rule.[1]

Miracles that can be conclusively studied by investigators using hard scientific disciplines, such as chemistry and physics, are limited to physical miracles of a nonmedical nature, that is, those miracles that are visible to more than one observer are manifested as physical and paranormal phenomena, and do not involve healings.

The Roman Catholic Church has a long history of extensive investigation of miracles, but only in very few cases have physical miracles of a nonmedical nature been accepted as evidence for sanctity or as caused by a special divine intervention. Examples include miraculous images, weeping icons, and unexplained transformations of physical state (e.g., coagulated blood that liquifies).

The "weeping Madonna" in Siracusa, Italy, who reportedly shed tears in 1953, was declared by the local bishop to be a genuine miracle just four months after the phenomenon took place.[2] In other cases the church has traditionally been much more cautious, preferring not to express itself as to the authenticity of the event (which can, however, be declared of prodigious nature), while still allowing its cult, as long as this is doctrinally sound.

BLOOD MIRACLES

Among the religious relics of this type still venerated by the Roman Catholic Church are remains of the blood of early saints. In Italy alone,

Fig. 9.1. Dr. Luigi Garlaschelli. (Massimo Polidoro Collection)

particularly clustered near Naples, there are some 190 blood relics.[3] A small number of these samples become liquefied from their usual clotted state—in a purportedly paranomal manner—on specific occasions, generally during religious ceremonies.

When blood is drawn from a living body and poured into a container, the soluble serum protein, fibrinogen, forms a network of insoluble fibrin, which in turn binds the erythrocytes, resulting in a jelly-like clot. This clot can be mechanically broken down, but once this has been done, no further change of state can recur. Thus, the resolidification of a blood sample would be even more surprising than its first liquefaction.

The most celebrated of these miraculous relics is a vial containing a dark, unknown substance, considered to be the blood of St. Januarius, that has liquefied once or twice a year since 1389 in Naples.[4] St. Januarius was an early bishop of Benevento, and was beheaded during the persecution by the emperor Diocletian in 305 C.E. The relic representing his blood appeared in Naples more than ten centuries later, around 1389. Other relics of this kind, wherein the phase transition is evident and genuine, are the blood of St. Pantaleone in Ravello (Avellino) and that of St. Lorenzo (St. Lawrence) in Amaseno (Frosinone), whose visual properties and behavior appear extremely similar.[5]

Some years ago we proposed that thixotropy may furnish an explanation for the properties of the Januarian blood.[6] Thixotropy denotes the property of certains gels to liquefy when stirred or vibrated, and to solidify again when left to stand. The very act of handling the relic during the ceremony, repeatedly turning it upside down to check its state, can provide the necessary force to trigger its liquefaction. In support of our hypothesis we also succeeded in preparing thixotropic samples, closely resembling the Januarian relic, using materials and techniques available in the fourteenth century.

Although the Januarian relic is subjected to many mechanical stresses, however, the large vial containing the blood of St. Pantaleone (which liquifies around July 27) is never moved, since it is locked behind a grating; and that of St. Lorenzo is gently moved only once, on August 10, from its niche to the altar. In these cases, then, thixotropy cannot be the explanation. Moreover, it appears that the liquefaction begins days before the feast day, and ends much later (precise day-to-day records are lacking).

The Blood of St. Lorenzo

St. Lorenzo was martyred on August 10, 258 C.E., under the Roman emperor Valerian, by being charred on a grill, and his popularity as a saint was always great during the Middle Ages and up to our days.[7] The most famous of the relics of St. Lorenzo still existing is a small flask which allegedly contains his blood and which is venerated in the collegiate church of St. Maria in the small town of Amaseno (Frosinone). The relic is normally locked in a silver tabernacle in the right wing of the church. A few days before the saint's feast the niche is sometimes unlocked and the state of the relic inspected. On the morning of August 10, the relic is brought near the altar, put onto a baroque stand, and locked into a glass cabinet. There, any further transformation of its state can be witnessed by the worshipers. A ceremony is held on that same day in the presence of the bishop from Frosinone; in the evening the relic is locked again in its niche, and sometimes further changes in the following days are checked by opening the safe a few times. No physical, chemical, or spectroscopical tests have ever been performed on this relic.

On August 10, 1996, I had permission to examine the small flask during a TV documentary filmed by a crew of the Italian state television, Rai 2. I had brought with me various equipment in order to perform a few simple tests: a camera, a caliper, an electronic balance, a test-tube spinner, chemist's clamps, laboratory metal stands, thermometers, beakers, and so forth.

Tests on the Relic

The relic consists of a small glass flask, 15.3 cm high and weighing 141.8 g (the mean of three measures on an Acculab electronic balance). It is shaped like an inverted cone connected to a long neck with a diameter of 2.5 cm. The bottle is closed with a cork that cannot be removed because it is secured by red strings, red wax seals, and an old, discolored bishop's label. However, the cork is clearly not airtight.

The vial contains an estimated 35 ml of a mixture of substances. On the bottom there is a lumpy, tan layer, possibly containing sand or earth. A very tiny piece of darker material in this layer was traditionally interpreted by believers as a particle of the coal on which the saint was martyred. A few observers even claim to see a piece of the saint's charred skin.[8] A second layer, normally in the solid state and also brownish, is topped by a third, thin, more amorphous layer. When liquefied, the middle layer becomes transparent, changes to ruby red, and flows freely if the flask is tilted slightly. The bottom layer always remains solid and the top one sometimes becomes partly liquefied. When I examined the relic, the middle layer was liquid while the other two layers were still opaque and solid.

I whirled the ampoule for ten seconds on a Maxi Mixer test-tube mixer to check for a possible stress-induced thixotropic phase transition, but the only result was that the two uppermost layers became slightly mixed. The bottom layer remained unchanged, and a further ten-second whirling failed to alter the fluidity of the viscous contents.

I then cooled down the small flask by clamping it at the neck and immersing its lower part in an ice-water bath. After a few minutes, the entire contents solidified into an opaque, tan-colored mass.

Finally, I slowly rewarmed the water bath to the initial room temperature (29–30° C) by placing a hair dryer under it, while monitoring its temperature by a chemistry thermometer. At 29–30° C the contents of the flask melted again, and its color turned red, thus clearly demonstrating that the observed change is simply a temperature-related effect of a low-melting-point compound.

Conclusions

The red substance cannot possibly be blood, since whole blood is typically opaque; even a clear hemoglobin solution would have decomposed and lost its bright red color over the centuries; a water solution would have dried up from the imperfectly sealed flask, and would not freeze at 30° C.

The softening temperature and the overall look suggest that the relic consists of fats, waxes, or mixtures thereof, possibly containing an appropriate oil-soluble red dye. As a matter of fact, this relic is described in the church consecration act scroll (1177) as *reliquia de pinguedine St. Laurentii Mart.* (relic from the fat of the martyr Saint Lorenzo). The liquefaction phenomenon was not observed until the seventeenth century, when it became dubbed "fat and blood" and finally just "blood." This fact might even raise the suspicion that the early relic was at that time substituted for the present one (possessing evident liquefying properties).

It is interesting to notice that one of the hypotheses to explain the behavior of the blood of St. Januarius was that the unknown substance is simply a mixture with a low melting point. Solid when stored in a somewhat cooler place, it would melt when taken to the warmer altar, near burning candles, amidst a fervent crowd. This hypothesis was first recorded as early as 1826 and was quickly supported by numerous recipes, mostly based upon waxes, fats, or gelatins (plus suitable dyes).[9] A practical, not anachronistic one, was recently suggested by Nickell and Fisher.[10] In any case, mixtures such as these have a constant melting point, whereas the blood-liquefaction ceremony can be performed at different room temperatures (May, September, December). Thus, in the case of the Januarian blood, the thixotropic hypothesis seems more plausible.

However, contrary to the Januarian relic, the "blood" of St. Lorenzo is not contained in a sealed flask. A tiny drop of the substance, extracted with a syringe through the somewhat loose cork, might easily be analyzed by standard spectroscopic and chromatographic methods (UV-VIS and IR spectrophotometry, GC-MS, HPLC, etc.) and the nature of the red dye and that of the low-melting-point mixture could be identified.

Almost any substance melting in that range would do; it is tempting, however, to think of fats or waxes. Fats, in particular, could be analyzed rather easily. The type and the relative amount of the different fatty acids obtained by hydrolysis of triglycerides (fats), in fact, are a sort of "fingerprint," often allowing the identification of the specific oil or fat, and distinguishing, for example, among sunflower, linseed, or coconut oils, tallow, etc.

What now can be said, by way of speculation, is that the "blood" of St.

Lorenzo looks very similar, for example, to the so-called red palm oil, a vegetable fat extracted from the plants *Elaeis guineensis*: this alimentary fat contains reddish-orange carotenes, is yellowish when solid and deep orange when liquid; this color change, and its exotic origin, might well have elicited fantasies about its miraculous properties. Its melting point (around 17° C), however, is lower than that of the unknown "blood," and its color seems to be more orange than red. Thus, unless it was mixed with other higher-melting compounds, better candidates might exist: coconut butter, tallow, etc. These fats are colorless and would call for the addition of suitable dyes.

Chemically, a preponderance of saturated fatty acids in the triglycerides leads to substantially higher-melting fats. Saturated fats are also more resistant to oxidation, bringing to rancidity. Since the relic's substance appears to have been fairly stable for centuries, one should suppose a large amount of saturated fatty acids in it. Even more stable are waxes, which, however, generally have a higher melting point.

The first fat-soluble red dye that comes to mind, which has the right red hue and was widely used during the Middle Ages,[11] is "dragon's blood," a vegetable resin extracted from the plants *Daemonorops propinquus*,[12] *Dracoena draco*,[13] or *Calamus draco*.[14]

Clearly, these are just speculations. As stated above, the relic representing the blood of St. Pantaleone in Ravello also seems to behave in an exactly similar manner, and has the same visual properties. So, it would be even more interesting to obtain exact data on both these maybe-not-so-miraculous substances.

The simplest check that we have recommended to the relic's keepers is a regular daily record of the state of the substance as well as the temperature. Conclusive analysis, of course, should be of a chemical and instrumental nature.[15] The permission to perform such tests, however, has not, so far, been given by church authorities.

NOTES

Reprinted with permission of the editors from the *Journal of the Society for Psychical Research* 62, no. 852 (July 1998). Copyright 1998 by the Society for Psychical Research.

The author wishes to thank Father Italo Pisterzi, Church of St. Maria, Amaseno, for permission to examine the relic; Rai 2 and director Gianni Romano for making this investigation feasible; his colleague Franco Ramaccini for bringing the properties of red palm oil to his attention, and for useful discussions and suggestions.

1. See P. E. Damon et al., "Radiocarbon Dating of the Shroud of Turin," *Nature* 337 (1989): 611–15; and J. Nickell, *Inquest on the Shroud of Turin* (Amherst, N.Y.: Prometheus Books, 1987).

2. See D. S. Rogo, *Miracles: A Scientific Exploration of Wondrous Phenomena* (Chicago: Dial Press, 1983); and my "You Can Get Blood from a Stone," *Chemistry in Britain* 31, no. 7 (1995): 534.

3. G. B. Alfano and A. Amitrano, *Notizie storiche ed osservazioni sulle reliquie di sangue dei martiri e dei santi confessori ed asceti che si conservano in Italia e particolarmente in Napoli* (Historical News and Observations on the Blood Relics of Martyrs and of Confessing and Ascetic Saints Preserved in Italy and Especially in Naples) (Napoli: Arti gafiche Adriana, 1951).

4. G. B. Alfano and A. Amitrano, *Il miracolo di S. Gennaro: documentazione storica e scientifica* (The Miracle of St. Januarius: Historical and Scientific Documentation) (Napoli: Scarpati, 1924).

5. Alfano and Amitrano, *Notizie storiche.*

6. Luigi Garlaschelli, Franco Ramaccini, and Sergio Della Sala, "Working Bloody Miracles," *Nature* 353 (1991): 507, and "A Miracle Diagnosis," *Chemistry in Britain* 30 (1994): 123.

7. G. Boccaccio, *Decameron*, bk. 6, v. 10.

8. E. Giannetta, *Il sangue miracoloso di S. Lorenzo martire* (The Miraculous Blood of St. Lawrence Martyr) (Frosinone: Tecno Stampa, 1964).

9. E. Salverte, *Des sciences occultes ou essai sur la magie, les prodiges et les miracles* (Of Occult Sciences, or Essay on Magic, Prodigies, and Miracles) (Paris: Bailliere, 1826).

10. J. Nickell and J. Fisher, *Mysterious Realms* (Amherst, N.Y.: Prometheus Books, 1993).

11. C. Cennini, *Il Libro dell'Arte* (The Book of Art) (14th century; reprint, Vicenza: Neri Pozza, 1971), p. 43.

12. *Merck Index*, 11th ed. (Rahway: Merck & Co., 1989).

13. D. Thompson, *The Materials and Techniques of Medieval Painting* (London: George Allen & Unwin, 1936), p. 124; H. G. M. Edwards, D. W. Farwell, and A. Quye, "'Dragon's Blood': Characterization of an Ancient Resin Using Fourier Transform Raman Spectroscopy," *Journal of Raman Spectroscopy* 28 (1977): 243–49.

14. Gerolamo Villavecchia and Gino Eigenmann, *Nuovo Dizionario di Mercelogia e Chimica Applicato* (New Dictionary of Merceologia and Applied Chemistry) (Milano: U. Hoepli, 1977).

15. Edwards, Farwell, and Quye, "'Dragon's Blood."

PART 3

INVESTIGATING
PSYCHICS TODAY

CHAPTER TEN

THERE BE
POLTERGEISTS!

*T*he very first case I investigated took place on January 22, 1989, right after the founding of CICAP (the Italian Committee for the Investigation of Claims of the Paranormal). It was a case of poltergeist. TV news and newspapers in Italy suddenly devoted lots of space to the strange case of Marco, a twelve-year-old living in Milan with his parents, who seemed to be at the center of some very mysterious happenings: furniture moved around the house, frames fell from the walls, books flew. An exorcist was called, and also a psychic healer, a medium, and some parapsychologists, but no one was able to restore peace to the house. Since the birth of our committee had attracted some attention only a few weeks before, we were immediately called upon by journalists to investigate the matter. However, it was only when the family itself called us in distress that we decided to step in.

We knew, from previous experience of other skeptic groups and investigators like James Randi, that most similar cases revealed that the paranormal was not involved. One of the most significant such cases was that of the

Resch family in Columbus, Ohio, where the adopted child, Tina, caused strange phenomena, very similar to that of the Italian case we were going to investigate. It was thanks to a video camera, left on inadvertently, that the girl was filmed in the act of throwing a lamp in the air and the case was closed.[1]

REVEALING FACTS

We met with Marco's family on February 2 and decided on the following procedure: while a few members of the committee would talk with the parents, have them describe the whole story, and try to outline their psychological profile, I would spend time with Marco, let him play with his toys, and try to understand what was going on.

We spent three days with Marco and his family and, while nothing supernatural happened, several interesting facts came to light. First of all, the family appeared to be quite open to psychic phenomena: there were several books on the subject on their shelves; Marco had seen many movies that might have influenced him (*Poltergeist*, *The Exorcist*, *Nightmare on Elm Street*), and the parents had attended séances and consulted palm readers, psychic healers, and occultists. Furthermore, there appeared to be some tension inside the family because of the parents' many work committments and the child's need for their presence. The most revealing fact, however, was that some members of the family had, more than once, caught Marco in the act of throwing something.

"Oh, but that was nothing!" said the parents, explaining this revelation away. "Those times he was only playing, but all the other times the phenomena were real."

"What *other times*?" we asked. "Did anyone ever see a book take flight or a frame fall off the wall?"

Well, it appeared that nobody, except Marco, had ever seen any phenomenon from the start. At most, they had seen something when it touched the ground, but only because Marco had yelled to attract attention. However, usually the phenomena only happened in the presence of Marco and when he was alone in his room.

The Flying Glass

The three days I spent with Marco showed me that he was an intelligent boy with a good sense of humor, but also very alert in watching all my movements. I was very careful never to leave him unobserved and this resulted in no phenomena. The parents told us clearly that those were the first three days devoid of phenomena and could not explain it. Had the poltergeist run its course, they asked?

On the last day, however, something did happen. I wanted to see if, given the opportunity, Marco would seize it, and so I relaxed my attention on him. I let him play and frequently turned my back to him. At one point in the evening, while we were playing a computer game, he suggested that I keep on playing while he prepared his books for school. "Oh, don't worry," I said. "I can help you." "No, no! Please," he insisted, "keep on playing; I'll be done in a second."

Okay, I thought. I turned around but managed to keep an eye on his reflection in the window. I saw him put some books in his bag and look frequently at me; then he took something out of his bag and, with a sudden move, threw it against a wall. It was a glass and it shattered with a loud bang! I immediately turned around and asked: "Why did you do that?"

He looked at me quite puzzled: "What? What do you mean?"

"I saw you in the reflection," I explained. "Why did you throw that glass?"

"I . . . I . . ."

He could not finish his sentence, however, because his father arrived, excited, in the room. "Did it happen? Did something happen? And you witnessed it, right?"

"No," I said. "I am sorry, but I clumsily bumped the glass and broke it."

"Oh, is that what happened?" he asked, a bit frustrated.

"Yes. I am very sorry."

The boy didn't look me in the face, but kept on putting his books in the bag, silently. I had not wanted to embarrass him in front of his father and so had invented that excusable lie.

Our conclusions were that Marco was a normal boy who needed more attention from his parents. He found that if he threw things around while nobody could see him he got a lot of attention, not only from his parents but also from the TV and from a lot of strange and funny people who came to visit him. When I played with him and his toys he couldn't care less about psychic phenomena and poltergeists and, in fact, nothing ever happened. Only when we announced that we were leaving did Marco "cause" something: was it because he did not want his family to be thought liars? Or because he did not want me to leave? I don't know the answer to this; however, I know that from the day we left all phenomena disappeared.

OTHER SPIRITS

This was not the only time we had to deal with apparent poltergeist cases. In a case that took place shortly after that of Marco, a girl was thought to be a "firestarter," just like in Stephen King's novel: when she was angry things around her could catch fire. It turned out that her mother had announced that a new baby was on its way and she was not at all happy about it. She had found a lighter around the house and used it to set fire to curtains, clothes, and blankets, to the horror of her parents. The whole family finally decided to consult a psychologist and was able to overcome their problems.

Both in this case and in that of Marco—as with some others of a similar nature—we did not reveal the full facts to the media. We thought that it was only fair to let the families resolve their problems, without the nosy curiosity of the media.

At other times, however, the explanation had nothing to do with troubled children. Once we received news of a strange occurrence: in the house of a friend, a big panda bear made of crystal moved from its place during the night. The owner was quite sure about it: after noticing that the bear seemed not to be in the place were he had put it, he drew a circle around it with a pen. On the following day he found that the bear had moved again a few inches out of the circle.

It could not be some practical joke because he lived alone, and we were quite sure that he was not playing a trick on us (although we never completely excluded that possibility). He tried to ascertain if the movement was caused by trucks or trains passing close to his house, or by the vibrations of his own hi-fi equipment or other household appliances. Nothing seemed to explain the phenomenon. The wardrobe on top of which the panda stood was quite steady and was nailed to the wall.

Then, one day, he told us that he had seen the panda move. It slid slowly and silently toward the center of the wardrobe, which was slightly curved toward the center. No noises were heard or vibrations felt. He told us that he had tried to discover if the cause for the movement was low frequency vibrations and he even applied Hall-effect sensors to the walls of his room. These sensors respond to the presence or the interruption of a magnetic field, such as those produced by household appliances. He suspected, in fact, that the movement was caused by some appliance in one of the apartments close to his. He was right: the cause of the "poltergeist" was finally located in the new, super-silent washing machine of the apartment upstairs!

There have been many other examples of natural phenomena that were wrongly thought to be paranormal in origin. Also, in various other situations, the real cause of phenomena turned out to be the need to get attention or revenge. In one case, we found that an employee of a business agency was setting fire to documents, jamming photocopier machines, sabotaging computer lines, and causing other technical problems because he thought that his pay was unjustly low. What we have never seen so far, however, but would love to, is some real poltergeist manifestation.

NOTE

1. James Randi, "The Columbus Poltergeist Case," *Skeptical Inquirer* 9, no. 3 (spring 1985): 221–35.

CHAPTER ELEVEN

ROLL UP
FOR THE
MYSTERY TOUR

*T*he announcement a few years ago of a million-dollar prize established by the James Randi Educational Foundation for any psychic ability demonstrated under scientific conditions has generated quite an interesting reaction in Italy. At CICAP we have received dozens of requests from self-proclaimed psychics to be tested; very few, however, offered actually testable claims.

THE ELUSIVE COLD-READER

There was one man, quite resolute, who wanted to be addressed as Doctor, although from his speech we suspected he didn't possess any degree. He claimed that he was able to know everything about a complete stranger within a few minutes.

However, he said that in order for him to be successful there were a few conditions he wanted us to observe: he had to be able to speak to the subject, he needed to look him in the face, and he had to receive feedback from the subject regarding his guesses. He told us he might start on the wrong track but, following the subject's reaction, he would eventually be able to ascertain the correct information. In other words, the claimant was adamantly telling us that he used classical "cold reading" techniques and wanted to do so without interference.[1]

We explained to him that there was nothing paranormal about such demonstrations, whereupon he said he could do the same thing on the phone. We saw a possibility here and suggested the following experiment: he was to be in a room with a telephone and an experimenter. In another building, a dozen people, unknown to the subject and to the experimenter that was with him, were to go to the telephone one at a time and just say a few words. They were not allowed to talk with the psychic. The psychic claimed that just by listening to the voice, he could guess the kind of studies that the subject had done, the color of her hair, and the appearance of her clothing. We are still waiting for him to give us a date on which to perform the test.

I HEAR VOICES!

A lady wrote us that she was in contact with an "entity." She told us that she honestly did not know whether it was a spirit or just her imagination. This entity, she said, appeared to be omniscient and could predict earthquakes and plane crashes. She only had to write a question and the entity would reply through her, writing "yes" or "no." Therefore, before setting up a possible experiment to formally test her claims, we wrote a few questions, the answers to which she could not know, just to see if the entity was really omniscient or not. Judging by the answers we received, it appears it is not.

There were other people who claimed they heard "voices": some of them stated that the voices could predict the future, and so we asked them to write their predictions for us; others thought the voices were telepathic commands from some unknown entities. In these cases we suggested they visit a good psychiatrist.

In one case, however, I was quite frightened. I always turn down re-quests for private meetings and consultations, but one man, through common friends, insisted that I meet him. When we did meet he looked very tired and had a sorry smile. He told me he felt he was being psychi-cally monitored by someone who could direct a "magnetic field" around him. Also, he said, this person who was "controlling" him always insulted him, drained his energies, and he felt weaker and weaker. He couldn't go on much longer with this burden and wanted us to do something.

I explained that the best thing for him was to visit a psychiatrist; he told me he had already been to three different ones and had also been to seven electroconvulsive sessions, but to no avail. He said that he had been able, through complicated calculus, to track down the source of the mag-netic field and had come to believe that his "controller" lived in a house in a nearby town. One day, he said, he went there and waited in his car for the controller's arrival; he knew he would be able to "psychically" recog-nize him. He had a gun with him and was ready to shoot the one who he thought was his enemy. However, no one appeared and he returned home.

We contacted his psychiatrist but we couldn't do much to help him, and we haven't heard from him again. But from that time to the present, I have been even more cautious before meeting with strangers who "need" to consult with me.

THE INSISTENT TIME-SENSER

If I had needed more evidence to convince me to be cautious, I would have gotten it through "Mr. Tops," the most insistent of all the psychic claimants we have had so far. This man somehow got my private cell phone number and called me to say he wanted to be tested because he had to buy a new house with the million-dollar prize. He blabbed on for about half an hour, never saying exactly what he could do and without letting me say anything. Finally, he explained that he was able to "sense," without looking, when the second hand of a watch was on the numbers 3, 6, 9, or 12. He insisted this was actually an extraordinary new scientific discovery which, however, he could not yet present as such, since he wanted first to win the prize. I told him to send me a description in writing of his abilities and asked him to accept the terms of Randi's challenge.

During the next few months Mr. Tops called many times, left up to fifteen messages in a row on the answering service when I was not reachable, and sent me pages and pages of faxes. He even called a few times in the middle of the night. I am not sure that I was always polite on those occasions. He became euphoric and suggested plans on how we could present him to the world once he had won the prize. He suggested that we should rent an auditorium and invite the prime ministers of various countries and all the living Nobel Prize winners. We always tried to calm him down, explaining that he hadn't won the prize yet, but he just laughed.

When we finally met for the test, he warmed up like a gymnast, but following an odd ritual: he wore very heavy clothing, stretched a few elastic bands between his fingers, and ate some honey. We had various timers available. He examined them all and chose the one he felt most attracted to. We started the timer at random in another room, then we brought it face down into the presence of Mr. Tops. He concentrated to "feel" the numbers and told us when to stop the timer. The test took a full day, and on a very long run of trials, he only guessed correctly once or twice. He was quite surprised at the results and made up all kinds of rationalizations to explain his failure. He wanted us to agree that this was only a trial and not the real experiment, but we insisted that this was it, and that we were not going to perform any other test. We suggested that he find a friend to work with and publish his results in a scientific journal, and that after that we would be interested in testing him again. He still calls us every now and then to see if we have changed our minds.

A TABLE-LIFTER AND A STRANGE CALLER

A Mr. Salvatore recently wrote us that he could levitate tables, in full view, at any time. This looked quite interesting and we asked him to return to us the completed participation form and also to send us a videotape of his performance. He did send the form and also a videotape: a new one, still sealed! We thought he had clearly misunderstood our request: did he think we collected blank videotapes? However, he later explained to us that the video actually contained his demonstration but that he had the tape resealed "for protection." In the video, Mr. Salvatore simply presses down on the table and raises it on two legs. We suggested he try to repeat his demonstration with two sheets of paper under his hands and are now waiting a reply.

We are very curious about another claimant who displays strange behavior. He usually calls after office hours and explains—on our answering machine—that he can receive telepathic messages. He goes on and on detailing his various successes but never leaves a number where we can call him back. A few days ago, a member of CICAP was in the office working late and received a call. He answered, but no one spoke. Then a man asked if this was CICAP and my colleague recognized the voice of the "mysterious" psychic. He invited him to speak freely but the man said he preferred to talk to the answering machine and would have to call back.

These are examples of the people we sometimes have to deal with. Besides these, however, we are currently examining the possibility of testing more conventional candidates who claim to be dowsers and clairvoyants, and even one metal bender. So far, we have always been approached by people who appear to sincerely believe that they possess some strange power or people who seem disconnected from reality. Only rarely has some faker tried to trick us, as we shall see later.

NOTE

1. The term *cold reading* refers to a set of techniques used by professional manipulators (psychics, salespersons, hypnotists, advertising pros, faith healers, con men, and some therapists) to get a subject to behave in a certain way or to think that the cold reader has some sort of special ability that allows him to

"mysteriously" know things about the subject. To know more about cold reading see Ray Hyman, "'Cold Reading': How to Convince Strangers That You Know All About Them," *Skeptical Inquirer* (spring/summer 1977), reprinted in Ray Hyman, *The Elusive Quarry: A Scientific Appraisal of Psychical Research* (Amherst, N.Y.: Prometheus Books, 1989). For a quick guide to cold reading by Ray Hyman see: http://www.skeptics.com.au/journal/coldread.htm.

CHAPTER TWELVE

SECRETS
OF A
RUSSIAN PSYCHIC

*F*or years, owing to the aura of secrecy that surrounded it, psychic research in the USSR has been regarded as some kind of myth. It was said, for example, that the Russians were far ahead in parapsychological discoveries and that the West had better invest lots of money in the field in order to avoid a "psi-gap." The sparse information that reached the West hinted at extraordinary faculties being scientifically demonstrated by amazing psychics. During the early 1960s, interest in Soviet paranormal claims was first aroused by newspaper articles describing the astonishing abilities of Rosa Kuleshova, a twenty-two-year-old Russian woman who could apparently read print while blindfolded.[1] However, the loose conditions in which Rosa operated allowed for very easy methods of deception to be used.[2]

In 1968, films of Nina Kulagina apparently moving objects with her mind (psychokinesis, or PK) were shown at the First Moscow International Conference on Parapsychology and were also observed by some

Western scientists. Finally, the general public became aware of the varied work in parapsychology carried out in the USSR with the publication of Sheila Ostrander and Lynn Schroeder's *Psychic Discoveries Behind the Iron Curtain* (1970), followed by various other similar publications on the subject.[3]

Films of Russian psychics at work have now been seen on Western TV shows and documentaries. The most popular are those that show apparent PK in action. We have seen Nina Kulagina apparently moving compass needles and light objects, Boris Ermolaev "levitating" small objects, and Alla Vinogradova willing round objects to roll on flat surfaces.

RUSSIAN PK STARS

As for Nina Kulagina, the conditions under which she operated were far from acceptable by basic scientific standards. Tests were frequently carried out at her own home or in hotel rooms; no tight controls were ever applied, owing in part to the fact that a demonstration might take several hours of preparation (i.e., concentration by Nina), which, of course, was no guarantee of success. Also, when watching these films, anybody who has a background in magic cannot avoid the feeling that she is using standard conjuring techniques: magnets hidden on her body to move the compass needle; threads or thin hair to move objects across the table; small mirrors concealed in her hand to read signs with numbers and letters being held behind her. Unfortunately, no expert in conjuring techniques was ever present at Kulagina's demonstrations.

Boris Ermolaev, a Russian film director, became relatively famous during the 1970s for his apparent ability to suspend objects in midair by concentrating on them. Ermolaev didn't perform on stage, but showed his demonstrations "only to serious scientists of his own choosing or to close friends."[4] He was tested by various experimenters, among them Prof. Venyamin Pushkin, who stated: "The experiments were conducted under the strictest controls, and no devices of any kind were used."[5] However, in a 1992 *World of Discovery* documentary called "Secrets of the Russian

Psychics," Ermolaev's method was finally revealed. He would sit on a chair and place the objects to be suspended between his knees; unfortunately for him, the light conditions when the documentary crew was filming were probably not what he was accustomed to. The TV crew was able to capture a fine thread fixed between his knees to which he attached the objects; the whole unmasking procedure was filmed and shown during the documentary.

Alla Vinogradova is another story.

VINOGRADOVA'S MOVING OBJECTS

A child psychologist, teacher, and wife of Russian psi-researcher Victor Adamenko, Alla Vinogradova saw a 1969 film of Kulagina in action and suspected that she too could move objects without touching them. In fact, trained by Adamenko, she discovered she could really move objects placed on transparent surfaces. Films of her demonstrations were shot in the early 1970s and, a few years ago, the already mentioned *World of Discovery* documentary on Russian psychics had an interesting section devoted to her. Here she was presented as she is today, still demonstrating the same abilities for the camera. She took such objects as cigarettes, aluminum cigar tubes, and pens and put them on a Plexiglass plate suspended between two chairs; in such conditions she was able to make them rotate, roll, and move just by having her hand approach, but never touch, them. The demonstration was quite puzzling. It did appear very natural and repeatable, and it seemed that the usual tricks (like secretly blowing on the surface to have the object move thanks to the air current) were unlikely.

Some time ago, I visited James Randi in Florida; he had recently returned from Russia, where he had gone for some filming to be included in *Nova's* 1993 documentary about his work: "Secrets of the Psychics." Randi told me that, while he was there, the TV production staff had approached Vinogradova, and asked if she would agree to demonstrate her abilities on camera. She agreed; however, she made the condition that Randi had to be kept away from the room where the filming was to take place. This was quite an inappropriate request, considering that the documentary was dedicated to Randi's investigations. Nonetheless, Randi accepted her veto. She would present her demonstration as she always did, that is, not under controlled conditions. It was, in any event, an occasion to film her from different angles and to have better video material for study.

The segments filmed with Vinogradova were not included in the final documentary; however, Randi had copies of the original unedited footage that he showed me. Vinogradova was seen speaking in Russian with the operators, then walking back and forth on the thick carpet, combing her hair, and rubbing with a towel the surface of Plexiglass plate placed on top of four glasses turned upside down on a table. It was a cold, crisp, winter day.

She started to demonstrate her abilities with various objects: cigarettes, pens, plastic rings, a small wooden matrioska doll, a small hairspray bottle, and a glass. All the objects moved quite freely, as seen in the other films; only the spray bottle and the glass, being the heaviest objects, moved little or only wobbled back and forth as she passed her hand over them. Suddenly, while moving the nesting doll, a white thread that was on the table, under the Plexiglass, was seen to be moving too, following the doll. I pointed this out to Randi and he told me that the cameraman, after shooting the film, told him that he had seen the moving thread, but didn't realized that he had actually zoomed in on it and had caught it on film. Randi himself hadn't yet had a chance to examine the film so he was quite interested too. "That thread," he told me, "was from the torn end of a cloth-based duct tape used to hold tiny microphones to the edge of the Plexiglass. The microphones were there to detect if she was doing any blowing to move the objects. The thread was not placed there purposely. It was just a loose thread. But, of course, it proved to be the indicator needed."

A NEGLECTED EXPLANATION?

Randi and I discussed the possibility of static electricity being solely reponsible for the phenomena. In the *World of Discovery* documentary, this possibility was mentioned as an explanation proposed by skeptics, but it was immediately discarded since Vinogradova said that she could move objects weighing up to two hundred grams. She claimed that it was impossible to do this using only static electricity. We thought we should try to repeat her performance with a Plexiglass plate but, owing to other things we were involved in at the time, we didn't have a chance to get around to it before my departure.

Once back in Italy, I discussed the subject with my collegues Luigi Garlaschelli and Franco Ramaccini, and soon we tested the theory of static electriticy. Ramaccini found a Plexiglass plate and showed us how easy it was to move any kind of round object on top of it only by making use of the repelling forces caused by static electricity. Of course, the effect was much better if the surface was electrically charged, by rubbing a towel (or even just a hand) on it. Heavier objects, like glasses and spray bottles, could be as easily moved. Everything shown on Alla Vinogradova's films, then, now seemed to have a very simple and rational explanation.

We then wondered whether others had already discovered this very interesting and counterintuitive phenomenon. No mention of Vinogradova's abilities appeared in the skeptical literature of the paranormal, or in popular science "magic" books, and some of the best-known skeptics didn't know much about her.

I then got in touch with some of today's leading parapsychologists and was more than pleased to discover that they had a lot of information on Vinogradova and, above all, had solved the mystery years ago.

THE HELP OF PARAPSYCHOLOGISTS

Stanley Krippner, a psychologist at Saybrook Institute in San Francisco and past president of the Parapsychological Association, whom I had met some years before during the taping of the "Exploring Psychic Powers Live!" TV show, told me that he had dealt with Vinogradova in his book *Human Possibilities* (1980). In it he writes that, when he was in Russia, he observed Vinogradova in action with an aluminum tube: "She picked it up and rubbed it for a few seconds—suggesting to me that she was simply producing an electrostatic charge that would cause her hand to repel the tube. As expected, the object moved across the table."[6] He was able to reproduce the effect back in the United States. In his book, Krippner quotes a Canadian parapsychologist, A. R. G. Owen, who in 1975 wrote: "Anyone can produce this effect. . . . It is entirely due to static electricity."[7]

Richard Broughton, director of the Rhine Research Center in Durham, North Carolina, explained: "Adamenko had a notion that he could train people to produce Kulagina-like effects by starting them out moving objects by static electricity, and then gradually moving them to objects that would not be susceptible to static electricity effects."[8]

A LESSON TO BE LEARNED

Although the more impressive feat of moving objects not susceptible to static electricity hasn't so far been publicly demonstrated by Vinogradova or others, I think there's a lesson to be learned. Serious skeptics and serious parapsychologists should establish more occasions for mutual cooperation. Parapsychologists shouldn't be generally thought of by skeptics as more gullible than other researchers (although there have been many examples of such cases) simply because they may have a more open attitude toward psi. Some of the best skeptical investigations in early psychical research were carried out by members of the Society for Psychical Research. More important, however, is the fact that today parapsychologists are quite aware of the pitfalls of experimenting with self-proclaimed psychics, and they either make use of experts in psychic fraud or, like Richard Wiseman of the Perrot-Warrick Research Unit at the University of Hertfordshire, England, they have themselves developed an expertise in this field.

I hope the era of hard fights between proponents and critics of parapsychology is over. The time has come for a new era of cooperation, where there may be agreement on some basic points, namely, that it is in both sides' interest to get rid of superstition and charlatans and examine the claims, rather than just argue over them. I am not saying that there may be real psi to be discovered, but at least there may be something inter-esting to be discovered about human psychology.

POSTSCRIPT

During a lecture tour of North America, in which I discussed some of the investigations presented in this book, I had a chance to lecture at the Rensselaer Polytechnic Institute in Albany, New York, at the invitation of Mike Sofka, vice president of the Inquiring Skeptics of Upper New York. A couple of weeks after the lecture, I received an e-mail from Mike, who had thought about the Vinogradova investigation and had some further comments to make on the performance of the effect and the explanation of the phenomenon:

> Last week I was visiting my father, and he had a nice piece of Plexiglass. My wife also happened to be near a cigar store and purchased a mod-estly priced stogy in a metal humidor. There are a few extra steps to take to get the effect (and it is a cool effect—good for the next Skeptic fair or Friday the 13th gathering). First, the Plexiglass should be insu-lated. A couple of books do nicely, a wooden table frame would look sharper. Second, use a wool cloth. Cotton doesn't charge the Plexiglass. Third, keep yourself insulated from the Plexiglass after it is polished. To complete the effect, put the humidor dead center of the Plexiglass. Then, using your hand, hold it near the table and humidor, but not touching either. It will roll away from your hand.
>
> Here is why.
>
> The Plexiglass is uniformly charged. The humidor, being a con-ductor, picks up that charge. Same charges repel, so the humidor moves towards the center of the Plexiglass. Of course, if you put it in the center this movement doesn't happen. But put it near the edge and the first thing it will do is roll towards the center.
>
> When you place your hand near the Plexiglass you change the center of charge by grounding some through your hand. You can feel this on the hairs of your hand (if you have hair on your hands). This causes the humidor to roll toward a new center of charge. The effect is, of course,

strongest on a dry day. We've been having about 60–70 percent humidity and it works. But on the day with 40 percent humidity the tube flew away from my hand. I can't wait to see what happens in January.

I wish to thank Mike not only for his insights but also for taking me to visit Albany's Rural Cemetery, where we had a chance to stop by the burial place of Charles Hoy Fort, the famous collector of anomalies, and clean away the overgrown weeds.

NOTES

Reprinted with permission of the editors from the *Skeptical Inquirer* 21, no. 4 (July/ August 1997). Copyright 1997 by the Committee for the Scientific Investigation of Claims of the Paranormal.

I thank the following persons for their kind help and cooperation with this research: Carlos S. Alvarado, Richard S. Broughton, Luigi Garlaschelli, Stanley Krippner, Franco Ramaccini, James Randi, and Nancy Zingrone. Thanks also to the following persons for their useful suggestions: Eberhard Bauer, John Beloff, Susan Blackmore, Ray Hyman, Lewis Jones, Robert L. Morris, and Marcello Truzzi.

1. Ms. Kuleshova appeared in the January 25, 1963, issue of *Time* and the June 12, 1964, issue of *Life*.

2. Martin Gardner, "Dermo-Optical Perception: A Peek Down the Nose," in *Science: Good, Bad and Bogus* (Amherst, N.Y.: Prometheus Books, 1981).

3. See also M. Ullman, "PK in the Soviet Union," in *Research in Parapsychology, 1973*, ed. W. G. Roll, R. L. Morris, and J. D. Morris (Metuchen, N.J.: Scarecrow Press, 1974); and H. Gris and William Dick, *The New Soviet Psychic Discoveries* (Englewood Cliffs, N.J.: Prentice-Hall, 1978).

4. H. Gris and William Dick, "Soviet Psychic Ermolaev . . . Master of Mind over Matter," *Fate* (April 1986).

5. Ibid.

6. Stanley Krippner, *Human Possibilities* (New York: Anchor Press, 1980), p. 20.

7. Ibid.

8. Richard Broughton, personal communication with the author, 1996.

CHAPTER THIRTEEN

THE MYSTERY
OF THE
WATCH THAT
WAS "ALIVE"

One can have many opinions on Uri Geller, but even skeptics have to agree that what he does to his cutlery is done very nicely. Whether he bends spoons with simple manipulations or special powers, he must be credited with showmanship: humor, timing, presence, and a sense of the venue, whether it's stage or TV.

If you watch his TV appearances closely, you might notice how media savvy he is. He really seems to make use of the TV monitors and knows which camera is on. However, after you have seen him two or three times on TV, it becomes easier to guess what he's going to do or say next: his act hasn't changed very much in the last thirty years.

I watched an old tape of Geller on an Italian TV show called "Alla ricerca dell'arca" ("Search for the Ark," taped on March 18, 1989). The show, as usual, had been broadcast live. A few weeks before, they'd had James Randi on their program. During the course of that program, Randi showed simple tricks that mirrored what you might see a psychic do: how to take a picture of your "thoughts," how to make a compass needle move, how to break a spoon, and how to move the hands of a watch. The host was clearly amused and warned the people at home never to trust psychics appearing on TV who claimed these kinds of simple tricks were "the real thing."

Then Geller appeared on the same show. He was on a world tour promoting a book, *The Geller Effect* (which, as it happens, has never been published in Italy), and agreed to do some demonstrations: moving the hands of a watch and bending a key.

WATCH THE WATCH!

As usual, Geller explained how incredible it was that every time he went on TV strange things happened in the houses of viewers. He urged the people at home to bring their watches and household appliances close to the TV set and do as he did. He asked the host for his watch and promised not to bend it. The angle of the camera remained wide, showing both

Fig. 13.1. Uri Geller on Italian TV shows the host's wristwatch.
(Massimo Polidoro Collection)

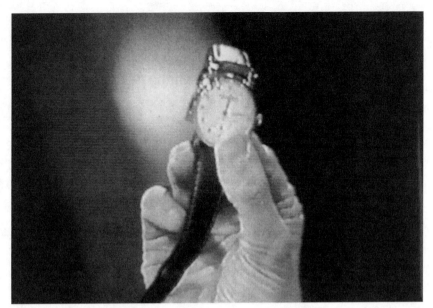

Fig. 13.2. A close-up of the watch: the stem is definitely sticking out. (Massimo Polidoro Collection)

Geller on the left of the TV screen and the host on the right (see fig. 13.1). Geller took the watch with both hands and, asking: "What's the time?" held it with his fingers for a second or two; then he asked: "Can I show it to the camera?" and held it upright, slightly turned, showing the face of the watch. The hands of the watch were on 12:15 P.M., but on rewinding the tape, you could see something else: the stem of the watch was clearly pulled out (see fig. 13.2)! One could theorize that when Geller took the watch with both hands, he pulled the stem out with a fingernail while checking the time.

The watch remained on the screen for only a few seconds; then Geller took it off the screen saying: "Now, please look here, look." The camera focused on nothing while Geller was saying this (and holding the watch out of the picture) and then opened its angle to show Geller putting the watch face down on his right palm. He began stroking it gently and during this procedure urged the people at home to "want your watch to work! Say

Fig. 13.3. A close-up of the watch after a while: the stem is back in its place. (Massimo Polidoro Collection)

'work'!" (Here, Geller seems to have slipped into the script for his starting-watches-at-home demonstration, not the moving-watch-hands miracle!) Some more stroking, some fist clenching: "And there are no magnets," he said, "I don't touch the stem. . . ." Well, yes, he wasn't touching the stem then, but what about a few seconds before? Then (as if suddenly recalling which demo he was supposed to be doing), Geller said, "Move!" and slowly turned the watch: "Look!" he exclaimed, and showed the watch again upright, holding it by the straps. It had moved almost an hour ahead, but . . . something was wrong. When we had seen the watch that close just a minute before, the stem was clearly sticking out of the case; now it was back in again (see fig. 13.3)!

If you were cynical enough not to believe Geller, you would probably suspect that there was something fishy going on, the exact kind of thing that has been suggested for many years by skeptics. The psychic asks for a watch and takes it with both hands; he asks a question so that the owner looks him in the face and, at the same time, with a fingernail, the psychic pulls the stem out. Then he takes his hands away from the watch and shows its face openly: "What time does it say?" Then comes another question or phrase like, "Now, please look here, look," while staring into the eyes of the owner and, at the same time, giving the stem a quick turn and pushing it back in. This description strangely fits perfectly with what Geller was doing on screen.

THE KEYS

Still unconvinced? Geller then asked people in the audience to take out their keys. He took from a table a bunch of keys and said: "These are not my keys," but nobody said where they came from or if Geller had been near them before. He invited people to hold the keys in their hands and, with their minds, to say to the key: "Bend! Bend! Bend!" The camera showed people holding keys and when it went back on Geller he was already stroking one key: unfortunately, his fingers were covering half of the key. Still stroking, he slowly took his fingers away, and the key was bent slightly upward. "Now, check your keys, maybe yours are bent too!" he said. More people from the audience on the screen, checking their keys. Then back to Geller. He was standing, holding the key with both hands and saying, "This is impossible to bend by sheer force, impossible!" While saying this, he made the motion of bending the key with his hands and when he had finished he very clearly took the point of the key out of the bunch of other keys.

Why did he have to hold so many keys in his hands? He had at least two key-holders filled with keys. It would certainly have been more comfortable to keep only the one with the key he was bending. But now he took the key again and very quickly, stroking it again, showed it had bent some more.

Suppose that you inserted the point of a key into the hole of another. A little pressure would create a bend in the tip of the first key. When you extracted the bent key from the other, the motion would look exactly like the strange movement Geller made while plucking his key out from among the others.

The ever-present cynic could now say that when Geller began stroking the key, it was already bent, maybe through muscular pressure during the commercial break, and then Geller proceeded to reveal the bend slowly, pretending it was bending at that moment. Secondly, while showing how hard it was to bend a key with the fingers, he could have been bending it some more.

CONCLUSIONS

This probably was not the best apperance for Mr. Geller; indeed, it appears to be one of the few TV shows where Geller had little control over the cameras and monitors, very much like a 1980s program I remember in Baltimore with American TV host Oprah Winfrey, where Geller could be clearly seen bending a spoon with his hands. This is a fact which, at least, seems to disprove the claim made by Mr. Geller in *The Geller Effect*, that after some "youth mistakes" he has never presented "any other kind of deliberate deception."[1]

NOTE

Reprinted with permission of the editors from *Swift: The Newsletter of the James Randi Educational Foundation* 2, no. 1 (1998). Copyright 1998 by the JREF.

1. Uri Geller and G. L. Playfair, *The Geller Effect* (1986; reprint, London: Grafton Books, 1988), p. 204.

CHAPTER FOURTEEN

MIRACULOUS OIL INSIDE A GLASS TUBE

Testing a Miracle by Means of Tamper-Proof Containers

by Luigi Garlaschelli

and Massimo Polidoro

When testing psychic claimants, the need often arises to let the person take away some target material from the laboratory to try to obtain a psi effect on it in his or her own home. Until a short time ago, the importance of using foolproof containers when conducting this kind of experiment was not fully recognized. Consider, for example, the naiveté with which some parapsychologists have investigated the claimed PK powers of children and teenagers in the past.[1] Since children or teenagers were considered unable to cheat, they were all too readily left alone with target material—for example, spoons or pieces of metal to bend—and when bends were found in these, psychic investigators immediately assumed that some kind of psychic force was at work. Further investigations have shown these suppositions to be false and now stricter controls are (or should be) used in this kind of experiment.[2]

One of the problems encountered has always been that of preparing foolproof containers (e.g., bags, envelopes, or boxes); that is, containers which do not allow the psychic access to the item inside.[3] However, we believe that it is not so important to prevent access to the item (as would be the case with a steel safe) as it is to make sure that the container is "tamper-evident," that is, prepared in such a way that any improper attempt to open it could be easily detected. Special security items are now used to this end. The old sealing wax, for example, has been replaced by self-adhesive labels that show signs of physical tampering, such as attempts to peel them off and the application of heat or solvents. These strips also carry unique identification numbers to prevent the container being opened and the strip being replaced by a duplicate one.[4]

EXPERIMENTAL SUBJECT

We wish to report here on the investigation of a purported macro-PK case, in which an important role was played by a simple, homemade tamper-evident container. Debora Moscogiuri is a twenty-two-year-old mystical seer living in Manduria (Taranto) in southern Italy. During ecstatic periods, she can supposedly see the Virgin Mary, and receive messages from her to Italian worshipers. Other phenomena are said to take place in and around the seer's home; for example, religious icons (pictures and statues) allegedly weep blood. None of these phenomena has been carefully investigated or documented, however, nor have DNA tests been performed to ascertain the origin of the blood.

In 1995 it was said that a statue of the Virgin Mary had started to drip olive oil. In addition, closed containers, such as small bottles or jars, left in the proximity of the statue were later found to be partially filled with oil. These had been tied with ribbons, taped, sealed with wax, and further sealed inside polythene bags. As requested by the claimant, some olive leaves were placed inside the bottles before sealing them.

The phenomena produced by the young lady were also followed by Dr. Gagliardi, a physician from Milan (northern Italy), who prepared two such wax-sealed containers: one was kept in his office in Milan, while a second, identical, one was sent to Manduria.[5] Weeks later this was returned to him with some oil in it—and still sealed. Nothing had happened inside the jar in Milan. Realizing that wax-and-tape sealing was inadequate, Dr. Gagliardi contacted us, asking for secure, "tamper-evident" containers.

METHODOLOGY

We confirmed that the kind of seals he had used could be easily opened and replaced.[6]

Therefore, we prepared a set of sealed test tubes as follows:

1. An olive leaf was put into each glass test tube.
2. The tubes were flame-sealed on a Bunsen burner, taking care not to scorch the leaf inside.
3. Each tube was numbered in several positions using a vibrating glass-etching instrument.
4. Each tube was checked for invisible gaps by holding it under water; in such conditions small air bubbles would escape from those imperfectly sealed.
5. The tubes were weighed on an accurate laboratory balance (calibrated just prior to this operation), recording all digits with milligram precision.
6. Each tube was then photographed with additional close-up lenses, in such a way as to record the etched number and the shape of the sealed tip where the glass had been melted.

It was noticed that when these tubes were slightly heated, a few tiny droplets of water were given off by the leaf inside. The general look was quite different from that of oil, the total weight of course did not change, and the droplets were reabsorbed after a few days. Thus we decided not to worry about this detail. Each tube could now be identified by its weight and photograph, and was "tamper-evident," as there is no way that glass can be melted and resealed in exactly its original shape.

Eight of these phials (numbered 1, 2, 3, 4, 6, 7, 8, and 10) were delivered to Ms. Moscogiuri through Dr. Gagliardi and Father Civerra, a Catholic priest who follows the seer. We had no idea of the whereabouts of the sealed tubes, nor about what was happening to them at the other end of Italy.

Two notable events followed: we received a fax from Fr. Civerra, wherein Moscogiuri reported a mystical vision of the Blessed Virgin: a large tongue of flame (of the Holy Ghost) had approached the tubes, taking one of them away and leaving just seven (the number of the Virgin's sorrows). Later, rumor was heard that some of our tubes contained oil. So, again through the intermediacy of Dr. Gagliardi and Fr. Civerra, we managed to have our tubes brought back to be checked. The meeting was attended by Fr. Civerra and Dr. Gagliardi, videotaped, and a statement of the results was then signed by all participants. Fr. Civerra had put the tubes we had prepared into a jar and then into a plastic bag; each of these containers had been wax-sealed. For the reasons given above, we disregarded these extra security measures, and requested that only our tubes be taken out and checked. It should be noted that, when asked, Fr. Civerra admitted that he had no way of verifying whether his wax seals had been tampered with and replaced.

RESULTS

It turned out that:

1. One of the eight tubes (no. 3) was missing.
2. Tubes nos. 1, 2, and 7 were intact and did not contain any liquid.
3. Tube no. 4 had a broken tip that had produced a small gap; no liquid was present.
4. Tubes nos. 6, 8, and 10 did contain a yellow, viscous liquid.

A comparison with the photographs of the original showed that the tips had been melted and resealed. The shape of the tips was quite clearly different. One of the tubes had been tampered with on the side, and the glass was deformed, leaving a large bubble. One tip was also slightly cracked. In all of these three phials there were traces of a black substance, and the leaf was partially or completely carbonized.

Conclusions

We deemed it evident that some crude tampering had occurred, and that this was indicative not of a miracle but, on the contrary, of some sort of fraud carried out by somebody in Moscogiuri's group. Fr. Civerra's reaction was different: he did not accept such a conclusion, claiming that he placed more trust in his own external wax seals, and that if the tubes were deformed it had been due to the "Holy Ghost's flame." In conclusion, we believe that these flame-sealed glass test tubes—with these few simple control procedures—can be a useful tool in the hands of researchers testing psi abilities, in particular, macro-PK or clairvoyance.

Notes

Reprinted with permission of the editors from *Journal of the Society for Psychical Research* 61, no. 846 (January 1997). Copyright 1997 by Society for Psychical Research.

1. See, for example, John Taylor, *Superminds* (New York: Viking Press, 1975); and J. B. Hasted, *The Metal Benders* (London: Routledge and Kegan Paul, 1981).

2. See John Hanlon, "But What about Children?" *New Scientist* (June 5, 1975); and James Randi, *Flim-Flam!* (Amherst, N.Y.: Prometheus Books, 1982).

3. T. Besterman, S. G. Soal, and I. Jephson, "Report on a Series of Experiments in Clairvoyance Conducted at a Distance under Approximately Fraud-proof Conditions," *Proceedings of the SPR* 39: 375–414, quoted in Paul Kurtz, ed., *A Skeptic's Handbook of Parapsychology* (Amherst, N.Y.: Prometheus Books, 1985), p. 102.

4. Richard Wiseman and Robert Morris, *Guidelines for Testing Psychic Claimants* (Hatfield, England: University of Hertfordshire Press, 1995), p. 72, and references cited within.

5. Dr. Gagliardi is a member of the "Centro studi e recerche sulla psicofisiologia degli stati di coscienza," Via Villoresi 5, 20143 Milano, Italy.

6. J. M. Harrison, ed., *CIA Flaps and Seal Manual* (Boulder, Colo.: Paladin Press, 1975).

CHAPTER FIFTEEN

THE GIRL
WITH
X-RAY EYES

*S*ome time ago, while I was trying to put some order into my video library, I came upon a videotape without any label to suggest its content; so, I put the tape in the VCR to find out what it was. It was the recording of a TV show on the paranormal, called "Incredible," aired a few years ago by RAI-TV, the Italian network. I had never seen it and I later found out that my sister taped it while I was living in the United States, studying with James Randi.

The discovery proved to be most interesting.

A SPANISH MINI-GELLER

I had read and heard about the achievements of a young Spanish girl named Monica Nieto. According to newspapers and books on the paranormal, she appeared to bend metal and see through solid objects. From the descriptions, she seemed to be another mini-Geller, as the imitators of self-proclaimed psychic Uri Geller are called; enthusiastic reports told of her ability to bend metal rods in sealed glass tubes, and spoons and forks under the eyes of the onlookers. Others said that the bending never occurred when anyone was looking (anyone remember the "shyness effect" of Professor John Taylor?), but a long time after Nieto had taken the object in her hands and played with it. Sometimes she would leave the room with a tube for a while and then return, hiding its content with her hands and revealing later that the metal inside it had bent; other times she would dance, holding the object in her fists and close to her body, which precluded anyone's seeing it. Jose L. J. Pena, the former vice-president of the Sociedad Espanola de Parapsicologia (SEDP), who conducted an investigation of Nieto's claimed powers, said that he believed she could bend the lighter strip of metal enclosed in the glass tube by shaking it vigorously while dancing, and that any sound would be covered by the loud music she played "for concentration."[1]

Besides these more conventional effects, Nieto was noted for another special ability—reading messages inside closed containers. The descriptions were very vague and did not allow any speculation. That's when the videotape came to my aid.

Suspicious Bendings

The "Incredible" show was on PK, and after interviews with some parapsychologists who attempted to explain what PK was supposed to be, there was a documentary on Monica Nieto. It had been shot in her own house in Caceres, Extremadura (Spain), and showed an adolescent girl who was obviously enjoying the attention. The hostess of the show, actress Maria Rosaria Omaggio (a would-be Shirley MacLaine), said that Nieto had never before shown her abilities on television and that she was very happy to do so for Italian TV.

Nieto then proceeded to demonstrate metal bending—well, almost. In the first demonstration, one sees the hostess walking in the streets of

Caceres with Nieto, who is holding a glass tube with a metal rod inside it; a voice-over tells Nieto's story. At the end of the walk, the metal is taken out of the tube and shown to be bent: incredible!

Next we are in Nieto's house. Here a parapsychologist explains how Nieto was thoroughly studied by a commission that included a physicist, a biologist, an engineer, a priest, and a parapsychologist—no conjurors— and all of them had been convinced of the psychic nature of her powers. Nieto is then asked to bend a piece of metal in front of the camera; the rod is placed in the tube and a cork placed on top of it—not sealed, only placed; she holds the tube in both hands and suddenly the image on the screen freezes and fades away! After a while (how long, we don't know) Nieto's image returns; she is still seated with her hands on the tube, but now the metal inside it is bent.

What happened during the interval? Was it possible for her to leave the room or do something else that didn't appear important enough to be included in the documentary? Did she go on and on sitting with the tube, thus forcing the cameramen to stop taping? Who knows? They don't tell us.

WHAT'S IN THE BOX?

Finally comes the most revealing part of the show, the x-ray eyes demonstration. The hostess shows a few pieces of paper with names of colors or Spanish phrases written on them. A handmade cardboard box is introduced, and one of the pieces of paper, chosen at random, is placed inside the box, face down. A lid is placed on the box, which is then given to the girl.

Seated in an armchair with a long back and wings at the sides of her head, she manipulates the box very close to her face, rotates it, turns it upside-down, and presses it; most of the time she is not looking at the box but at the experimenters' faces. What is very clear in the film is that she raises the lower part of the box with her thumbs and reads the note while she misdirects the attention of the spectators with sudden moves and requests like: "May I turn the music on? It helps me." After a while she announces her guess, obviously correct.

Nieto had finally demonstrated that she resorted to trickery. She surely enjoys all the attention she gets from the media; in an interview she says: "I like very much to be in the magazines, with pictures and all the rest."[2] In her view there is surely nothing wrong with fooling some adults and gaining popularity. What is certainly wrong is the attitude of those who present the case as inexplicable and don't suggest that there could be an alternative explanation for it. A correct procedure would have been to call a professional conjuror to comment on the video. Well, incredible as it may seem, they did; but this proved to be more confusing than anything else.

The conjuror was very popular with TV audiences in Italy, and was known for his attempts to be credited as a Geller-like psychic. He asked where the box came from and if it was transparent; when the hostess answered that she herself had brought the box and that it was not transparent, he declared that the only possible explanation was clairvoyance. A conjuror, he explained, could do the same thing, but only if he could control the game (which was exactly what Nieto had done). He then proceeded to perform his version of the trick, which in reality was nothing like the one used by Nieto. This, I think, is the kind of thing that persuades people of the reality of psychic phenomena. Here was a famous conjuror declaring that there was no possible trick, *ergo* the girl really did it by psychic powers!

NOTES

Reprinted with permission of the editors from the *Skeptical Inquirer* 18, no. 2 (1994). Copyright 1994 by the Committee for the Scientific Investigation of the Claims of the Paranormal.

1. Jose Pena, "Las Capacidades Prodigiosas de Monica Nieto" (Monica Nieto's Wonderful Abilities), *Psi Comunicacion*, nos. 31–32 (1990): 55–60.

2. Alfonso Montecelos, "Una Dolce Mirada Que Dobla El Acero" (A Gentle Look that Bends Steel), *Ya Rivista* (1987): 15.

CHAPTER SIXTEEN

AN EXPERIMENT
IN
CLAIRVOYANCE

Some years ago at CICAP, we received a letter from a lady, R. G., who said she could see inside a sealed box and could describe what objects were inside it; she wanted us to test and verify her powers. We accepted her proposal and invited R. G. to the University of Pavia where, with the help of my colleague Luigi Garlaschelli and of Prof. Adalberto Piazzoli, we usually test psychics. In letters and by telephone she had explained to us that we could use any kind of box and any object we liked; she claimed a 60 to 70 percent rate of success. Once in Pavia, she agreed that the situation was ideal, that the people there were not hostile, and that she was confident that she would succeed. We read her the protocol we had prepared for the test, to which again she agreed.

THE TEST

We had previously selected twelve objects, each one different from the others in shape, color, and material; these objects were taken by the experimenters to a different room from the one where the test was going to take place and randomly numbered from one to twelve. During the test, an experimenter would choose a random number, then take the corresponding object, wrap it up in paper to avoid any clue by noise (the psychic said beforehand that paper didn't block her visions), put it in a wooden box kept closed by two rubber bands, and then bring it in view of R. G. This would happen for each object, and each object could be chosen only once.

When she saw the box for the first time, R. G. asked to take off the rubber bands around it, because they could confuse her images. We accepted only on the condition that nobody could get close to the box after the experimenter had entered the room.

We then gave her a list of the twelve objects in order to help her to remember what to look for. We explained to her that she had to concentrate on the box and then, instead of giving vague visions that we had to associate with an object, that she herself had to point on the list to the object that would best match her visions. If she wished, she could change her mind and switch one guess for another before the end of the test. The correct answer for every guess would be given only at the end of the session. The person who placed the objects in the box was kept away from the lady so as to avoid any involuntary nonverbal communication. As usual, we videotaped the whole test.

"I SEE SOMETHING SQUARED . . ."

R. G., sitting six feet away from the box, with her husband beside her, would concentrate for a few seconds and then give her perceptions: "I see something squared . . . a bit thick . . . something dark . . . straight . . ."; having to choose an object on the list, she pointed, in this case, to the rubber stamp. The test went on until the last object was reached: "It's something rigid," said R. G., "straight . . . not a cube . . . has only one color . . . looks like a pen, a tube . . . could be the key."

At the end of the test, we took the list with the order in which the objects were presented and compared it to her guesses. Out of twelve objects, she had got one right: exactly what one would expect by chance.[1]

R. G. tried to justify her unsuccessful performance by saying that the conditions (to which she had agreed before the start of the test) were unfamiliar and then tried to accommodate her descriptions to the objects actually presented. For example, the object she had indicated to be the "key" turned out to be a mirror. "Well, I was right after all," she said. "It was something straight, not a cube and only had one color . . ."; she seemed to have forgotten that she had also said that the object looked like "a pen, a tube."

AN INFORMAL TRIAL

We had designed our protocol on the basis of what she said she could do and under what conditions and we had tried to accommodate her needs; however, she insisted that this was not the procedure that she used at home. Usually, she said, she needed two series of objects: one for the test, the other to be kept in front of her so that she could compare her visions with a replica of the actual object and not with a word on a list.

Even though we considered the test finished, we agreed to an informal trial after we found twelve double objects in the laboratory. We proceeded then as before and, as before, the result was one hit on twelve trials.

R. G. still wasn't convinced, and repeated that at home she could usually get six or seven objects out of ten. She indicated two more differences with our test: at home, her husband could use the same object more than once, and this gave her more freedom of choice; furthermore, she needed some encouragement, which meant that she needed to know if she was right or wrong immediately after each guess.

Some of us were against performing a new test and again changing the protocol; however, after clearly stating on camera and on paper that that test was not to be considered scientific and that it was only done as another informal trial, in view of future and more rigorous tests, we agreed to try.

Since this demonstration proved very quick to prepare for, we did twenty-eight trials with a choice of the same seven objects for each trial; R. G. was right in six cases. Even this demonstration was not considered to be significant.[2]

At the end of our meeting, we suggested R. G. repeat at home the test as we had performed it that day; in this way, in fact, she might have realized that, once the possibility of adapting one's "visions" to the correct object in the box is ruled out, the results can only be random (unless she really possessed psychic powers, that is). We invited her back if, following this procedure, she could still obtain a 60 to 70 percent success rate.

A few years have passed, but we never heard from her.

NOTES

1. This procedure corresponds to the one used by Susan Blackmore for a test on an English psychic; see *JSPR* 60, no. 840 (July 1995).

2. According to the literature (e.g., M. Rýzl, chapter 9 of *ESP Experiments Which Succeed* (Copyright 1976 by M. Rýzl), in order to have a minimum of significance ($p = 0.02$), with seven objects and twenty-eight trials, nine to ten hits are required.

CHAPTER SEVENTEEN

THE STRANGE CASE
OF THE
CREEPING DOORS

by Francesco Chiminello

In almost fifteen years of research and experimentation we have never found any real proof of psychic phenomena. Most of the time the explanations for what happens are very mundane, but sometimes they surprise even us. This was the case, for example, with an episode investigated by my friend and CICAP member Francesco Chiminello, a Ph.D. physicist working at the University of Padua on the Antarctic atmosphere, and an amateur conjurer. I will let Francesco tell you the story personally.

MP

*I*n October 1996, Marino Franzosi, administrator of CICAP, told me about a call he received from a man living in the northeastern town of Vicenza, not far from Venice. Marino suggested I investigate the case, since I live close to Vicenza.

The man, Dario Tancredi, had asked the help of CICAP in order to explain a phenomenon that he and his son, Giulio, were able to perform: they appeared to be able to produce a small movement of the doors in their house, barely perceptible but still visible, without touching them. Such a phenomenon, should it really happen, would prove psychokinesis, one of the few phenomena that skeptics usually put under the category of "hard" paranormal. That's an almost correct description of the phenomenon. However, in this case, the remote movement was not produced by the mind but by some other part of the body, as we shall see.

It is important to stress that Mr. Tancredi, during his initial call to Marino and always thereafter, made it clear that he and his family did not claim psychic abilities; they were simply not able to explain what was happening. They called us since our committee was known for investigating strange events.

I called the Tancredis and arranged an appointment with them. A date was chosen that was convenient for both father and son. Giulio, now working full-time, said he originally discovered the phenomenon when he was fifteen years old.

POSSIBLE EXPLANATIONS

In the days leading up to the appointment, helped by useful discussions with other members of CICAP, I considered four possible explanations.

The first and most obvious one was that it was a trick or a joke started by the son years earlier and growing bigger ever since. In this case, Giulio should always be present for the phenomenon to happen, even when it was apparently produced by his father.

The second theory was that a wooden floor, or more generally an elastic floor, deformed when stepped on and applied a force to the door.

The third one was that the subject could move the air around himself during the performance.

The fourth and last possible explanation, sadly, was self-deception: the idea was that the door moved anyway, every now and then, due to air currents, trucks on the road, or something else. But the people present would notice it and give it a meaning only during the performances: it is actually quite unusual for anyone to stop and stare at a door, seeking barely perceptible movements. This last hypothesis included an even sadder version, that is, the door did not move at all, except in the mind of the performer looking at it with muscles contracted and maybe even without breathing.

It is apparent that each of the above theories portrays the performer in a bad light: the trick theory assumes he cheated; the wooden floor theory and the air-movement theory imply that he was not able to make the simplest counterproofs; and finally, the self-deception theory indicates a very high degree of gullibility.

You can understand why I went to the meeting without very great expectations. I took with me a friend, Erika, who was very amused by the story. She was not intended as just a generic witness: I was certainly not going to investigate a mysteriously moving door without somebody checking both its sides!

"Abdomenkinesis"

We arrived at the Tancredi's house at about nine o'clock in the evening. I must admit that, just after ringing the doorbell, I experienced a few moments of panic as the fifth and saddest possible explanation suddenly came to my mind: the Tancredis might be completely insane. I imagined being surrounded by the entire family, who stared at me ominously, and one of them asking: "Did you see the door moving? You saw that, DIDN'T YOU?"

Luckily, such last-minute fears were dispelled by the warm welcome of the family, whose members were positively sane and kind. After a coffee and a chat, I began a short interview on the phenomenon. The Tancredis explained that the door did not accomplish single movements, as I imagined, but a series of oscillations. Mr. Tancredi said that the door, set ajar, during performances moved rhythmically in a barely visible way. At each oscillation, however, the sound made by the lock touching the doorpost could be clearly heard. Finally, he informed me that some of the family's relatives, too, had learned to produce the phenomenon.

Then the most interesting part of the evening started: the demonstration. Apparently, the door's movement was wider in the case of small rooms, so Giulio and I went into the bathroom; everybody else stayed outside. Giulio took a deep breath and then, holding it, he alternatively contracted and relaxed his abdominal muscles. The interval between contractions was about half a second; he repeated the act about twenty times. Finally, he breathed out. Perhaps, a better a posteriori description is that he compressed the air in his lungs by means of the diaphragm, just like a singer or a wind instrument player would do. At the same time, and with the same rhythm, the door—initially set ajar—opened a bit and then moved back until it touched the doorpost, a movement of a few tenths of a millimeter but still clearly visible, and which produced a sharp series of clicks.

UNDER PRESSURE

To discover that the phenomenon did really take place, at first glance without tricks, made me quite uneasy, but on the other hand pushed me to think really fast. For a few minutes I was very suspicious about everything and everybody: I even suspected that Erika, from the other side of the door, could have quickly arranged with the Tancredis to play a joke on me. After dispelling this somewhat paranoid idea and discarding—for obvious reasons—the hypothesis of self-deception, I began to countercheck the hypotheses of the wooden floor and of air movement. The result was exactly the same one that the Tancredis had predicted to me during the interview: no result. It was possible to perform a series of standing jumps on the floor or to vigorously wave two large magazines without obtaining the faintest reaction from the door.

At this point, the only initial theory that had survived was that it was a trick, but after several performances, observed from different points of view and with Giulio in different positions in the room, I estimated that to be very unlikely. Then I asked Giulio if any particular condition was required for the phenomenon to happen, and he told me two very interesting necessary conditions: the first one was that the air taken in should not be breathed out at each contraction, but kept in the lungs; the second one was that the room's windows had to be closed. At this moment, I became certain that the door movement was caused by the air in the room: not by movements of the air but by a variation of air pressure inside the room.

This is the line of my reasoning. When Giulio contracts his muscles, he compresses the air in his lungs, whose volume lessens by a certain quantity which we will call x. The volume occupied by his body also diminishes by x. Therefore, the volume available to the air inside the room correspondingly increases by x. Thus the air pressure of the room is diminished by $\_P = x/V$ atm, where V is the volume of the room. The pressure drop in the room causes a force $DF = \_PS$ to act on the door, opening it slightly, where S is the surface area of the door. When Giulio relaxes, everything returns to the previous conditions; the door closes a bit, touches the doorpost, and produces a click.

Although qualitatively reasonable, the validity of this explanation cannot be assumed until the volumes, pressures, and forces in play are estimated. The volume V of the room, 11.9 m^3, and the surface S of the door, 1.8 m^2, were quite easy to measure. I just needed to estimate x, but this was a difficult step: I obviously could not put Giulio into a giant graduated measuring tube! I tried to estimate x by some rule of thumb, underestimating it in the dubious steps. I estimated the volume of the air in the lungs to be five liters, but how much can we compress it? I considered the following fact. It is common, in Italy, to buy wine in large glass containers, called *damigiane* (demijohns), whose capacity ranges from a few liters up to sixty liters. The wine is then poured into normal bottles by means of a siphon, which is activated by blowing into the *damigiana* through a pipe. I remembered having raised a column of wine up to at least half a meter, which corresponds to a hydrostatic pressure of one-twentieth of atmosphere, which in turn corresponds to a volume decrease of a quarter of liter of the air inside the lungs. Now all the quantities needed to calculate the force on the door were available, and the result was a force equivalent in weight to 400 grams, enough to move the door.

Furthermore, from the known quantities, a rough estimate of the corresponding extension of the movement of the door (if considered as a cylindrical perfect piston) gave a result of three-tenths of a millimeter, which was quite in agreement with direct observation.

A Wall of Skepticism

I was suddenly aware that, during the last ten minutes, I had done nothing but scribble on my notepad, without paying any attention to anything else. So I discussed my hypothesis with the Tancredis, explaining that some quantity estimates were far from certain, and then we departed for that evening.

At the next local CICAP meeting, everyone was very curious about the investigation. At first, I just described the phenomenon to them, without giving any explanation, and then listened to their questions and their attempts at explanation. Finally I revealed my explanation and—would you believe it?—I hit a wall of skepticism.

One group, led by Francesca Guizzo, defended various trick hypotheses, ranging from invisible threads to remotely activated hidden electromagnets. She was so clever that she nearly made me doubt my conclusion. After long discussions, the majority of the people present tended to accept my theory, but not everybody. Only at the next meeting, after they saw me moving a door, were they all convinced. Massimo Albertin, a physician, told me that, in the average adult man, the air inside the lungs after a deep inspiration is about six liters (one liter more than I had estimated). Massimo, however, had no idea about the maximum pressure obtainable from the diaphragm.

From Theory to Experiment

About one month later I visited the Tancredis again with a friend who owns a video camera. Unfortunately, the door movements were too small for her handycam's resolution in low artificial light, so Mr. Tancredi and

I designed and quickly made an amplifier of the door movements with a wooden tablet, some iron thread, and some paper. The result, due to a simple lever mechanism, surpassed our best hopes: the movement of the door was amplified to several centimeters.

After that, we tried to reproduce the phenomenon by mechanical means. We tried with a bicycle air pump first, closing its outlet, but the volume change was way too small. We tried with a volleyball and then with a balloon, but none of them worked. Apparently, the volleyball was too small, while the balloon was too soft: pushing it on one side just made it expand on another one. Obviously, it would be easy to design, for instance, an apparatus with a big steel cylinder, a sealed piston, and a hydraulic engine, but it would be too expensive to build. It was only months later, recalling the whole affair by chance, that I happened to find a cheap solution to the problem.

The balloon volume is certainly enough, but its membrane is so soft and elastic that it cannot hold a large difference in pressure between the internal and external side of the balloon: pressing the balloon, initially almost spherical, just changes its shape. When its shape changes, however, the membrane is compelled to increase in surface, because the sphere is the solid which, given a certain volume, has the minimum of external surface. Pushing the balloon, it becomes less spherical but the volume of the air inside is not changed. This implies that the surface increases. To compress the air inside the balloon efficiently, it is sufficient to find a workaround to keep its surface area constant.

I moved from theory to experiment. I bought a fairly strong party balloon, at the price of about a half-dollar U.S., and inflated it thoroughly until it assumed a spherelike shape. Then I wrapped it in a large cloth, whose loose ends I twisted together until the cloth was stretched. Now the balloon surface could not expand any more. Pushing it against a wall reproduced excellently the original movement of the door (to my joy and satisfaction).

This story still holds one secret, which probably will never be revealed. Not even the two friends of mine who took part in the investigation were able to convince Giulio to say how he discovered the phenomenon for the first time, nor if the discovery was casual or intentional.

CHAPTER EIGHTEEN

INVESTIGATING TABLE TIPPING

*R*ecently, an Italian Spirit medium approached us and said he wanted his "powers" tested. His name was Teodosio Lavinia, aka "Mago Matheus Faust," from Potenza, and he claimed he could move any three-legged table without touching it, using only his psychic powers. "Table tipping" has been a standard of séance mediums since the mid-1800s, but the hands-off claim was a new twist.

IN SEARCH OF A ROOM

The Italian national network, RAI-TV, considered the occasion sufficiently spectacular to film the test live. The site for the test was going to be the usual laboratories of the Department of Chemistry at the University of Pavia, where we often conduct tests on psychics.

The medium arrived that morning to examine the conditions of the test. We provided five different three-legged tables at his request, and he would choose one of the five that he felt was best suited for his demonstration. He examined them all, touching and looking, and finally he chose one for the test.

But something was wrong: the problem, he told us, was not in the tables, but in the floor. It was not sufficiently smooth: the small cracks between the tiles might prevent the table from sliding. We suggested placing the table on top of a large, wooden platform. After we did so, he waved his hands on the table a few times, examined the platform and then shook his head. The wood, he explained, stopped the "spiritic fluid," which apparently came from the ground, and the table could not move.

When examining people who claim to possess psychic powers, it is essential that the test conditions be as favorable as possible to the claimant; in this way, any possible failure cannot be attributed to unfavorable conditions or the skepticism of the experimenters.

We thus looked for another room in which to perform the test, but the only apparently suitable room we could find, the only one without cracks between tiles, was a space under a staircase. Psychic, table, and crew moved to the new location, but alas, nothing could be done there either.

The space was "too gloomy," the psychic explained.

Back again in the original room, the psychic agreed to try the test. He claimed he felt pretty confident of his success. Psychic powers work in mysterious ways.

LIGHTS, CAMERA . . . ACTION!

Before starting the official test and the filming we asked the psychic, as we usually do, to give us a demonstration without the constraint of control conditions: this was needed to be sure that his powers would work well in that particular room, and that the lights, the cameras, or the people present did not affect his sensibility. In case of a failure under test conditions, such elements could not then be blamed as the possible source of the fiasco.

We sat around the table and the psychic asked us to place our fingers on the surface of the table after he did the same. Suddenly, without even attempting to hide it, he started to press on the table, making it slide. When we informed him that we could see the "move" quite clearly, he replied that it was not him pushing the table, but the "fluid" exuding from his fingers. However, he still hadn't shown us his ability to move the table while not touching it, which was the most interesting part of the demonstration. He said that since it required incredible concentration, he would only attempt that during the official test.

All was ready for the live experiment. We took our places around the table and placed our fingers in the usual way. After a few seconds, the psychic started to push and we observed an interesting twist on the trick: after he had tilted the table on two legs, the psychic removed his hands from it and left it in that precarious state. It was quite clear now how he usually succeeded: he would claim that any movement caused by us in the attempt to keep the table from falling was, actually, produced by the fluid emanating from his hands, which he kept waving in the air. We did not give him a chance to try that on us, but put the table back on the floor and asked him to move it from that position, even only for a few millimeters. Evidently surprised, the psychic appeared to concentrate for awhile, but then stopped and said that was enough. Before the end of the program, we explained to the TV viewers how the psychic had been able to incline the table by pressing on it.

When asked about his failure during the test, the psychic answered: "It's *their* fault! They lack enough psychic energy." That makes sense: he was the psychic, but if we wanted to see real psychic power at work we'd better provide it ourselves.

CHAPTER NINETEEN

THE CASE
OF THE
HUMAN MAGNETS

One of the relatively new paranormal claims that has recently attracted much interest in various parts of Europe is the one for so-called human magnets. According to magazines and TV shows, there are people whose bodies behave like magnets and attract metallic (and nonmetallic) objects.

The first examples of such phenomenal people came from Russia, then some appeared in eastern European countries, and soon more were cropping up all over Europe.[1] Italy was no exception. We, too, had our share of "human magnets" and at CICAP we examined four of them on separate occasions.

MAGNETIC DELUSIONS

First was a very deluded woman, Ms. L., who believed she could "magnetically" keep a pen or a Bic lighter attached to her inclined hand; the fact that the objects fell off as soon as her hand reached a critical vertical angle didn't mean much to her.

Second were Mr. and Mrs. Baroni, professional "psychic healers" and amateur "magnets." I met these two people on a TV show, but despite the inadequacy of the setting for a scientific test, it became quite evident that they, too, were only fooling themselves. Mrs. Baroni offered exactly the same demonstration that Ms. L. had previously given for CICAP. As for her husband, it was very clear to the audience that the pieces of cutlery that he kept putting on his chest only stayed there because of the natural friction offered by his skin; his large stomach helped, too. When I asked him to bend forward, he began to do so, but as soon as spoons and forks began sliding off his body, he stopped, saying that in such a position the "psychic force" weakened.

Fig. 19.1. The author examines the demonstration of a "magnetic man" during a TV show. (Massimo Polidoro Collection)

A "STICKY" CASE

The last "human magnet," Ms. Rita Cutolo, was a woman who gained a lot of publicity for her psychic healing business by giving demonstrations of her magnetic powers on TV talk shows. Her demonstration consisted of holding two bottles full of water apparently attached to her open hand. My friend Luigi Garlaschelli and I had a chance to watch her perform before us; however, we weren't allowed to properly examine her hands or to institute stricter control conditions.

This case would need much more space to be fully told. Suffice it to say that: (a) all of the witnesses (including Dr. Piero Cassoli, Italy's leading parapsychologist) agreed that her demonstrations didn't present any psychic aspect and were patently due to some physical action; (b) Dr. Garlaschelli clearly had the sensation, when shaking hands with her, that her hand was "somehow sticky"; (c) when she was asked to put talcum powder on her hands the phenomena ceased; (d) the phenomena only worked on smooth surfaces, not on cloth or fabric; (e) when it was proposed to conduct a chemical analysis of the surface of the skin and, subsequently, to wash her hands with solvents, the proposal was rejected; and (f) once we were at home with our colleagues, we were able to reproduce all of her demonstrations by natural means.

We requested another chance to meet with Ms. Cutolo, at which time we intended to conduct a complete chemical analysis of her hands and then observe her performing under various test conditions. A meeting was promised by Ms. Cutolo, but it never materialized. In the end, we were told that Ms. Cutolo didn't want to meet with us again, because such meetings appeared to be very stressful for her health. Oddly enough, we recently read an interview with Ms. Cutolo where she stated that CICAP's investigators had examined her "under the strictest controls" and even "washed her hands with trychloroethylene," but were unable to explain her phenomena. Now, this would have been something! We only wished we had been present when such a demonstration took place!

NOTE

Reprinted with permission of the editors from *Swift: The Newsletter of the James Randi Educational Foundation* 1, no. 1 (1997). Copyright 1997 by the JREF.

1. James Randi, "A Report from the Paranormal Trenches," *Skeptic* 1, no. 1 (spring 1992): 27–28.

CHAPTER TWENTY

SECRETS
OF
INDIAN GOD-MEN

*One good method of solving puzzles is to reduce the
apparent enigma to its lowest and simplest ingredients.*

James Randi

Some of the most astonishing feats ever accomplished (or supposedly accomplished) are the incredible demonstrations of Indian
fakirs and gurus. The word "fakir" brings to mind the image of a thin, old
Indian man lying on a bed of nails or walking on hot coals. It is said that
years of practice and meditation are needed to master these peculiar abilities and that they are denied to regular mortals.

Since this is just the kind of claim that provokes the curiosity of
people like me and my friend Luigi Garlaschelli, some years ago we
decided that we were going to test on ourselves all the fakirs' demonstrations that it was possible to perform.

The episode that sparked our curiosity and desire was a meeting with famed Indian skeptic Basava Premanand. Premanand, who was born in Calcutta in 1930, is an Indian magician and leader of the Indian Skeptics; he has devoted his abilities and time to the investigation of supernatural claims in India and the subsequent revelation of the tricks and frauds he found. CICAP has twice invited Premanand to Italy in order to present to the Italian public the results of his work. Both Luigi and I spent hours discussing with him Indian fakirs and gurus; he is a very likeable fellow, kind and helpful in all of his descriptions, and he has a good sense of humor, especially when relating some of the more bizarre episodes he was involved in.

"Have you ever seen a real 'miracle'?" we asked him almost as soon as we met him.

"I've seen a lot, but unfortunately, not one of them was authentic; they were all accomplished by trickery."

"What kind of trickery?" we wanted to know.

"You see, there are four different ways to obtain a 'miracle': by sleight of hand, by the use of chemical compounds, by mechanical means, and finally, using some little-known facts about the human body." Premanand then went on to describe all of the tricks he had found and that we, subsequently, put in practice. We wanted to know more about him and his work.

"When I was a kid," Premanand told us, "I believed in miracles. I was fascinated by stories of magic powers and yogis. Being a Hindu boy, I too wanted to possess these powers and so I set forth looking for a guru willing to teach me. My search took me to various gurus: among the first was Swami Sivananda Maharaj, then the only living disciple of Ramakrishna Parmahansa, the guru that claimed he had seen God and had shown It to his disciples. I went to the Swami and asked him to show me God, exactly like Parmahansa had shown It to him; he confessed he hadn't really seen It. In those days, furthermore, I observed a recurring fact: while yogis kept on explaining to others how to obtain perfect health, they themselves had various kinds of health problems: rheumatism, liver deficits, asthma, diabetes, cancer. I asked one of the gurus about this and he said: 'I could instantly be healthy if I want to, but I am voluntarily paying for the sins I commited in a previous life.' It was quite clear even then that my attitude was not welcome and, usually, when I started questioning what I saw I was asked to leave the temple."

One of the most famous "targets" of Premanand's investigations has been Sai Baba. This Indian figure is more than just another guru; he claims to be God on earth and to "prove" it he exhibits various singular demonstrations. Among other things, he "materializes" objects, sometimes jewelry for rich visitors or political leaders, but usually some kind of sacred sand (called "vibuthi").

"I was one of Sai Baba's disciples for about three years," Premanand told us. "I lived in his ashram, and I was there for my research, obviously, not because I believed in him. This specific investigation cost me quite a lot, though. I was asked to give his entourage two million rupiahs (about eighty thousand dollars) in order to be admitted inside the ashram. I had to sell ninety acres of my father's soil to get the money. In the end, however, I knew all of his tricks, which were not much different from those of the other gurus. Take his 'vibuthi,' for example: it looks like ash and smells of incense. You know what it is, in fact? It's cow dung, burned, dried up in small pellets, and then aromatized with incense! You hold a pellet between your thumb and second finger; then, show your hand empty and rotate it above the ground, Sai Baba style. Finally, with a swift movement, you bring down the pellet to the fingertips, crush it, and let the ash fall into the praying hands of your disciples and faithfuls. Should you ever meet Sai Baba, ask him to repeat this miracle holding up the palm of his hand, I would be very curious to know his reply."

There is another kind of materialization, however, that is said to take place in the homes of Sai Baba's devotees.

"Yes" said Premanand. "It's Holy Ash forming inside framed photographs of Sai Baba. You want to know how to obtain this miracle? Well, when you go to buy Sai Baba's pictures from the samiti, they first make a pretense of wiping the frame. Actually they are anointing it with a mercuric chloride solution. When an aluminum frame dabbed with this comes into contact with moisture, a gray powder mistaken for holy ash falls out."

> WARNING: Attempting to perform these dangerous acts will result in serious injury or death.

We wondered whether this kind of debunking work has ever damaged Premanand in some way.

"Of course it has!" was his prompt answer. "I have collected several death threats, some broken ribs, and quite a few visits to the hospital, but I have never stopped."

Premanand, who is also the author of thirty books in malayalam (the language of his country) and five in English, told us he had a strong desire "to build a research center in India where all the miracles and psychic phenomena will be exhibited and explained with a library on religion, magic, science, etc. But this costs money and, unfortunately, I cannot conjure up money from thin air!"

It was right after meeting this very peculiar and inspiring man that we decided to try his suggestions and see if we could turn ourselves into some sort of Occidental disciples of Premanand.

PLAYING WITH FIRE

Any demonstration that involves fire has quite a strong impact on the lay public, since everyone knows from childhood the kind of threat it represents. However, if it is handled very carefully and if one takes all the necessary precautions, it is possible to perform feats that appear to be more impressive and dangerous than they really are. *Before going any further, however, you should take note that we strongly discourage any attempt to reproduce the demonstrations described below unless you are being helped by an*

> This information is provided for educational and scholarly purposes only. It's not intended to encourage or instruct someone to attempt these dangerous acts.

> **WARNING:** Attempting to perform these dangerous acts will result in serious injury or death.

expert in the field, and that we cannot be held responsible for anything arising from an improper use of the information contained in these pages.

It is possible, for example, to light a torch and pass it close to the skin without getting burned. How? First, you prepare the torch: you need a wooden stick about an inch thick; wrap a rope at one end of the stick quite a few times and then immerse this end into kerosene. Let the excess liquid drop and then light the rope with a lighter or a match. With kerosene you obtain quite a large flame, with dark fumes, that you can pass under your forearm without burning your skin (but your hair probably will get burned). Always keep the flame in motion and never stop it close to the skin unless you want to get seriously burned. It takes about three seconds for the flame to burn you. You can start by moving the flame from your elbow and then finish by passing it under your hand and finally away.

Fire Eating

You don't really "eat" fire, but you can put a flame in your mouth without getting burned. You need a torch built as described above and some kerosene. Immerse the torch in kerosene, let the excess kerosene drip off, and then light it. Bend your head backward, open your mouth, and slightly breathe out. *Never* breathe in during this demonstration! Put the torch in your mouth, without rushing but also with no hesitation: instantly close your mouth. You won't feel any pain and the torch will extinguish itself: this happens because without oxygen the flame can't stay alive. Be careful only to use kerosene, never use alcohol, gasoline, or any

> This information is provided for educational and scholarly purposes only. It's not intended to encourage or instruct someone to attempt these dangerous acts.

> **WARNING:** Attempting to perform these dangerous acts will result in serious injury or death.

kind of solvent: their flames are way too hot and can easily burn you. Premanand also showed us how you can keep a piece of flaming camphor in your mouth (the kind used to keep insects away from your clothes) or toss it from one hand to the other without damage.

Camphor Eating

"In 1977," said Premanand, "a film artist of Kerala published an article challenging me to burn camphor on the hand and wave it before the idol in the temple. He said that his godman, Swami Satyananda Saraswathi, the International President of Vishwa Hindu Parishad, burns camphor on his hand and waves it before the idol of Shri Rama in his temple. This was considered to be a miracle. I told him that this stunt is done by children of five. And in the end they even eat the fire. If this godman really has supernatural powers let him keep the camphor in his beard, light it, and wave it before the idol without getting his beard singed. The godman did not accept the challenge."

For this demonstration you need a large camphor cube (pure and not synthetic) and a matchbox. Hold the camphor cube between thumb and index finger and light it. You can keep the burning camphor on the palm of your hand as long as it never remains in the same place but is moved about on the palm as you wave your hand. When your palm gets hot transfer the camphor to the other hand and wave it as before. Later, when both hands have absorbed enough heat and might burn, place the burning camphor on your tongue. When you feel the tongue getting hot, blow out

> This information is provided for educational and scholarly purposes only. It's not intended to encourage or instruct someone to attempt these dangerous acts.

> WARNING: Attempting to perform these dangerous acts
> will result in serious injury or death.

the fire by breathing out, or close the mouth and the fire will get extinguished by itself.

GLASS EATING

This is a demonstration which my friend Luigi has mastered, but which I have always refused to perform (like the two that follow); on the other hand, there is at least one fakir stunt that he won't perform but I do, as we'll see. You take a light bulb, the kind with a transparent glass (other kinds, like fluorescent tubes, could poison you), envelop it in a napkin, and then smash it on the floor. When you re-open the napkin, the bulb is obviously in pieces: you choose one that is roughly the size of a quarter and temporarily place it on the middle of your tongue. This is to show that it is really a piece of the light bulb and not some piece of ice, plastic, or something else that might only resemble a piece of glass. With your tongue you then place it between your molars and carefully, but without fear, you crush it. Chew it for a while until you reduce it to a fine powder: it's as nice as munching sand, but it doesn't hurt. When the whole piece of glass is reduced to a powder you can swallow it without fear. There's no risk of cutting your insides: it is a fact that all of the alimentary canal from start to finish is a mucous membrane, soft and pulpy, and it is not easily cut. Eat a piece of banana after this; it helps to collect the grains of powder. Never attempt this demonstration if you have caries in your teeth: if you do it could be very, very painful.

> This information is provided for educational and scholarly
> purposes only. It's not intended to encourage or instruct
> someone to attempt these dangerous acts.

> WARNING: Attempting to perform these dangerous acts will result in serious injury or death.

Lifting Weights with Your Skin

This seems to be quite a popular item with some fakirs. "Actually," Premanand told us, "a common sight near South Indian temples is that of mendicants piercing their skin and stitching lemons, fruits, and vegetables all over their bodies. In Kerala there is a temple where the oracle puts two hooks into his back and hangs himself on a pole. Others pierce their tongues and cheeks with tridents. Muslim babas pierce their necks and chests with swords. There was even a Naga Baba that walked in a recent Kumbh mela with a hook on his penis skin dangling a thirty-five-kilogram stone! People seeing these ghastly miracles are filled with awe and devotion, but are they real miracles? No, they can be done by any courageous person with minimal pain."

For an easy start, let's begin with stitching a lemon on the skin of a forearm. First, thread a no. 8 needle with twelve inches of sewing thread. Put the needle through the lemon and knot the ends of the thread so that the lemon does not fall from the thread and the needle is in the center of the thread. Pinch your skin two or three times, pull it, pass the needle through the outer epidermis, and insert the needle into the lemon. Now the lemon will be hanging on the skin without tearing it.

"The sensation of pain," explained Premanand, "can be known only when the pain symptom is registered in the brain. That is how surgery is performed without pain through anaesthesia. When the skin is pinched the nerves are numbed and so the pain sensation does not reach the brain. The outer epidermis can easily take a weight of about 500 grams without tearing, while three layers of skin can take a weight of eighty kilograms."

> This information is provided for educational and scholarly purposes only. It's not intended to encourage or instruct someone to attempt these dangerous acts.

> WARNING: Attempting to perform these dangerous acts will result in serious injury or death.

A NAIL IN THE BRAIN

Well, not really in the brain but close. You need a five-inch-long nail and a hammer. To all appearances you push the nail all the way inside one of your nostrils! Quite disgusting, right? That's why I really prefer not even to watch Luigi when he (too frequently, I am afraid) performs this feat in public. First, you file any sharp edges or points the nail might have, then clean it with a disinfectant. Place the point of the nail at the entrance of the nostril, and carefully push it in for half an inch. The first time you must be very careful, since not all noses are alike and what works for one might not work for another. Tilt your head slightly backward and slowly push the nail inside the nose until it touches anything: stop when it does. This, of course, is just how you would do it the first few times, in order to get familiar with the proceedings: in order to perform publicly this feat in an impressive way, you can use a hammer to push the nail inside the nose. It's just an illusion, of course, you are not really hammering the nail into your head, but be careful to hold it in place with the other hand and never let it slide in too quickly. This demonstration works because there is an empty channel that connects the nose with the throat and it is this channel that the nail goes into. Sometimes the channel is not straight and you cannot push the nail inside it without injuring yourself. Never mind, there are so many other wonderful things you can do in this life.

> This information is provided for educational and scholarly purposes only. It's not intended to encourage or instruct someone to attempt these dangerous acts.

254 INVESTIGATING PSYCHICS TODAY

> WARNING: Attempting to perform these dangerous acts
> will result in serious injury or death.

SLEEPING ON A BED OF NAILS

Maybe you won't really want to sleep on one of these, but you can certainly rest on a bed of nails for a while without too much pain. Luigi took two wooden boards, linked them together with a hinge—in order to bend the "bed" in two and take it around more easily—and hammered a few dozens nails into it (about the same size as the one used in the previous demonstration). What's the trick, here? No trick, actually: the fact is that the more nails there are, the less pain you'll feel. Let's say, for example, that on a "regular" size bed-o-nails (like the one Luigi built) the nails are about two inches apart; a man resting on the bed covers about eighty nails with his body. This means that, if he weighs seventy kilograms, he has less than a kilogram on each nail, a feat almost anyone can do without feeling too much pain.

"It occured to me," James Randi told me a little while ago, "that if one of the tatty Orientals who I saw represented performing this miracle had chosen, rather than a board studded with hundreds of nails, just one single spike to recline on, we would have been spared the idiocy altogether."

STOP YOUR HEARTBEAT

This is a very old stunt, but it never fails to astonish. You give someone your wrist to hold in order to feel your heartbeat. You then concentrate and the observer will feel the beat slowly fading and finally stopping!

> This information is provided for educational and scholarly purposes only. It's not intended to encourage or instruct someone to attempt these dangerous acts.

> WARNING: Attempting to perform these dangerous acts
> will result in serious injury or death.

Quite spooky, but there's nothing to worry about. The trick (for this is just a trick) lies in a ping-pong ball that you hide under your armpit. Whenever you want to create the illusion of your heart stopping, you press on it with your arm; this will slowly stop the flow of blood to your arm, which means that what the observer feels is the blood slowing down, and not the heart stopping! James Randi used this illusion quite effectively when our friend José Alvarez successfully impersonated the "channeler" Carlos in Australia. Carlos appeared on various Australian TV shows and performed this same stunt any time he was in the process of channeling a spirit from beyond. Not even the physicians who examined him were able to guess how he did it.

WALKING ON FIRE

And now, for something that (amazingly) Luigi said he won't ever attempt . . . firewalking! We are all familiar with the sight of fakirs walking on beds of hot coals without getting burned. Nowadays, however, it is not something that only Indians or people from other Oriental cultures perform, you can easily see managers and executives fire-walk in order to "increase their mental energies," "transcend their boundaries," or "improve their brain potential." There are people, in fact, willing to spend hundreds or thousands of dollars in order to learn to do something that any twelve-year-old street kid in India could do. Which, I think, should tell quite a lot about the actual cerebral potential of these managers.

> This information is provided for educational and scholarly
> purposes only. It's not intended to encourage or instruct
> someone to attempt these dangerous acts.

WARNING: Attempting to perform these dangerous acts will result in serious injury or death.

Fig. 20.1. The author walks on hot coals.
(Massimo Polidoro Collection)

"But in India everyone has superior powers!" some believer might protest. "An Occidental needs the right preparation in order to succeed." Quite unlikely. In any case, it is really possible to walk on hot coals without getting burned and without possessing any kind of supernatural powers or spending hours in meditation: I know because I did it.

A few years ago, in order to test the scientific facts according to which it is possible for anyone to "fire-walk," at CICAP we decided to build a firewalk ourselves. First of all we met in the open, on the property of Giovanni Baschiera, a friend of mine, and burned quite a lot of fireplace logs. When, after a few hours, the fire subsided and there were only red-hot coals burning, we used a rake to distribute them for a length of about

---

WARNING: Attempting to perform these dangerous acts
will result in serious injury or death.

---

three to four meters. The coals were still very hot (they turned out to be
burning at about 1,600 degrees Fahrenheit).

As I said, I was the "willing" volunteer who was going to defend scientific reasoning. To tell the truth, I was a bit scared at the prospect of
placing the soles of my bare feet on those red, yellow, and white glowing
embers! I knew that physics was on my side, but even if Einstein was
standing on my side, it would not have made me feel safer. Finally, I took
my shoes and socks off, took a deep breath, and stepped quite resolutely
onto the coals. One, two, three, four, five steps I think and I was out in
the cool moss. My feet were unharmed and I felt quite relieved.

But how is this possible? The fact is that, though the coals can reach
such high temperatures, they still are quite "slow" to conduct heat. What
does this mean? Imagine you want to bake a pie: you heat the oven to
about 350° Fahrenheit; after a while, everything inside the oven is at
350° F: the cake, the metal dish that holds the cake, the air inside the
oven. However, you can place your hand inside the oven and feel that the
air is hot without getting burned; you can also touch the cake without
burning yourself. If you touch the metal pan, even for just a second, however, you immediately get a blister on your finger. This is because different
materials conduct heat at different speeds: they are all at the same temperature, but the air takes more time to burn your skin than does a metal
plate. In a similar way, hot coals—though very hot—take a little time
(two or three seconds) to burn you. This means that as long as you walk
resolutely, without slowing down or stopping, it is unlikely you will get
burned. I said "unlikely," and not "impossible," because it is in fact still

---

This information is provided for educational and scholarly
purposes only. It's not intended to encourage or instruct
someone to attempt these dangerous acts.

> WARNING: Attempting to perform these dangerous acts
> will result in serious injury or death.

possible to be burned: maybe just a small blister, but you could get it, even
if you are very careful.[1]

LICKING RED-HOT RODS

"While talking to the District Education Officers at Delhi," Premanand told
us, "one of them from Gharwal district told me he had seen an oracle, possessed by the deity, licking a red-hot poker until it was cold. He wondered
how a person could lick a red-hot iron unless he had supernatural powers."

This time, I didn't need to wait for Premanand to tell us the solution
to this mystery. When I was living in Florida and working with Randi, he
told me a very revealing story: "In my youth, I worked Saturdays at an aluminum foundry in Canada. It was my delight to watch and speak with
some of the old-timers there, and one chap used to astonish me by
washing his hands, scooping the dross from the surface of some molten
metal, then splashing his hands in it! Told by him that I could do another
related stunt, I got my nerve together and alone one afternoon in the
garage of my home, I heated a soldering "copper" in a blow-torch flame,
and when it was glowing brightly red, I licked it with my bare tongue. As
I brought the thing close to my face, I felt the extreme heat of it on my
face, to the point where it was almost unbearable. But I did the dumb
thing, and rushed indoors to examine my tongue in the bathroom mirror.
It was intact, and hasn't stopped moving since. There was no trace of any
burn, and I was ecstatic. My mother never found out."

> This information is provided for educational and scholarly
> purposes only. It's not intended to encourage or instruct
> someone to attempt these dangerous acts.

FROZEN IN A BLOCK OF ICE

On the opposite extreme from walking on hot coals or licking hot pokers, is the ability to resist extreme low temperatures. Recently, magician David Blaine set a new record by resisting more than sixty-one hours inside a six-ton block of ice. He wore only a pair of pants, boots, a shirt, and a hat to protect himself from his frigid temporary home. To help insulate his body, he also wore the same type of gel that swimmers of the English Channel wear, and he took a blood thinner to prevent blood clotting. All this notwithstanding, when he was pulled out he was clearly disoriented, unable to walk on his own, and complained of severe foot pain. However, after a few days he was back to his usual health and ready for new stunts.

This feat, however, was not invented by Blaine. Houdini himself had a similar idea but death prevented him from trying it. However, in December 1927, his wife, Bess, announced plans to take on the road the illusion, titled: "Freezing a Man in a Cake of Ice." At a press conference, an Indian in a rubber suit was lowered into a metal container. A ton-and-a-half block of ice was apparently frozen around him, using a carbon-dioxide and cold-water mixture. The ice was chopped so the man's face could be seen inside. The top was then chopped and the man lifted out of the icy prison.

In any case, it seems that the first world record for resisting a block of ice belongs to Randi. "Yes, that's right," Randi confirmed. "In March of 1979 I established the world's record for being frozen into a block of ice. For the first time, I was beating someone else's mark in this endurance stunt, since the previously established times—43.5, 47, and 49 minutes—were my own, and only the latest—51.5 minutes—was earned by my colleague Jim Pyczynski. The *Guinness Book of Records* listed my first record, but never got to list Jim due to their dropping such 'dangerous' marks of recent years."

Randi's record of 51.5 minues was established in Amsterdam during a TV special. A box was built using twelve 300-pound blocks, each measuring 12" × 18" × 3.5" each: two half-blocks were used to seal the ends. Randi ended up enclosed in a 60" × 17" × 12" space, wearing only a pair of trunks. "It isn't easy," said Randi, "but it can be done."

At the end of the lengthy discussions we had with Premanand on the mysteries of the East, which didn't appear very mysterious anymore, there was one more thing that Basava Premanand told us: "You know, I told you I had one desire: to create a research center in India for the investigation of psychic phenomena. Well, to tell you the truth I also have one other wish."

"And what is it?" we asked.

"It's simple; I'd like to witness a real miracle before dying."

I think that is a wish many of us would subscribe to as well.[2]

NOTES

1. If you plan to do a firewalk, it would be helpful to read an interview with David Willey, a science educator who is better known as the "physics instructor who walks on fire." He recently performed a firewalk at Buffalo's CSICOP headquarters and explained what it takes in order to succeed. You can read the interview on CSICOP's Web site at this address: http://www.csicop.org/genx/firewalk/index.html.

2. For further reading, see S. Dalal, ed., *Swami and Mantra* (Washington, D.C.: Kaufman and Co., 1997); J. Fisher, *Body Magic* (New York: Stein and Day, 1976); D. Lever, *Stranger than Fiction* (Bideford: Supreme Magic Co., 1961); J. Ovette, *Miraculous Hindu Feats* (Pomeroy, Ohio: Lloyd & Jones, 1947); and B. Premanand, *Science versus Miracles* (Podanur, India: Indian CSICOP, 1993).

INTRODUCING ITALY'S VERSION OF THE GREAT HOUDINI

An Interview with
Massimo Polidoro

by Matt Nisbet

At the age of thirty-one, Italian paranormal investigator Massimo Polidoro is the author of fourteen books, performs and lectures to standing-room-only crowds across the globe, runs a national organization of Italian skeptics, and is a hit with the Italian media. A life that may seem very complex to most is very simple to Polidoro: he is merely leading a life inspired by his boyhood hero Harry Houdini.

Ithaca, N.Y.; August 31, 2000

Most ten-year-olds growing up in Italy dream of feats of national heroism on the soccer field, with visions of professional soccer stardom dancing in their heads. But as a young boy Massimo Polidoro dreamed of magic. It all started when Polidoro saw the 1953 Tony Curtis classic, *Houdini*. A romanticized version of the life and times of the legendary escape artist and debunker, the film chronicles Harry Houdini's early beginnings in show business as a dime museum performer to his ultimate, and inaccurate, death on stage in the Chinese Water Torture Cell. Amazed by the story of Houdini, young Polidoro developed a fascination with the paranormal. He tried bending metal like popular 1970s television personality Uri Geller, and delved into books about telepathy and spiritualism.

Fantasy turned to skepticism at the age of fifteen when Polidoro came across the book *Journey into the Paranormal World* by well-known Italian journalist Piero Angela. The book introduced Polidoro to the adventures of American magician James "The Amazing" Randi. The teenage Polidoro wrote to both Angela and Randi, with Randi responding by sending books to Polidoro on skepticism and the paranormal. A short time later when Randi visited Italy on a lecture tour, Polidoro met with the magician and Angela. Randi recruited Polidoro to serve for the next year as his "sorcerer's apprentice," traveling the globe testing psychics and dowsers, and working in front of television cameras to unmask mystery and trickery for global audiences.

Today, at the young age of thirty-one, life is no less exciting for Polidoro as he has built an international profile as an author, journalist, lecturer, and professional skeptic. He is cofounder and executive director of the Italian Committee for the Investigation of Claims of the Paranormal (CICAP—Comitato Italiano per il Controllo delle Affermazioni sul Paranomale), has published fourteen books, and draws standing-room-only crowds at public appearances across the globe. In mid-August, I traveled to Amherst, New York, to meet and interview Polidoro, who spent the month on a speaking tour of the United States. His first stop was the Center for Inquiry-International, headquarters for the Committee for the Scientific Investigation of Claims of the Paranormal (CSICOP), and the *Skeptical Inquirer* magazine.

About two inches short of six-feet tall, slender, with a well-groomed Don Quixote goatee, Polidoro speaks fluent English, looks younger than his years, and unlike many international celebrities, lacks the slightest trace of hubris or arrogance. Polidoro and I sat down for about an hour before his evening lecture to discuss his career and insights on the world of the paranormal.

After spending a year abroad with James Randi, Polidoro returned to Italy in 1990, and began to shop around to Italian publishers the manuscript for his first book *Viaggio tra gli spiriti* (Journey into the Spirit World). Polidoro encountered difficulty in convincing publishers that a book skeptical of the paranormal would interest readers, but *Viaggio tra gli spiriti* finally made it into print in 1995, and experienced strong sales. Polidoro was then able to follow with a series of books, all in Italian, that included *Misteri* (Mysteries) (1996), *Dizionario del paranormale* (Dictionary of the Paranormal) (1997), *Sei un sensitivo?* (Are You Psychic?) (1997), *La maledizione del Titanic* (Curse of the *Titanic*) (1998), *I segreti dei fachiri* (Secrets of the Fakirs) (1998), *L'illusione del paranormale* (The Paranormal Illusion) (1998), *Il sesto senso* (The Sixth Sense) (2000), *Il grande Houdini* (The Great Houdini) (2001), *Investigatori dell'occulto* (Psychic Investigations) (2001), *Grandi misteri della storia* (Great Historical Mysteries) (2002), and *Enigmi della Storia* (Historical Enigmas) (2003). His first book in English, *Final Séance*, devoted to the strange friendship between Harry Houdini and Sir Arthur Conan Doyle, was published by Prometheus Books in the spring of 2001.

In 1989, Polidoro also teamed with Italian scientist Luigi Garlaschelli to found CICAP, and, in the first years, the duo worked tirelessly to recruit members and subscribers to the CICAP newsletter. The newsletter soon grew into the glossy bound magazine *Scienza & Paranormale* (Science and the Paranormal), reached bimonthly status in 1998, and today boasts about 2,500 subscribers. Since 1989, Polidoro has contributed over 200 articles and papers, not only to *Scienza & Paranormale* but also to such periodicals as the *Journal of the Society for Psychical Research*, the *Skeptical Inquirer*, *Skeptic*, and *Swift*. As a chief spokesperson for CICAP, Polidoro delivers about four lectures a month to crowds as large as several thousand. Polidoro earned a degree in psychology from the University of Padua in 1996 with his thesis devoted to the study of the reliability of eyewitness reports of unusual events.

Polidoro views his work with the Italian media as one of his most important achievements. "Before CICAP, the Italian media were absolutely pro-paranormal, and rarely critical, but now CICAP has

Fig. A1. Massimo Polidoro. (© Roberto Spampinato)

grown into a friendship with many journalists," Polidoro said. He and CICAP have tried to adopt a media-relations approach that fosters a partnership with the Italian media, and makes covering paranormal claims from a critical view easy. CICAP maintains a media e-mail list and a state-of-the-art organizational Web site. "There are skeptical journalists and they are certainly supportive of our cause," Polidoro said. "But most are looking for a nice story. So if we find a way to present ourselves in a more interesting light, it can be very important."

Polidoro names alternative medicine (especially homeopathy), UFOs (specifically the ancient astronaut claims of Robert Hancock), crop circles, and various miracle claims as the most frequent paranormal topics he encounters among the Italian media and public. On the miracle front, Polidoro believes that the canonization by the Catholic Church of stigmatic Padre Pio has helped reignite widespread belief in miracles. "In Italy, almost every actor or celebrity claims to have been healed, saved, or comforted at some time by Padre Pio," Polidoro said. "I think the Catholic Church might be following the New Age and coming up with more miraculous events."

Polidoro envisions CICAP's main role as "letting people have all the facts, so they can make up their mind. We are not trying to convert people. Often people are asking questions about cases that have already been solved. We are trying to give information to people." Current efforts by CICAP include increased involvement with schools, initiating programs with teachers to teach critical thinking and science via paranormal topics, and to provide books and tapes as educational resources. CICAP is also expanding its Web resources, building a Skeptic's Web dictionary in Italian, and offering the sale of books and other materials through the CICAP site. CICAP sponsors eleven regional Italian skeptic organizations, and has held a national conference every two years that features international leaders in science and skepticism. In October 2000, CICAP unveiled in the city of Padua its new national headquarters. Occupying two floors of an office building, CICAP now employs three full-time staff members, several part-time staff, and dozens of volunteers. The organization bases its operations on a growing annual budget of $150,000, raised mostly through subscriptions and donations.

I asked Polidoro if living a life inspired by Harry Houdini ever struck friends his age as a bit strange or eccentric. He claims it doesn't cause any problems. "Though my work is a very important part of my life, I have other interests. I play the piano and the guitar, and I am a big fan of the

Beatles, of cinema, and of authors like Michael Crichton, Jeffrey Deaver, and Stephen King. Very rarely do I talk about paranormal subjects with my friends. Sometimes they see me on television, and they say they didn't know I do these things."

I also asked him about women his age. Did he have any thoughts on the notion that women might be more prone to belief or fascination with the paranormal? "It is possible," he answered carefully, remarking that his fiancée might have something to say about his answer. "Maybe women are less likely to be attacking, and are not as cynical. Maybe men are interested as well but don't manifest their belief in the same way." Hmmm . . . stated like a true escape artist.[1]

MATT NISBET is a graduate student in the department of communication at Cornell University. His research interests include science and political communication, public opinion, and public policy. From 1997 to 1999, he worked as public relations director for CSICOP and the *Skeptical Inquirer*. Nisbet lives year-round in Ithaca, New York.

NOTE

Reprinted with permission of the editors from the *Skeptical Inquirer* 25, no. 2 (March/April 2001). Copyright 2001 by the Committee for the Scientific Investigation of Claims of the Paranormal.

1. Some recommended Web resources are the Massimo Polidoro Web site (in English and Italian), www.massimopolidoro.com; and the CICAP Web site (in English), www. cicap.org/en/.

THE SEARCH
FOR
MARGERY

An Interview with
the Medium's Granddaughter

W hile researching material for my book *Final Séance: The Story of the Strange Friendship Between Houdini and Conan Doyle*, I made several attempts to locate some of the relatives of the medium "Margery" (Mina Crandon), whose fame was so prominent when Houdini and Doyle were friends and later enemies. I knew that Margery had a son and that he was probably still alive, but though I tried many times to contact him, I never had a reply. The deadline for the book finally came and I closed it without the information I wished to include.

Then, in March of 2002, I received an e-mail from Anna Thurlow, who introduced herself as Margery's granddaughter. Was this real or a joke played by some friend of mine? I soon found out it was for real. She wrote me because she had read a review I wrote for *Skeptical Inquirer* on Ken Silverman's book on Houdini.[1] She thought the book was "superb" but wanted to "point out, though, that it was not ever proven that Mina provided 'sexual favors' to members of the séance circle. Ken is careful to point this out himself. Bird later made that claim, but I would argue that a man desperate to salvage his own reputation and is willing to do so by commenting on such personal matters is perhaps not the most trustworthy source of information."[2]

I was quite excited to get a chance to speak to someone who had had Margery as a grandmother and I thought it would be very interesting to hear the perspective of a member of the family, who was not as involved in the case as Dr. Crandon. To me it seemed almost as if, eighty years later, the contemporary "representatives" of Margery (Anna) and Houdini (myself) had a chance to meet and discuss what went on during those famous séances in Boston.

Massimo Polidoro: Anna, I must say that I am an admirer of Margery and I think that the idea of her faking the phenomena was probably more a matter of a difficult relationship with her husband than an attempt to deceive the public or others. What do you think?

Anna Thurlow: Please, do not feel any anxiety over offending me regarding whether she was "authentic" or not—I do not believe in supernatural phenomena. I am, however, fascinated with the pageantry and ritual of it. I know that for whatever reason she started it (and I agree with you, I do not think it was with intent to deceive but rather for reasons more psychologically complex), it conquered her mentally in the end—after Dr. Crandon died (even though he was my great-grandfather, we've always called him "Dr. Crandon") she continued automatic writing on her own, as if it was the only company she had, which I find very sad.

MP: Did you have a chance when you were a kid to know Mina personally?

AT: I never knew Mina, nor did my mother, as Mina drank herself to death so early on. But my grandfather, John Crandon (Mina's son and my mother's father), was greatly influenced and shaped by her. He was a very unhappy man and both obsessed with and ashamed by her. She was rarely spoken of in the family but my mother gathered many stories and passed them on to me. I've been worried about the veracity of the stories, but where I've been able to verify them, they've turned out to be true. More immediately, however, the psychological impact of my great-grandparents' dysfunctionality and the conflict with Houdini was deeply imprinted on the family.

MP: Is John still living?

AT: Yes, my grandfather is still living although not mentally competent; even before, however, he rejected anyone's attempt to contact the family—which is why you wouldn't have been able to find any of us. My mother, on the other hand, was fascinated by Mina and was preparing to write a book about women, spirituality, and class in Boston, with Mina as the central figure. My mom died of cancer in 1995, just before Ken's book came out—she would have been thrilled to read it, as he uncovered so much more than we knew. I've been very grateful to him for answering so many of the questions that my grandfather never would.

MP: Do you think you will finish your mother's writings?

AT: I have thought of continuing my mother's work (to be more exact, she made me promise I would finish it for her). I am still in the process of sorting through the materials my mom gave me. I try to attend the annual Houdini séance, and that has been very interesting, and, after having sat through both very good and very bad séances, I now appreciate the skill Mina must have had to cultivate the right atmosphere.

MP: What other members of your family are still alive?

AT: There is only myself and my mother's brother.

MP: Can you help me to build a better picture of Mina's and your family?

AT: I'd be happy to. As a warning, this is a long reply! I find that my family tree tends to confuse people, so I will start there. Mina was married to Mr. Rand, who was a working-class grocer in Boston. They had a son named Alan Rand. Mina had to have her appendix removed and the surgeon was Dr. LeRoy Crandon. She and Dr. Crandon fell somehow for each other, and she divorced her husband to marry Dr. Crandon. Dr. Crandon had been married and divorced once before. He had a daughter named Mary, who he at some point disinherited and no one on my side of the family knew what happened to her. When Mina and Dr. Crandon married, Alan was about nine or ten years old. His name was changed to John Crandon and he was legally adopted by Dr. Crandon, who had always wanted a boy. John Crandon married Dorothy Tebbe. They had two children, Mary and Alan. John Crandon continued in Dr. Crandon's steps, as Dr. Crandon wanted; he also became a surgeon. Mary is my mother. However, she hated the name Mary and has always been called by anyone except my grandparents, "Libbet." Then there is my uncle, who currently lives in Boston with my grandfather (my grandmother died in 1991). I am guessing he wouldn't want his or his family's name in the press. I don't think it was a conscious decision to repeat the names from generation to generation. However, I am not named after anyone in my direct family—my mother named me after her and my uncle's nanny.

MP: It must not have been easy for a kid like John, your grandfather, to live in a house where all those strange things went on. What did he think about his mother's fame?

AT: It made my grandfather very angry to talk about Mina (the Rand side of the family only knew her as Mina; people outside of the family or Houdini specialists always refer to her as Margery; my mother and I refer to her as both). I asked him several years ago what he thought about the whole thing, and he said that he knew when she started the séances that something was not right with her mentally. However, a few minutes later he turned to me and said in a way that made my hair stand on end: "They didn't know what they were playing with. It was a very dangerous game." His room at 10 Lime Street was right next to the séance room, and he could hear everything. They locked him in every night (as well as the servants) to prove to the sitters that the séance circle was controlled. I think he was around twelve years old. So I imagine, for him, however much of a rationalist he was, it must have nonetheless been absolutely terrifying. Seeing him relive that was chilling enough for me not to ask again. My mother told me that the public outcry on this arrangement was such that Mina had to send my grandfather away; which they did—to Andover (a boarding school). When I asked him once about how it was done, he said, "mirrors." But he didn't explain more than that.

MP: Did you have other chances to talk about Mina with John?

AT: I've asked my grandfather about Mina over my whole life, but he really didn't like to talk about it. The conversation I relayed to you took place in 1997, I think, just before he really slipped mentally; he must have been in his early 80s, and I was in my late 20s. The question about the mirrors was the same day—I asked him if he believed in it ("no"), how they did it ("mirrors"), and how he felt about being in the room next door (wouldn't say). He was very rattled and the nurse told me that he had nightmares all that night. Sid Radner (of the Houdini séances) was very interested in talking with him, but after that, I really felt that he couldn't remember enough for it to be worth the emotional turmoil it obviously caused him.

MP: Dr. Crandon died in 1939 (by the way, do you know how he died?) and Mina in 1941. However, we know that she went into depression and drank quite heavily. What was it like for her during those two years alone?

AT: After Dr. Crandon died (I don't know how, I think of natural causes) Mina had an affair with their lawyer, Mr. Button, and I believe she moved in with him in New York City. However, my mother and grandmother (my grandmother was rather horrified by the whole thing and never really knew how to handle Mina) always hated him. I am not sure why, but I think my grandfather felt Button stole Mina's money or he otherwise took advantage of her. Button certainly supported her continued "experiments" so I wouldn't be suprised if he was hoping to recreate some of her past notoriety. However, I haven't found a thing about him that confirms that he was a bad person, so I have to reserve my judgment. But Mina did drink herself to death by her early 50s (although the toll of drink and depression, as I gather, made her seem much, much older). But yes, my grandfather was terribly ashamed of her, as I think most children of alcoholics are, even without having had the whole world know very intimate things about her. By the time she died, my grandfather was already married.

MP: Could this Button you are referring to be W. H. Button, once president of the American Society for Psychical Research?

AT: You are right! I was shocked to realize that he was the head of the ASPR—my mother had thought he was a lawyer. All of the papers I have from later in Mina's life were archived, sorted and stored by him—the envelopes all have his name and address on them. I am now curious as to what date he starts the archiving as opposed to Dr. C.—I never really thought about it, but Dr. C.'s papers seem to peter out around 1926 (presumably around the time that Dr. C. no longer believed in Margery?) even though he didn't die until 1938. I wonder if Button "took up the cause" and perhaps that is how Mina and he became involved with each other. She moved to New York to be with him. Coincidentally, she lived on West 116th Street, and of course Houdini had lived on West 113th Street. My mother and I also lived on West 113th Street for almost fifteen years, only two blocks away!

MP: Since you are talking about houses. . . . While on my search for material and information for my book, I went to Boston and tried to locate the house where Mina lived and where the famous séances with Houdini and the *Scientific American* team took place. However, due to time constraints, I was not able to find it. Does the house still exist, I wonder?

AT: Yes, 10 Lime Street is still there. I have written to the owners to ask if I could meet them but they've never responded. My mother was born there and I'd like to see it for personal history, but no luck. I am dying to find out if they found any secret passages, etc. As an interesting note, the photo of her most often reproduced (standing in a doorway) was actually of the building next door. 10 Lime doesn't have a recessed doorway. I understand that the photo was taken by Houdini, and I saw a note somewhere asking him to keep that fact rather secret, for fear of their "reputations"—I presume to keep it a secret that they actually got along long enough to take a picture! I do suspect that they were quite similar in the aspect of having been working class and yet outsmarted a lot of very self-satisfied people. Plus, they each had some aspect that society used to dismiss them—he being Jewish and she being female. Neither of which were qualities held in high value by many of the participants, from what I can tell. As to my mother, I thought she was born there but the address on her birth certificate is different—but they moved from 10 Lime around that time. My uncle might have been born there. They didn't move from 10 Lime Street until around that time (early 1940s). I was hoping it would be

Fig. B.1. Margery stands next door from her home at 10 Lime Street. (McManus-Young Collection, Library of Congress, Rare Books and Special Collections Division, LC-USZ62-99115)

an acceptable reason for wanting to see the house, without getting into the whole séance thing, as I find that often freaks people out.

MP: Talking about pictures and old documents, on September 2000 there was a very interesting collection put on sale on eBay: it was an archive on Margery which included 350 original photographs (including six never before seen of Houdini) and many others taken during the *Scientific American* experience. Furthermore, there were numerous rare books and pamphlets, probably all that existed on Margery. When I sent my bid, the collection had already been sold! Do you know anything about it? It seemed to come from a very close member of Mina's family.

AT: I don't, but I definitely will try to find out more about it. I confess it was a bit of a shock at first when I read the document you sent me—my grandmother often gave things away out of the house when she became senile (in the late 1980s and early 1990s) and my first thought was that she may have given this away. However, I realize that all the major players from *Scientific American* must have had similar scrapbooks so it likely is from a source like that. Or perhaps it was Prince's? As he moved to Boston and I see the seller lives near there. But I am very, very interested to learn more—it certainly is an unusual collection—thank you so much for the reference!

MP: Was Houdini and the *Scientific American* investigation ever talked about in your family?

AT: I didn't know anything about the *Scientific American* episode other than it had been a scandal, until I read Ken's book. Houdini was a respected name in the household but his name also held a great aura of sadness and shame—I remember my mother telling me that when the *Boston Globe* stated that Houdini announced Mina to be a fraud, my grandfather went out and bought all of the newspapers so that Mina wouldn't read it. While I agree with Houdini that one can only explain the séances as a combination of theater and audience participation, the séances he was at were pretty simple. I would really like to know how they managed the more complicated séance events. I also don't feel that Houdini was quite up-front himself—he seemed to be playing his own games. However, he was treated terribly by Dr. Crandon and some of the others and that pretty much entitles Houdini to act however he wanted, to my mind.

MP: Are there any mementoes, letters, or other souvenirs that you have inherited from Mina?

AT: One of the strangest things to me is that in all of the scrapbooks, letters, and notes that I have, there is very, very little in them that has anything in Mina's own words. Dr. Crandon often even answered her fan mail on her behalf. What she left even to her own family is much like what she left to the rest of the world—many questions, and very few satisfactory answers. I have a necklace of hers (which I always wear at the séances), her wedding ring, and one of her skirts, but very little else. Mina also (like my grandmother) gave away many things before she died, sometimes to people on the street that she didn't even know.

MP: You said that after 1926, Dr. Crandon presumably no longer believed in Margery. What do you think of him? Did he help her in some of her trickery or was he really a complete believer?

AT: I think Dr. Crandon must have been convinced of the experiments—I don't think anyone can write so consistently to intimate friends for so many years and have it be a lie. I think that Conan Doyle (whose friendship was dearly valued by my great-grandparents) and Dr. Crandon truly thought they were foraging at the frontiers of science, as strange as that seems now. The fact that we all still refer to him as "Dr. Crandon" even though he was my great-grandfather says something about his personality—I suspect he was capable of great anger. He wasn't a horrible person, but he was greatly flawed. My grandfather both loved and admired him as well as was terrified of him—I think he appreciated all of the opportunities Dr. C. gave him (my grandfather became a very well-known and respected surgeon and continued Dr. C.'s practice) but was aware that Dr. C.'s anger could be devastating (as I said, he disinherited his biological daughter because he didn't approve of her husband). And Dr. C. had been divorced before marrying Mina—so I imagine she must have cared very much about keeping peace in the home. This is one reason why I take Bird's testimony regarding a sexual relationship with a grain of salt. He strikes me as a rather charming but unbalanced and not entirely trustworthy person—tragic, too, as he disappeared (from what I know) after all this—probably not a person it would be wise to get too intimately involved with. Would she even dare get involved with such a person, if her highest priority was to keep Dr. C. happy? Of course, relationships do not always make sense, but Bird sets off alarm bells even for me, eighty years later.

MP: As with many of those who have studied the Margery story and the *Scientific American* investigation, you don't seem to have a great opinion of Malcolm Bird.

AT: I think he was a rather duplicitous person himself. He basically moved in to 10 Lime Street, and I suspect may have been given money by my great-grandparents (although I can't prove that—there is just a reference to a blank check to him from Mina, about which he teases her: "what would it look like if certain people saw this?" [see Bird's letters below]) and there may have been plenty of personal reasons for them to all grow quite tired of each other's company. I find, however, I am quite curious to know what happened to him. He strikes me as a rather sad person as well, not quite able to handle the demands of the situation he found himself in, although I suppose the situation got the better of most of the participants.

(Anna did not know about my book but finally got hold of a copy.)

AT: I am enjoying your book very much. . . . I have some thoughts to share with you on questions and points you raise. By the way, the picture in your book of Mina in the doorway is the picture I was referring to earlier—I believe it was taken by Houdini and she asked him not to reveal that fact (a collector at one of the Houdini séances showed me the same picture and told me Houdini had taken it, and I have a copy of a letter from Mina asking Houdini to not tell anyone he was the one who took pictures of her). It is of her standing in the doorway of 11 Lime Street, not 10 Lime.

MP: On reading about the story from some of the original documents, what do you think now of Dr. Crandon's role and character?

AT: I'm pretty sure I know what Dr. C.'s problems at the hospitals were—women. He was a philanderer. I suspect that in combination with too many sexual escapades with the female staff, he was argumentative with his peers. Plus, I think Ken Silverman may have mentioned that Dr. C. was not as wealthy as he appeared to be. This also makes sense to me, as he had been divorced and was likely to have some financial pressures on that end, which may have complicated things. There have been disappointments for me in learning more about my great-grandfather—he was a racist and a sexist (which my grandfather inherited). However the both of them hid it fairly well under the veneer of upper-class manners and propriety, but when pushed or angered, you can see it, and it is ugly. But there have also been two things of which I am surprised to say I am rather proud: one, he was staunchly atheist and did not let social mores pressure him into believing certain things. I believe his belief in spiritualism to be genuine, and to be based in a combination of hope and science, but not in religion. Which must have made his disappointment later all that more devastating. The second thing I am proud of him for is mentioned in your last chapter. I don't know that he assisted women with abortions for a fact, but had heard it before, and it makes sense to me, and I am proud to think that one of my ancestors did something that gave women more autonomy over themselves, particularly in a time when women had so few choices. Sexism I find not an absolute quality, but it exists by degrees, and although I think he thought of women as less capable than men, I think he also thought women should have some autonomy over their bodies or minds. To his credit, he warmly welcomed my grandmother into the family—a doctor herself, and the only woman to graduate from McGill Medical School in 1939.

MALCOLM BIRD'S LETTERS

Anna also sent me a couple of previously unpublished letters by Malcolm Bird which are quite revealing of Bird's character.

AT: Here is the letter from Bird that I referred to (it is actually two letters—neither are dated but they appear to go together. I am not sure in which order they go). He used *Scientific American* letterhead when he wrote formal letters to my great-grandparents, and often included typed personal notes to either Dr. Crandon or Mina on distinctive, half-size yellow paper. These are two of those personal notes. There is something about the tone/presentation which I find a bit unsettling (a hint of betrayal of Houdini in letter no. 1; a reminder that he is also in the position to betray Mina in letter no. 2). Perhaps he was finding himself a bit drunk on all the publicity. By the way, I have no idea who "cousin Carl" is—a new name for me to research. I don't know who Alfred Grey is either.

Letter No. 1

Dear Doctor:

It seems to me that your next point to be considered is just where you stand with the Cttee, and just what you want to do about them. Do you want to make any demands of any description (for decision, for sittings, for anything else); or do you want to lie quiet until the Cttee makes a move? Do you want to file any formal allegations against Houdini, to protest his presence or membership, or anything of the sort? If you do, do you not think it best to wait until his Boston engagement has given him all the opportunity that it will give to say or do something objectionable that will give further force to your position? All this has doubtless occurred to you, but it will do no harm for me thus briefly to review it.

And dont forget that with the present alinement [*sic*], I can stand much more definitely on your side than I could before. I dont know that any emergency will arise calling for public display of this fact, but if it arises, it will be met.

(UNSIGNED)

Letter No. 2

Later:—

Have just seen clippings from Hearst papers, *Journal* and *Mirror*. "Houdini prevents Margery from Landing $2,500 Prize" is the head and the burden of the story in both. Of course we dont give a damn what these papers say—I dont know whether the Hearst organ in Boston is held in sufficient contempt by decent folks to serve as a basis for comparison for what such people think of the NY Hearst papers.

Had a call a few minutes ago from Margery's cousin Carl (Gray). He was announced by last name, and I had Alfred on my mind; and when he walked in he looked enough like Alfred's photo to preserve the deception. He wanted to know what I thought of the case, and I told him.

By the way: how much would a certain member of the Cttee give for a photo of a blank check drawn to my order by Margery? Just as a measure of sensible precaution, I cashed it here in the office, so that when it comes thru [*sic*] it will carry the endorsement of Munn & Co.

(UNSIGNED)

NOTES

Reprinted with permission of the editors from *Skeptical Inquirer* 26, no. 6 (November/December 2002). Copyright 2002 by the Committee for the Scientific Investigation of Claims of the Paranormal.

1. See Massimo Polidoro, "Review of Houdini!!! The Career of Ehrich Weiss, by Kenneth Silverman," *Skeptical Inquirer* 21, no. 3 (May/June 1997); Kenneth Silverman, *Houdini!!! The Career of Ehrich Weiss* (New York: Harper-Collins, 1996).

2. Anna Thurlow, e-mail communication, March 1, 2002. The following interview is actually compiled from e-mail correspondence between Anna Thurlow and the author between March 1, 2002, and June 9, 2003.

BIBLIOGRAPHY

Abell, G. O., and B. Singer, eds. *Science and the Paranormal*. New York: Scribner's, 1983.

Abbott, D. P. *Behind the Scenes with the Medium*. Chicago: Open Court, 1907.

Adare, L. *Experiences in Spiritualism with D. D. Home*. Privately printed, 1869. Reprint, vol. 35 of *Proceedings of the SPR*. London: Society for Psychical Research, 1924.

Adler, I. *Monkey Business: Hoaxes in the Name of Science*. New York: John Day, 1957.

Alcock, J. *Science and Supernature*. Amherst, N.Y.: Prometheus Books, 1990.

Alfano, G. B., and A. Amitrano. *Il miracolo di S. Gennaro: documentazione storica e scientifica* (The Miracle of St. Januarius: Historical and Scientific Documentation). Naples: Scarpati, 1924.

———. *Notizie storiche ed osservazioni sulle reliquie di sangue dei martiri e dei santi confessori ed asceti che si conservano in Italia e particolarmente in Napoli* (Historical News and Observations on the Blood Relics of Martyrs and of Confessing and Ascetic Saints Preserved in Italy and Especially in Naples). Naples: Arti grafiche Adriana, 1951.

Angela, Piero. *Alfa & Beta*. Rome: Garzanti Editore, 1984.

———. *Viaggi nella scienza* (Journey in Science). Rome: Garzanti Editore, 1982.

———. *Viaggio nel mondo del paranormale* (Journey in the World of the Paranormal). Rome: Garzanti Editore, 1978.

Anneman, T. *Practical Mental Effects*. New York: Max Holden, 1944.

Aveni, A. *Behind the Crystal Ball*. New York: Random House, 1996.

Baker, R. A. *Hidden Memories*. Amherst, N.Y.: Prometheus Books, 1992.

———. *They Call It Hypnosis*. Amherst, N.Y.: Prometheus Books, 1990.

Barnum, P. T. *Humbugs of the World*. New York: G. W. Carleton, 1865. Reprint, Detroit: Singing Tree Press, 1970.

Barrett, W. F. *On the Threshold of the Unseen*. London: Kegan Paul, 1908.

———. *Psychical Research*. London: Williams & Norgate, 1911.

Basil, R. *Not Necessarily the New Age*. Amherst, N.Y.: Prometheus Books, 1988.

Beloff, J. *Parapsychology: A Concise History*. London: Athlone Press, 1993.

Beloff, J., ed. *New Directions in Parapsychology*. London: Elek Science, 1974.

Bender, H. *Unser sechster Sinn*. Stoccarda: Wilhelm Goldmann Verlag, 1972. Reprint, 1982.

Bender, H. *Zukunftvisionen, Kriegsprophezeiungen, Sterbeerlebnisse*. Monaco: Piper, 1983.

Besterman, T. *Collected Papers on the Paranormal*. New York: Garrett Publications, 1967.

Black, S. *Mind and Body*. London: William Kimber, 1969.

Blackburn, D. "Confessions of a Telepathist: Thirty-Year Hoax Exposed." *London Daily News*, September 1, 1911.

Blackmore, S. *The Adventures of a Parapsychologist*. Amherst, N.Y.: Prometheus Books, 1986.

———. *Beyond the Body*. North Pomfret: David and Charles, 1983.

———. *Dying to Live: Near-Death Experiences*. Amherst, N.Y.: Prometheus Books, 1993.

Booth, J. *Psychic Paradoxes*. Los Alamitos, Calif.: Ridgeway Press, 1984. Reprint, Amherst, N.Y.: Prometheus Books, 1986.

Brandon, R. *The Spiritualists*. Amherst, N.Y.: Prometheus Books, 1984.

Broad, W., and N. Wade. *Betrayers of the Truth*. New York: Simon & Schuster, 1982.

Brookesmith, P., ed. *Incredible Phenomena*. London: Guild Publishing, 1984.

Broughton, R. *Parapsychology—The Controversial Science*. New York: Ballantine Books, 1991.

Browning, N. L. *The Psychic World of Peter Hurkos*. New York: Signet Books, 1971.

Buckman, R., and K. Sabbagh. *Magic or Medicine?* Amherst, N.Y.: Prometheus Books, 1995.

Burger, E. *Spirit Theater*. New York: Kaufman & Greenberg, 1986.

Burton, J. *Heyday of a Wizard: A Biography of Daniel Home the Medium*. London: George G. Harrap, 1948.

Butler, A. *Butler's Lives of the Saints*. Westminster, Md.: Christian Classics, 1981.

Cannell, J. C. *The Secrets of Houdini*. New York: Dover Publications, 1973.

Capaldi, Nicholas. *The Art of Deception*. Amherst, N.Y.: Prometheus Books, 1987.

Carrington, Hereward. *The American Séances with Eusapia Palladino*. New York: Garrett Publications, 1954.

———. *The Physical Phenomena of Spiritualism, Fraudulent and Genuine*. Boston: Herbert B. Turner & Co., 1907.

Carrington, H., and B. M. L. Ernst. *Houdini and Conan Doyle: The Story of a Strange Friendship*. New York: Albert & Charles Boni, 1933.

Chevreul, M. E. *De la Baquette Divinatoire, du Pendule dit Explorateur et des Tables Tournantes, au Point de Vue de L'histoire de la Critique et de la Méthode Expéri-mentale*. Parigi, France: Mallet-Bachelier, 1954.

Christopher, Milbourne. *ESP, Seers & Psychics*. New York: Thomas Y. Crowell Company, 1975.

———. *Houdini: The Untold Story*. New York: Thomas Y. Crowell Company, 1969.

———. *The Illustrated History of Magic*. 1973. Reprint, Portsmouth, N.H.: Heinemann, 1996.

———. *Mediums, Mystics and the Occult*. New York: Thomas Y. Crowell Company, 1975.

Cialdini, R. B. *Influence: How and Why People Agree to Things*. New York: William Morrow & Co., 1984.

———. *Le armi della persuasione* (Arms of Persuasion). Firenze: Giunti, 1989.

Committee on Techniques for the Enhancement of Human Performance, Commission on Behavioral and Social Sciences and Education, National

Research Council. D. Druckman and J. A. Swets, eds., *Enhancing Human Performance, Issues, Theories, and Techniques*. Washington, D.C.: National Academy Press, 1987.

Coover, J. E. *Experiments in Psychical Research*. Stanford, Calif.: Stanford University Press, 1917.

Corinda, T. *13 Steps to Mentalism*. Corinda's Magic Studio, 1958. Reprint, Bideford: Supreme, 1984.

Cortesi, P., ed. *Nostradamus: Le profezie* (Nostradamus: Prophecies). Rome: Newton, 1995.

Couderc, P. *L'astrologia*. Milan: Garzanti, 1977.

Croiset, G. *Croiset paragnost*. Naarden: Strengholt Televideo BV, 1977.

Crookes, William. *Researches in the Phenomena of Spiritualism*. London: Burns, 1874.

Culver, R. B., and P. A. Ianna. *Astrology: True or False?* Amherst, N.Y.: Prometheus Books, 1988.

Dalal, S., ed. *Swami and Mantra*. Washington, D.C.: Kaufman and Co., 1997.

D'Albe, E. E. F. *The Life of Sir William Crookes*. New York: D. Appleton, 1924.

Davenport, R. B. *The Death-Blow to Spiritualism*. New York, 1888. Reprint, New York: Arno Press, 1976.

De Heredia, C. M. *Los Fraudes Espiritistas y los Fenomenos Metapsiquicos*. Barcelona: Herder, 1962.

Dèttore, Ugo, ed. *L'uomo e l'ignoto* (Man and the Unknown). Milan: Armenia Editore, 1981. Reprint, *Paranormale: Dizionario enciclopedico* (Paranormal: Encyclopedic Dictionary). Milan: Mondadori, 1986 and 1992.

Dingwall, Eric J. *The Critics' Dilemma*. Sussex: Crowhurst, 1966.

———. *Four Modern Ghosts*. London: Gerald Duckworth & Co., 1958.

———. *How to Go to a Medium*. London: Kegan Paul, 1927.

———. *Very Peculiar People: Studies in the Queer, the Abnormal and the Uncanny*. New Hyde Park: University Books, 1962.

Di Trocchio, F. *Le bugie della scienza* (Lies of Science). Milan: Mondadori, 1993.

Douglas, A. *Extra Sensory Powers: A Century of Psychical Research*. Woodstock, N.Y.: Overlook Press, 1977.

Doyle, Arthur Conan. *The Coming of the Fairies*. London: Hodder & Stoughton, 1921.

———. *The Edge of the Unknown*. New York: G. P. Putnam's Sons, 1930.

———. *The History of Spiritualism*. London: Constable, 1926.

Dunninger, J. *Inside the Medium's Cabinet.* New York: David Kemp & Co., 1935.

Dunninger, J., and J. H. Kraus. *Houdini's Spirit Exposés and Dunninger's Psychical Investigations.* New York: Experimenter Publishing Co., 1928.

Ebon, Martin, ed. *The Amazing Uri Geller.* New York: Signet Books, 1975.

Edwards, I. G. *D. D. Home: The Man Who Talked with Ghosts.* New York: Thomas Nelson, 1978.

Eisenbud, J. *The World of Ted Serios.* New York: William Morrow & Co., 1967. Reprint, Jefferson, N.C.: McFarland, 1989.

Elliot, R. H. *The Myth of the Mystic East.* London: Blackwood, 1934.

Evans, C. *Cults of Unreason.* New York: Farrar, Straus, 1973.

Evans, H. R. *Hours with the Ghosts.* Chicago: Laird & Lee, 1897.

Eysenck, H. J., and C. Sargent. *Explaining the Unexplained.* London: Weidenfeld & Nicolson, 1982.

Fairley, J., and S. Welfare. *Arthur C. Clarke's World of Strange Powers.* New York: G. P. Putnam's Sons, 1984.

Feilding, Everard. *Sittings with Eusapia Palladino & Others.* London: University Books, 1963. Reprint of Everard Feilding, W. W. Baggally, and H. Carrington, "Report on a Series of Sittings with Eusapia Palladino," *Proceedings of the SPR* 23, pt. 59 [1909].

Ferraro, Alfredo. *Spiritismo, illusione o realtà?* (Spiritualism, Illusion or Reality?). Rome: Edizioni Mediterranee, 1979.

Festinger, L., H. W. Riechen, and S. Schachter. *When Prophecy Fails.* Minneapolis: University of Minnesota, 1956.

Fisher, J. *Body Magic.* New York: Stein and Day, 1976.

Fitzkee, D. *Magic by Misdirection.* San Rafael, Calif.: San Rafael House, 1945.

———. *The Trick Brain.* San Rafael, Calif.: San Rafael House, 1944.

Flew, Antony. *A New Approach to Psychical Research.* London: Watts, 1953.

Fodor, N. *Encyclopaedia of Psychic Science.* New York: University Books, 1933.

Frazier, Kendrick, ed. *Science Confronts the Paranormal.* Amherst, N.Y.: Prometheus Books, 1986.

Frikell, S. *Spirit Mediums Exposed.* New York: New Metropolitan Fiction, 1926.

Fuller, U. [Martin Gardner]. *Confessions of a Psychic.* Teaneck, N.J.: Karl Fulves, 1975.

———. *Further Confessions of a Psychic.* Teaneck, N.J.: Karl Fulves, 1980.

Gardner, M. *Fads and Fallacies in the Name of Science.* New York: Dover, 1952.

———. *How Not to Test a Psychic.* Amherst, N.Y.: Prometheus Books, 1989.

———. *The New Age: Notes of a Fringe Watcher*. Amherst, N.Y.: Prometheus Books, 1991.

———. *On the Wild Side*. Amherst, N.Y.: Prometheus Books, 1992.

———. *Science: Good, Bad and Bogus*. Amherst, N.Y.: Prometheus Books, 1981.

Garlaschelli, Luigi, and Massimo Polidoro. *I segreti dei fachiri* (Secrets of the Fakirs). Rome: Avverbi, 1998.

Gauld, A. *The Founders of Psychical Research*. London: Schocken, 1968.

Geller, Uri. *My Story*. New York: Warner Books, 1975.

Geller, Uri, and G. L. Playfair. *The Geller Effect*. New York: Henry Holt & Co., 1986. Reprinted and revised, London: Grafton Books, 1988.

Gettings, F. *Ghosts in Photographs*. New York: Harmony Books, 1978.

Giannetta, E. *Il sangue miracoloso di S. Lorenzo martire* (The Miraculous Blood of St. Lawrence Martyr). Frosinone: Tecno Stampa, 1964.

Giovetti, P. *I misteri intorno a noi* (Mysteries around Us). Milan: Rizzoli, 1988.

Gordon, Henry. *Extrasensory Deception*. Amherst, N.Y.: Prometheus Books, 1987.

Gresham, William Lindsay. *Houdini, The Man Who Walked through Walls*. New York: Henry Holt & Co., 1959.

Gris, H., and William Dick. *The New Soviet Psychic Discoveries*. Englewood Cliffs, N.J.: Prentice-Hall, 1978.

Gurney, E., F. W. H. Myers, and F. Podmore. *Phantasms of the Living*. London: Trübner, 1886.

Hall, T. H. *The Enigma of Daniel Home*. Amherst, N.Y.: Prometheus Books, 1984.

———. *New Light on Old Ghosts*. London: Duckworth, 1965.

———. *The Spiritualists*. London: 1962. Reprint, *The Medium and the Scientist*. Amherst, N.Y.: Prometheus Books, 1984.

———. *The Strange Case of Edmund Gurney*. London: Duckworth & Co., 1964. Reprint, 1980.

Hamilton, T. G. *Intention and Survival*. Toronto: Macmillan, 1942.

Hansel, C. E. M. *ESP: A Scientific Evaluation*. New York: Charles Scribner's Sons, 1966.

———. *The Search for Psychic Power*. Amherst, N.Y.: Prometheus Books, 1989.

Harlow, S. R. *Life After Death*. Rockport: Para Research, Inc., 1961.

Harris, Ben. *Gellerism Revealed*. Calgary, Alb.: Micky Hades Intl., 1985.

Harris, M. *Sorry, You've Been Duped*. London: Weidenfeld and Nicolson, 1986.

Harrison, J. M., ed. *CIA Flaps and Seal Manual*. Boulder, Colo.: Paladin Press, 1975.

Hasted, J. *The Metal Benders*. London: Routledge & Kegan Paul, 1981.

Hines, Terrence. *Pseudoscience and the Paranormal*. Amherst, N.Y.: Prometheus Books, 1988.

Hitching, F. *The World Atlas of Mysteries*. London: William Collins Sons & Co., 1978.

Hoggart, S., and M. Hutchinson. *Bizarre Beliefs*. London: Richard Cohen Books, 1995.

Hogue, J. *Nostradamus e il millennio* (Nostradamus and the Millennium). Milan: Mondadori, 1987.

Holms, A. C. *The Facts of Psychic Science*. New York, 1969.

Houdini, Harry. *Houdini Exposes the Tricks Used by the Boston Medium "Margery" to Win the $2,500 Prize Offered by the* Scientific American. New York: Adams Press Publishers, 1924.

Houdini, H. *A Magician Among the Spirits*. New York: Harper & Brothers, 1924. Reprint, New York: Arno Press, 1972.

Houdini, H. *A Magician Among the Spirits: The Original Manuscript*. New York: Kaufman & Greenberg, 1996.

Houdini, H. *Miracle Mongers and Their Methods*. New York: E. P. Dutton & Co., 1921. Reprint, Amherst, N.Y.: Prometheus Books, 1981.

Houdini, Harry, and Joseph Dunninger. *Magic and Mystery*. New York: Weathervane Books, 1947.

Humphrey, N. *Leaps of Faith, Science, Miracles, and the Search for Supernatural Consolation*. London: Basic Books, 1996.

Hyman, Ray. *The Elusive Quarry*. Amherst, N.Y.: Prometheus Books, 1989.

Inglis, B. *The Hidden Power*. London: Jonathan Cape, 1986.

Jones, K. I. *Conan Doyle and the Spirits*. Wellingborough, U.K.: Aquarian Press, 1989.

Kaye, M. *The Handbook of Mental Magic*. New York: Stein & Day, 1975.

Keene, L. *The Psychic Mafia*. Edited by Allan Spraggett. New York: St. Martin's Press, 1976. Reprint, Amherst, N.Y.: Prometheus Books, 1997.

Knight, D. C. *The ESP Reader*. New York: Grosset & Dunlap, 1969.

Korem, D. *Powers: Testing the Psychic and the Supernatural*. Downer's Grove, Ill.: Intervarsity Press, 1988.

Krippner, Stanley. *Human Possibilities, Mind Exploration in the USSR and Eastern Europe*. Garden City, N.Y.: Anchor Press/Doubleday, 1980.

Krippner, Stanley, ed. *Advances in Parapsychology 8.* Jefferson, N.C.: McFarland & Co., 1997.

Kurtz, Paul., ed. *A Skeptic's Handbook of Parapsychology.* Amherst, N.Y.: Prometheus Books, 1985.

Lever, D. *Stranger than Fiction.* Bideford: Supreme Magic Co., 1961.

Lodge, O. *Raymond Revised.* London: Methuen, 1941.

London Dialectical Society. *Report on Spiritualism of the Committee of the London Dialectical Society, Together with the Evidence, Oral and Written, and a Selection from the Correspondence.* London: J. Burns, 1873.

Lyons, A., and Marcello Truzzi. *The Blue Sense.* New York: Mysterious Press, 1991.

Manning, M. *The Link.* London: Colyn Smithe Ltd., 1974.

Marks, David, and Richard Kamman. *The Psychology of the Psychic.* Amherst, N.Y.: Prometheus Books, 1980.

Maskelyne, J. N. *Modern Spiritualism.* London: Frederick Warne, 1876.

Mishlove, J. *The Roots of Consciousness.* New York: Random House & The Bookworks, 1975.

Mulholland, John. *Beware Familiar Spirits.* New York: Charles Scribner's Sons, 1938.

————. *Quicker Than the Eye.* Indianapolis: Bobbs-Merrill, 1927.

Murphy, G., and R. Ballou, eds. *William James on Psychical Research.* London: Chatto & Windus, 1961.

Neher, A. *The Psychology of Trascendence,* Englewood Cliffs, N.J.: Prentice-Hall, 1980. Published in Italian as *La psicologia della trascendenza* (Psychology of the Transcendence). Padova: MEB, 1991.

Nelson, R. *The Art of Cold Reading.* Calgary, Alb.: Hades, 1971.

Nickell, Joe. *Inquest on the Shroud of Turin.* 2d ed. Amherst, N.Y.: Prometheus Books, 1987.

Nickell, J., ed. *Psychic Sleuths.* Amherst, N.Y.: Prometheus Books, 1994.

Nickell, Joe, and J. Fisher. *Mysterious Realms.* Amherst, N.Y.: Prometheus Books, 1993.

Nolan, A. *Healing; A Doctor in Search of a Miracle.* New York: Random House, 1974.

Ostrander, S., and L. Schroeder. *Psychic Discoveries Behind the Iron Curtain.* New York: Prentice-Hall, 1970.

Ovette, J. *Miraculous Hindu Feats.* Pomeroy, Ohio: Lloyd & Jones, 1947.

Owen, A. R. G. *Psychic Mysteries of the North*. New York: Harper & Row, 1975.

Panati, C. *The Geller Papers*. Boston: Houghton Mifflin Company, 1976.

———. *Supersenses*. New York: Quadrangle/New York Times Book Co., 1974.

Pearsall, R. *The Table Rappers*. London: Michael Joseph, 1972.

Permutt, C. *Photographing the Spirit World*. Wellingborough: Aquarian Press, 1983.

Podmore, F. *Modern Spiritualism*. London: Methuen & Co., 1902. Reprint, *Mediums of the 19th Century*. 2 vols. New Hyde Park, N.Y.: University Books, 1963.

———. *The Newer Spiritualism*. London, 1910. Reprint New York: Arno Press, 1975.

Polidoro, M. *Dizionario del paranormale* (Dictionary of the Paranormal). Varese: Esedra, 1997.

———. *Enigmi della storia* (Historical Enigmas). Milan: Piemme, 2003.

———. *Final Séance: The Strange Friendship Between Houdini and Conan Doyle*. Amherst, N.Y.: Prometheus Books, 2001.

———. *Il grande Houdini* (The Great Houdini). Milan: Piemme, 2001.

———. *Grandi misteri della storia* (Great Historical Mysteries). Milan: Piemme, 2002.

———. *L'illusione del paranormale* (The Paranormal Illusion). Padova: Franco Muzzio Editore, 1998.

———. *L'illusionismo dalla A alla Z* (Magic A to Z). Carnago, Va.: Sugarco edizioni, 1995.

———. *La maledizione del Titanic* (Curse of the *Titanic*). Rome: Avverbi, 1998.

———. *Misteri* (Mysteries). Varese: Edizioni Eco, 1996.

———. *Nel mondo degli spiriti* (In the World of Spirits). Padova: CICAP, 1999.

———. *Sei un sensitivo?* (Are You Psychic?). Rome: Avverbi, 1997.

———. *Il sesto senso* (The Sixth Sense). Milano: Piemme, 2000.

———. *Viaggio tra gli spiriti* (Journey Among the Spirits). Carnago, Va.: Sugarco edizioni, 1995.

———, et al. *Non ci casco!* (I Don't Fall Down!). Roma: Stampa Alternativa, 1996.

Polidoro, M., with Luigi Garlaschelli. *Investigatori dell'occulto* (Psychic Investigations). Rome: Avverbi, 2001.

Polidoro, M., with Mariano Tomatis. *Il trucco c'è!* (Here's the Trick!). Padova: CICAP, 2003.

Pollack, J. H. *Croiset the Clairvoyant*. New York: Doubleday, 1964.

Pratkanis, Anthony. *Age of Propaganda*. New York: W. H. Freeman and Co., 1992.

Pratt, J. G., J. B. Rhine, B. M. Smith, C. E. Stuart, and J. A. Greenwood. *Extra-Sensory Perception After Sixty Years*. Boston: Bruce-Humphries, 1940.

Premanand, B. *Science versus Miracles*. Podanur, India: Indian CSICOP, 1993.

Price, H., and Eric J. Dingwall, eds. *Revelations of a Spirit Medium*. London: Routledge & Kegan Paul, 1922.

Puarich, A. *Uri: A Journal of the Mystery of Uri Geller*. New York: Bantam Books, 1974.

Randi, James. *Conjuring*. New York: St. Martin's Press, 1992.

———. *An Encyclopedia of Claims, Frauds, and Hoaxes of the Occult and Supernatural*. New York: St. Martin's Press, 1995.

———. *Flim-Flam!* Amherst, N.Y.: Prometheus Books, 1982.

———. *The Magic of Uri Geller*. New York: Ballantine Books, 1975. Reprint, *The Truth About Uri Geller*. Amherst, N.Y.: Prometheus Books, 1982.

———. *The Mask of Nostradamus*. New York: Charles Scribner's Sons, 1989.

———. *Psychic Investigator*. London: Boxtree, 1991.

Randi, James, and B. R. Sugar. *Houdini: His Life and Art*. New York: Grosset & Dunlap, 1977.

Reed, G. *The Psychology of Anomalous Experience*. Amherst, N.Y.: Prometheus Books, 1988.

Rhine, J. B. *Extra-Sensory Perception*. Boston: Boston Society for Psychical Research, 1934. Reprint, Boston: Bruce Humphries, 1935.

———. *New Frontiers of the Mind*. New York: Farrar, 1937.

———. *New World of the Mind*. New York: Sloane, 1968.

Rhine, J. B., and J. G. Pratt. *Parapsychology, Frontier Science of the Mind*. Oxford: Blackwell Scientific Publications, 1957.

Rhine, L. E. *ESP in Life and Lab*. New York: Macmillan, 1967.

———. *Hidden Channels of the Mind*. London: Gollancz, 1961.

———. *Mind Over Matter*. London: Macmillan, 1970.

Richet, C. R. *Traité de Métapsichique*. Parigi: Felix Alcan, 1922. English version: *Thirty Years of Psychical Research; Being a Treatise on Metapsychics*. New York: Macmillan, 1923.

Richard, R., and R. Kelly. *Photographs of the Unknown*. London: New English Library Ltd., 1980.

Rinaldi, G. M. *Parapsicologia e TV: L'altra faccia del mistero* (Parapsychology and TV: The Other Side of the Mysterious). Manuscript, 1986.

Rinn, J. F. *Sixty Years of Psychical Research*. New York: Truth Seeker Company, 1950.

Roberts, H. *The Complete Prophecies of Nostradamus*. Great Neck, N.Y.: Nostradamus, 1969.

Rogo, D. S. *Miracles: A Scientific Exploration of Wondrous Phenomena*. Chicago: Dial Press, 1983.

———. *Parapsychology: A Century of Inquiry*. New York: Dell, 1975.

Roll, W. G., Robert L. Morris, and J. D. Morris, eds. *Research in Parapsychology, 1973*. Metuchen, N.J.: Scarecrow Press, 1973.

Sagan, C. *The Demon-Haunted World*. New York: Random House, 1995.

Salter, W. H. *Reminiscences of the Society for Psychical Research*, 1956. Unpublished manuscript preserved at the Trinity College in Cambridge, opened and transcribed for the first time in 1996 by G. M. Rinaldi.

Salverte, E. *Des sciences occultes ou essai sur la magie, les prodiges et les miracles* (Of Occult Sciences, or Essay on Magic, Prodigies, and Miracles). Paris: Baillière, 1826.

Schick, T., Jr., and L. Vaughn. *How to Think About Weird Things*. Toronto: Mayfield Publishing Company, 1994.

Seybert Commission. *Preliminary Report of the Commission Appointed by the University of Pennsylvania to Investigate Modern Spiritualism in Accordance with the Request of the Late Henry Seybert*. Philadelphia, 1887. Reprint, 1920.

Shepard, L. A., ed. *Encyclopedia of Occultism & Parapsychology*. Detroit: Gale Research, 1978. Reprint, Detroit: Book Tower, 1984.

Shermer, M. *Why People Believe Weird Things*. New York: W. H. Freeman & Co., 1997.

Silvan. *Arte Magica* (The Art of Magic). Milan: Rusconi, 1977.

———. *Il mondo dell'occulto* (The World of the Occult). Milan: Sperling & Kupfer, 1994.

Silverman, Kenneth. *Houdini!!! The Career of Ehrich Weiss*. New York: HarperCollins, 1996.

Smith, R. D. *Comparative Miracles*. St. Louis: B. Herder Book Co., 1965.

Soal, S. G. *Ciba Foundation Symposium on Extrasensory Perception*. Boston: Little, Brown & Co., 1956.

Soal, S. G., and F. Bateman. *The Mind Readers*. London: Faber & Faber, 1959.

————. *Modern Experiments in Telepathy.* London: Faber & Faber, 1954.

Somerlott, R. *Here Mr. Splitfoot.* New York: Viking Press, 1971.

Stearn, J. *Edgar Cayce: The Sleeping Prophet.* New York: Bantam Books, 1967.

Stein, Gordon. *The Sorcerer of Kings: The Case of Daniel Dunglas Home and William Crookes.* Amherst, N.Y.: Prometheus Books, 1993.

Stein, Gordon, ed. *The Encyclopedia of the Paranormal.* Amherst, N.Y.: Prometheus Books, 1996.

Stone, R. *Mysteries of the Mind.* Enderby, U.K.: Blitz Editions, 1993.

Tabori, P. *Harry Price: The Biography of a Ghost-Hunter.* London: Sphere Books, 1950. Reprint, 1974.

Targ, R., and K. Harary. *The Mind Race.* New York: Villard Books, 1984.

Targ, R., and H. Puthoff. *Mind Reach.* New York: Delacorte Press, 1977. Reprint, Dell Publishing, 1978.

Taylor, John. *Science and the Supernatural.* New York: E. P. Dutton, 1980.

————. *Superminds.* New York: Viking Press, 1975.

Tietze, T. R. *Margery.* New York: Harper & Row, 1973.

Time-Life Books, eds. *Mysteries of the Unknown.* Richmond: Time-Life Books, 1987.

Tomatis, Mariano. *Rol: Realtà o Leggenda?* (Rol: Reality or Legend?). Milan: Rome: Avverbi, 2003.

Truesdell, J. W. *The Bottom Facts concerning the Science of Spiritualism.* New York: G. W. Carleton & Co., 1883.

Ullman, M., and S. Krippner. *Dream Telepathy.* Baltimore: Penguin, 1973.

Wallace, A. R. *Miracles and Modern Spiritualism.* London: Nichols, 1985.

Ward, P. *A Dictionary of Common Fallacies.* New York: Oleander Press, 1978. Reprint, Amherst, N.Y.: Prometheus Books, 1989.

Waters, T. A. *The Encyclopedia of Magic and Magicians.* New York: Facts on File Publications, 1988.

————. *Mind, Myth & Magick.* Seattle, Wash.: Hermetic Press, 1993.

Weatherly, L. A., and J. N. Maskelyne. *The Supernatural?* Bristol: Arrowsmith, 1891.

Weiner, D. H., and R. D. Nelson, eds. *Research in Parapsychology 1986.* Metuchen, N.J.: Scarecrow Press, 1987.

Whaley, B. *Encyclopedic Dictionary of Magic.* Oakland, Calif.: Jeff Busby Magic Inc., 1989.

White, R. A., and L. A. Dale. *Parapsychology, Sources of Information.* Metuchen, N.J.: Scarecrow Press, 1973.

Wilhelm, J. L. *The Search for Superman*. New York: Pocket Books, 1976.

Wilson, C. *The Geller Phenomenon*. London: Aldus Books, 1976.

Wilson, Ian. *The After-Death Experience*. New York: William Morrow, 1987.

Wiseman, R. *Deception and Self-Deception*. Amherst, N.Y.: Prometheus Books, 1997.

Wiseman, R., and R. L. Morris. *Guidelines for Testing Psychic Claimants*. Hatfield: University of Hertfordshire Press, 1995.

Wolman, B. B. "Psi and Internal Attention States." *Handbook of Parapsychology*. New York: Van Nostrand Reinhold, 1977.

Zimbardo, P. G., E. B. Ebbesen, and C. Maslach. *Influencing Attitudes and Changing Behavior*. 2d ed. Reading, Mass.: Addison-Wesley, 1977.

Zorab, G. *D. D. Home il medium* (D. D. Home the Medium). Milan: Armenia Editore, 1976.

———. *Katie King donna o fantasma?* (Katie King: Woman or Phantom?). Milan: Armenia Editore, 1980.

Zöllner, J. C. F. *Transcendental Physics*. London: Harrison, 1880. Reprint, New York: Arno Press, 1976.

Zusne, L., and W. H. Jones. *Anomalistic Psychology: A Study in Magical Thinking*. Hillsdale, N.J.: Lawrence Erlbaum, 1989.

INDEX